Corporate Water Strategies

Corporate Water Strategies

William Sarni

publishing for a sustainable future

London • Washington, DC

First published in 2011 by Earthscan

Earthscan Ltd, Dunstan House, 14a St Cross Street, London EC1N 8XA, UK
Earthscan LLC, 1616 P Street, NW, Washington, DC 20036, USA

Earthscan publishes in association with the International Institute for Environment and Development

For more information on Earthscan publications, see www.earthscan.co.uk
or write to earthinfo@earthscan.co.uk

ISBN: 978-1-84971-185-2 hardback

Typeset by JS Typesetting Ltd, Porthcawl, Mid Glamorgan
Cover design by Rob Watts

A catalogue record for this book is available from the British Library

Library of Congress Cataloging-in-Publication Data

Sarni, William.
    Corporate water strategies / William Sarni. — 1st ed.
        p. cm.
    Includes bibliographical references and index.
    ISBN 978-1-84971-185-2 (hardback)
 1. Water resources development. 2. Water-supply—Economic aspects. I. Title.
    HD1691.S27 2010
    658.2'6—dc22
                                                                2010035170

This book is dedicated to the memory of Gary Bryner PhD,
a friend and colleague who inspired me during the early days
of my career in sustainability and who left a legacy of
innovative thinking, collaboration and leadership.
His contributions to advancing the economics and public
policy of environmental, energy and climate change were
only outshone by his humanity and generosity.
I am fortunate to have worked with Gary and to have
shared good times as we worked to evangelize
sustainability before it was mainstream.

Contents

Foreword

Tamin Pechet
CEO of Banyan Water and Chairman of Imagine H2O

When did you last think about water? Maybe water crossed your mind when you asked a waiter for a glass, waited for the shower to get hot, or dreamed of a beach vacation. But when did you last consider how water affects your life or your business?

Our most basic, precious and irreplaceable resource usually escapes our daily thinking. Water travels underground in an intricate system of pipes and pumps, and depending on your location, magically arrives at the taps of your home or business when and how you need it. In many places, the drop of water you need and the service to provide it carry a price so cheap you might not see or pay attention to your bill.

In fact, the chances are that you think about water only when there's a problem. As the saying goes, a plane that lands safely doesn't make a great story. Yet, when a water problem arises, everything stops. With the world's water challenges growing in frequency and severity, individuals, businesses and governments must now recognize, adapt to and address water needs.

What does a water problem look like? First, imagine you don't have enough water. Water scarcity affects one in three people on every continent,[1] from landowners who can't secure enough water rights to build homes in Boise, Idaho, to residents in Uganda who travel several hours a day to carry water to their homes.[2] Now, picture enough water in one place, but a system struggling to transport that water to points of use. Water infrastructure is crumbling globally, from breaks in water mains leaving residents of Boston on boiled-water alerts, to traffic jams in Washington, DC, to sewer spills in San Diego, California. There are almost a quarter of a million breaks in water mains each year in the US alone.[3] If you have enough water, and it reaches you when you need it, do you know what's in that water? Water quality is a daily concern for families from California's

San Joaquin Valley to urban Bangladesh. Globally, a child dies from a water-related disease[4] every 15 seconds. Even now, millions of Americans drink unhealthy water.[5] Finally, once water is used, where does it go? Used water must be treated, and either recycled or released back into the environment. Wastewater pollution is a top global environmental concern, and even today we are discovering new chemicals with unknown impacts in our wastewater streams.

The impact of these water challenges ripple through a society. Not only individuals, but governments and businesses also need to think about water requirements. Sufficient water, delivered in the requisite form and quality, is a business imperative. Yet, today, even some of the best-managed multinational companies are woefully unprepared to deal with water challenges, or the business opportunities they might present.

A few years ago, a renowned water resources attorney told me that the water industry wasn't desperate for an influx of innovative thinking. People had been purifying and moving water since the Egyptians, and we'd grown pretty good at it. That's true, but one need only look at the water problems we face right now to see how much better we can do. Where will we find new ideas, strategies and solutions? With only about 1 per cent of venture capital currently funding innovation in water, a variety of stakeholders, including entrepreneurs, government agencies and big businesses, need to develop new solutions to our water needs.

Fortunately, water is quickly becoming an important item on the general corporate agenda. The water industry itself, selling products and services to meet water needs, is already a half trillion dollar market. A variety of journalists and investors have called water 'the next gold'. The analogy serves a purpose. Like gold, water as a commodity carries commercial promise. But unlike gold, water is rarely measured or properly valued. Moreover, water poses as many risks as rewards.

Multinational companies depend on water as an input, and bear responsibility for its use as a resource. For some of them, this is easy to see. Beverage companies depend on water as the largest input for their products. For other major companies, the link is less direct, but no less crucial. Water is the critical variable in agricultural production. Yet most growers depend on their experience to estimate how to water crops, rather than using advanced measurement and control of water absorption to guide irrigation. Energy companies are among the biggest corporate water users. Electronics and pharmaceutical companies require specially treated ultra-pure water in their production processes. The challenges in supply, delivery and quality that affect individuals also pose a constant risk to the corporate community.

There is incredible potential mixed with the risks and problems of a water system. The pressures now transforming how we simultaneously think of and manage water present inspiring leadership opportunities. Innovation to address water needs, and thoughtful management of water as a resource, offer incredible opportunities to improve our personal health, and the health of our environment and our economy. It is hard to imagine a company today that does not have an energy policy and strategy. Soon we will think similarly about corporate water strategy.

This book provides a roadmap for companies committed to building a global water stewardship programme. Such a programme can assist companies in managing their physical, reputational and regulatory water risks. Moreover, for those forward-looking innovative companies it can provide a framework for developing new products and services, and a competitive advantage.

Notes

1 www.who.int/features/factfiles/water/en
2 http://hdr.undp.org/en/reports/global/hdr2006/
3 www.nytimes.com/2009/04/18/us/18water.html
4 http://water.org/learn-about-the-water-crisis/facts
5 www.nytimes.com/2009/12/17/us/17water.html

Introduction

Nothing in the world is more flexible and yielding than water. Yet when it attacks the firm and the strong, none can withstand it, because they have no way to change it. So the flexible overcome the adamant, the yielding overcome the forceful. Everyone knows this, but no one can do it.

Lao Tzu

Why Water and Why 'Corporate Water Strategies'?

I started my career as a hydrogeologist for Geraghty & Miller, one of the premier groundwater consulting firms in the United States at the time. It was there I first learned about water as an important public health issue. My early career encompassed managing water-supply projects (finding sources of groundwater) and the clean-up of contaminated groundwater at large Superfund sites. As a result, my youthful perspective was that there was no shortage of water – we just needed to look harder – and that we could clean up contaminated groundwater by applying the right technologies.

These early days of my career are in stark contrast to the past 12 years, which have been focused on sustainability. My sustainability consulting practice progressed from brownfields remediation, to sustainable land use, to green building, to climate change and, ultimately, to water. I have come full circle in my career, but I now look at water in an entirely new way. It is no longer a plentiful resource to be exploited or cleaned up. Instead, water is a resource that is becoming scarce and requires 'stewardship'.

This realization joined my long-standing belief that the private sector has the ability to quickly address big, complex issues. Water is such an issue (as are climate change, energy and land use), and the private sector is, indeed, addressing water as a critical business issue.

I also realized this story was not being told in an integrated fashion; hence my desire to write this book.

I was fortunate to have started with a foundational understanding of the technical aspects of water occurrence. In writing this book, I was also fortunate to have had access to thought leaders, and to companies that are addressing water as a critical business issue, as well as a public-policy and humanitarian challenge. The discussions I had with these professionals allowed me to explore their unique perspectives on water issues and solutions. The interviews and company 'snapshots' included in this book represent their stories, essentially in their own words, and provide valuable insight.

This book is a call to action for every company to move towards water stewardship and constructively engage all stakeholders in crafting 21st-century solutions to managing water sustainably. Moreover, it is a call for the public and private sectors to value water and integrate water stewardship into energy and climate policies and actions.

Acknowledgements

The more I write, the more I realize it is an impossible endeavour, without the help and support of many. There was no shortage of friends, family and colleagues who provided constant encouragement and support as the manuscript progressed.

I will never be able to find the words to adequately thank my wife, Maureen Meegan, who provided endless support and encouragement to take on the project and keep writing. She sacrificed precious weekends while I worked on the manuscript and I could not have written this book without her.

My sons, James, Thomas and Charles continue to provide encouragement for me to write. They now understand what I do for a living and why I am passionate about sustainability – I am very proud of them. They were always the first ones to ask, 'How is the book coming along?' when they knew I was dragging a bit.

Thanks to my sister, Celeste, who is one of my most vocal supporters and is now hooked on sustainability and almost all things 'green'; and to my parents, Josie and Mike, who instilled in me a love and curiosity for life, a strong work ethic and the belief that anything is possible. As always, thanks to the Aberman, Casey, Domijan and Zelkovich families, and to my nieces and nephews who provide ongoing encouragement.

My thanks also to Paul Aldretti, Lauren Hauptman, Jennifer Mich, Hillary Mizia, Kati Standefer, Deanna 'Drai' Turner, Jeffrey Weinberger and Andrew Winston for making significant contributions in helping me with the research, drafting and editing text, and preparing the graphics. Most importantly, they provided invaluable advice and perspective when it was critically needed.

My thinking about water strategies benefited enormously from my conversations with those who are working daily on addressing the global challenge of water scarcity. They were all generous with their time and support, and provided valuable insight into the way that multinational corporations and non-profit organizations are managing water risks and creating business opportunities. Thanks, then, to: Kate Brass, Mark Stoler and Jeff Fulghum from GE; Robert Berendes and Paul Minehart from Syngenta; Adam D'Luzansky and Josh Gilder from the White House Writers Group; Kevin McGovern from The Water Initiative; Dave Stangis from Campbell; Lisa Quezada from MillerCoors; Andy Wales from SABMiller; Alex McIntosh (formerly with Nestlé Waters) from Ecomundi Ventures; Bruce Lauerman from Nestlé Waters; Roberta Barbieri from Diageo; Jill Cooper from Encana US; Bart Alexander and Michael Glade from Molson Coors; Michael Law and Beth Haiken from Ogilvy PR; Tom Cooper from Intel; Janette Bombardier and Jeff Chapman from IBM; Tina Taylor from EPRI; Gregg Wagner from Rio Tinto Minerals; Sue Cischke from Ford Motor Company; Brooke Barton from Ceres; Bill Brady from Exelon; and Lisa Manley and Jeff Seabright from The Coca-Cola Company.

Also, a special thanks to Tamin Pechet, CEO of Banyan Water and Chairman of Imagine H2O, for writing the Forward for the book and being a driving force for innovation in the water industry; to Stan Laskowski, Lecturer/Advisor, University of Pennsylvania, Master of Environmental Studies program and President, Philadelphia Global Water Initiative for reviewing the manuscript and providing valuable insights; and to Greg Kelder, Vice President of Resolute Management Inc. and a Board Member of the Philadelphia Global Water Initiative who is always available to brainstorm about water issues and opportunities. All of them are making a difference in addressing water scarcity through innovative initiatives.

I also owe thanks to Don Smith from the University of Denver who was enthusiastic enough about the book idea to introduce me to his contacts at Earthscan; and finally to Tim Hardwick from Earthscan who provided the opportunity to write this book and offered guidance, encouragement and patience along the way.

Abbreviations

BIER	Beverage Industry Environmental Roundtable
BoP	base of pyramid
BSR	Business for Social Responsibility
CAP	Conservation Action Project
CCS	carbon capture and storage
CDP	Carbon Disclosure Project
Ceres	Coalition for Environmentally Responsible Economies
CESCR	Committee on Economic, Social and Cultural Rights
CSP	concentrated solar plants
CWP	Community Water Partnership
EIO-LCA	economic input–output life-cycle assessment
EPA	Environmental Protection Agency
EPCRA	Emergency Planning and Community Right to Know Act
EPRI	Electric Power Research Institute
EU	European Union
GE	General Electric
GEM	Global Emissions Manager
GEMI	Global Environmental Management Initiative
GETF	Global Environmental and Technology Foundation
GHG	greenhouse gas
GIO	Global Initiative Outlook
GRI	Global Reporting Initiative
GROW	Global Roundtable in Water
GWP	Global Water Partnership
GWR	Global Water Roundtable
HSAP	Hermosillo Stamping and Assembly Plant
IFC	International Finance Group
IGO	intergovernmental organizations
IHP	International Hydrological Programme
IPCC	Intergovernmental Panel on Climate Change

IPO	initial public offering
ISO	International Organization for Standardization
IUCN	International Union for Conservation of Nature
IWMI	International Water Management Institute
LCA	life-cycle analysis
LEED	Leadership in Energy and Environmental Design
MDG	Millennium Development Goal
NGO	non-governmental organization
NRDC	Natural Resources Defense Council
OECD	Organisation for Economic Co-operation and Development
POD	point of drinking
POU	point-of use
PUB	Public Utilities Board
PUC	public utility commission
REDA	Rural Empowerment and Development Agency
SAM	sustainability assessment matrix
SRP	Salt River Project
TCCC	The Coca-Cola Company
ToP	top of pyramid
TRI	Toxic Release Inventory
TVA	Tennessee Valley Authority
TWI	The Water Initiative
UNDP	United Nations Development Programme
UNEP	United Nations Environment Programme
UPW	ultra-pure water
USEPA	US Environmental Protection Agency
UV	ultraviolet
WBCSD	World Business Council for Sustainable Development
WEF	World Economic Forum
WFN	Water Footprint Network
WHO	World Health Organization
WMI	Water Missions International
WRC	Water Restoration Certificates
WRI	Water Resources Institute
WTO	World Trade Organization
WWC	World Water Council
WWF	World Wide Fund for Nature

Part I
Key Issues for Business in Water Stewardship

When drinking water, remember its source.

Chinese proverb

The Global Challenge of Water and Why it Matters to Business

In an age when man has forgotten his origins and is blind even to his most essential needs for survival, water along with other resources has become the victim of his indifference.

Rachel Carson

Introduction

Water is *the* global environmental and social sustainability issue both for businesses and society. While climate change and energy have gained increased recognition over recent years, it is the competition for water that poses a significant risk (and opportunity) to businesses and civil society.

In an age where the debate continues about how to move beyond oil dependency and towards a low-carbon economy, it is tempting to characterize water as the new oil or the new carbon.

It is neither. Water is unique.

I will repeat this theme throughout this book: water is unique, and as such represents risks and opportunities to global businesses that differ from those posed by energy and carbon. Moreover, water is intimately connected to humanity, unlike any other environmental issue and challenge.

This book will focus on how businesses are addressing the risks and opportunities from water scarcity. We will examine why water is a critical business issue and how it can effectively be managed. This is not to imply that water is an issue for businesses to manage alone.

On the contrary, solutions to water scarcity and sustainability will in general ultimately require close collaboration (not casual engagement but real partnership) with those who make public policy, non-governmental organizations (NGOs), investors and the local communities in which these companies operate. Water connects all of these stakeholders and it could be argued that water is the unifying sustainability issue.

Before we discuss the business drivers compelling companies to address water risk and opportunities, and to develop corporate water strategies, let's touch on the facts about global water use and scarcity. These facts make a compelling case explaining why companies are now addressing water as a strategic issue. We will get into greater detail on the global scenarios for water, but the current facts will frame the argument that water is a critical business issue. Facts about water scarcity from http://water.org are provided below.

- Less than 1 per cent of the world's fresh water (or about 0.007 per cent of all water on earth) is readily accessible for direct human use.
- 884 million people lack access to safe water supplies – approximately one in eight people.
- More than one-third of the world's population – roughly 2.4 billion people – lives in water-stressed regions and this number is expected to rise.
- 3.575 million people die each year from water-related disease and 98 per cent of water-related deaths occur in the developing world.
- Poor people living in the slums often pay five to ten times more for water than wealthy people living in the same city.
- Over 50 per cent of all water projects fail; fewer than 5 per cent of projects are visited; and far less than 1 per cent have any longer-term monitoring.

How do multinational companies operate in a world with these challenges impacting their potential consumers and the communities in which they operate? How do investors view water risk to businesses when supply chains may be disrupted? Who do businesses partner with to effectively address these challenges, and what is a smart global water strategy that addresses not just water scarcity, but business opportunities?

Let's look briefly at how businesses factor into this global water issue.

The Key Issues and Challenges

These facts highlight that companies can no longer take water for granted regardless of the industry sector they operate within.

One of the clearest and earliest discussions of the risk water represents to the private sector was published by the Pacific Institute (Morrison and Gleick, 2004). Business opportunities accompany these risks, for those companies that can deliver their products and services efficiently (low water use or no water use), or can develop technological solutions to provide clean water reliably to the public and private sectors.

First let's examine the risks to global businesses, with the most obvious being the *physical risk* to a business. Physical risk is essentially the pressure of decreasing water availability (water scarcity) and the reliability of supplies. The primary driver of physical water risk is increased population and resultant demand from urban and agricultural uses, coupled with the disparity of water availability.

With increased water scarcity there will be increased competition between businesses and local communities. It is likely that this potential for competition can be managed by effective engagement and planning, but, regardless, water scarcity is setting up this tension between the public and private sectors. If water scarcity is coupled with a notable *decline in water quality*, the physical risks to businesses can become acute. A decline in water quality can result in the need for pretreatment, which is an additional cost to businesses. This can be especially true when high-quality or ultra-clean water is required in the semiconductor, pharmaceutical, beverage and food processing sectors.

Water-quality standards (for surface and groundwater) have been established in developed countries and are emerging in developing countries. Businesses can expect increased regulation of water quality, and along with increased regulation come potential constraints on availability and higher costs for quality control. The increased costs associated with improved water quality may ultimately be borne by businesses operating in developing countries. Further complicating the challenge is that not all governments can provide water to 100 per cent of their populations, which means that there may be an inherent tension between communities and businesses for water availability. Furthermore, this tension impacts a company's licence to operate and brand on a global basis. (While there is no consensus on the definition of 'licence to operate', in general it means having the prior and informed consent from local communities in which a company is based, to operate its business.)

Physical water risk to businesses can be divided into:

- impacts on direct use; and
- disruptions within their supply chains.

While most companies are (to varying degrees) well prepared to manage direct water risk, supply-chain disruptions represent real and to a large degree unquantified threat. Companies are just coming to terms with the realization that they must quantify water use and risk within their supply chains. They have been grappling with this challenge with regard to their carbon risk and have made real progress in quantifying and reducing carbon in this portion of their footprint. Managing water risk within a company's supply chain will be no small task, as most companies that out-source manufacturing can only influence, and not control the behaviour of manufacturers.

So what does supply-chain water risk look like? Companies are just be-ginning to consider this, and investors are starting to pay attention. Water is an essential component in the production of apparel, food and beverage, forest and agriculture-based products. A few examples highlighted in the Pacific Institute report (Morrison and Gleick, 2004) underscore the issue. In 2001, Anheuser-Busch felt the impact of water shortages from a drought in the Pacific North-west of the United States within their sup-ply chain. This drought increased the costs of barley and aluminum (the aluminium manufacturing in the North-west relies on relatively low-cost hydropower). This was something of a perfect storm because two key components of their supply chain, barley, and aluminium for cans, were impacted. Both barley and aluminium production were competing for scarce water resources and costs increased for these key supply-chain products. Apparently, this experience resulted in Anheuser-Busch taking a comprehensive and strategic look at its water use.

Other risks that can threaten a business include reputational, regulatory and litigation risks. It is worth noting – it indicates how quickly our think-ing about water risk is maturing – that when the Pacific Institute report was released in 2004, reputational risk (the intangibles of a business) was not mentioned. However, the February 2010 Ceres report 'Murky Waters? Corporate reporting on water risk' (Barton, 2010) highlights reputational risks (along with litigation and regulatory water risk for companies). I will go into greater detail on this landmark report later, but first let's examine the reputational, litigation and regulatory risks from water.

Reputational and brand risk from water dovetail with the threat of physical risks. The linkage can be painfully obvious. As water scarcity increases, and competition for water between the public and private sectors increases, a company can either handle this 'competition' well or fail to proactively engage stakeholders. Reactive rather than proactive management of this competition is potentially more likely in areas where local communities lack access to clean water, or perceived or real inequities exist. Conflict with communities and other stakeholders seldom ends with a company's reputation and brand intact. This conflict and resultant reputational and brand damage can result in a loss of a company's licence to operate. At that point business disruption becomes real.

There is now an added dimension to the issue. The need for 'access to clean water as a human right' put forth by the World Health Organization (WHO) is increasingly recognized. Former UN Secretary-General Kofi Annan stated this clearly: 'Access to safe water is a fundamental human need and, therefore, a basic human right. Contaminated water jeopardizes both the physical and social health of all people. It is an affront to human dignity.' Some companies such as PepsiCo have adopted a policy of supporting this human right to water.

Further complicating the risk is the general failure of governments to provide not just water services to local communities but public services in general. In the mining sector it is increasingly common for private mining companies to bridge this gap and provide health services and basic infrastructure. Will this become more commonplace with other industry sectors, as water scarcity becomes an acute problem for businesses, and the communities in which they operate?

In addition to physical, reputational and brand risk there is the potential for regulatory and litigation risks. It is reasonable to assume that the world will see increased regulation of water quantity and quality. This trend will be both in the developing and the developed economies. For example, in the United States there is increased scrutiny of the effectiveness of the Clean Water Act in protecting US waters (*The New York Times*, 2009).

The US is not alone in re-examining regulations and directives. In China, the Water Pollution Control Law was revised following a release of benzene into the Songhua River in 2005 (Barton, 2010). The new act increased fines and included environmental regulation as a component of local government performance. The City of Beijing economic planning agency identified 12 international and local brewers, beverage and dairy companies on a 'List of Major Water-Polluting Enterprises' which subjects these companies to increased supervision and a requirement to submit plans to reduce energy use and water emissions (Barton, 2010). In the European Union (EU) the Water Framework Directive is designed to establish high water-quality conditions for all water bodies in all member countries by 2015. The EU Directive's approach is to improve water quality through an integrated basin-wide approach (Barton, 2010).

This represents a risk for those companies that are unprepared or poorly positioned for the forthcoming regulations. These regulations may consist of constraints on allocations (including caps), increased costs (cost does not currently reflect the value of water), and new or limited water-quality permits and standards. Increased regulation of both surface and groundwater should be expected.

With increased regulations come increased potential for litigation. This is especially true in the United States, where concepts such as joint and several liability are key to regulatory programmes such as 'Superfund' (Comprehensive Environmental Response, Compensation, and Liability Act, or CERCLA) and tort litigation is commonplace. Joint and several liability exists where a claimant may pursue an obligation against any one party as if they were jointly liable – it then becomes the responsibility of the defendants to sort out their respective proportions of liability and payment. All of these risks – physical, reputational, regulatory and litigious – are related, and as such pose unique challenges for global businesses as water becomes increasingly scarce.

What is the Current Understanding of the Risk (and Opportunity) for Businesses?

In short, the level of understanding is not well developed across industry sectors. Several surveys and benchmarking reports highlight the current level of understanding of water risk to businesses and how this risk is being managed.

Let's examine the findings and conclusions of these surveys and reports.

SustainAbility and GlobeScan

GlobeScan (a global public opinion and research company: www. globescan.com) routinely conducts surveys of opinions on various environmental topics. In January 2010 GlobeScan and SustainAbility released the 'Pulse survey on water' as part of their Sustainability Survey Research Program (SustainAbility and GlobeScan, 2010). This research programme is a comprehensive, consultative research agenda which connects corporations to the insights of leading global sustainability experts. At the time, the survey was the third of a series of polls conducted in 2009, and designed to better understand the critical issue of water scarcity and water-quality degradation. The water survey was developed with the participation of 1231 experts; respondents were asked to answer questions and rate their importance. On a scale of 1–5, 1 is 'not important' and 5 is 'very important'.

The key results of 'The sustainability survey: Pulse survey on water' are summarized below:

- Conservation and efficiency are the most critical aspects of the solution to water scarcity.
- Barriers to sustainable water management are public policy and public understanding.
- There is a strong preference for measures to reduce demand over increased supply.
- Changes across all industry sectors are expected due to water scarcity.
- It is important for companies to understand the full life cycle of products and services.

One of the key conclusions is that when asked the question: '*please rate the importance of each of the following issues in the transition to the sustainable and equitable management of fresh water globally*', respondents felt that the sustainable management of fresh water requires a multifaceted approach. Over 70 per cent of those surveyed believe that the following components are 'important' (ranked 4–5) in addressing this aspect of water:

- conservation/efficient use of water;
- universal access to fresh/potable water;

- ecosystem protection;
- universal protection of sanitation;
- education and awareness;
- ability of governments to supply water to citizens;
- involvement of local communities in water management;
- water for agriculture;
- pricing water appropriately;
- ownership/jurisdictional issues regarding water.

Only 16 per cent believed the privatization of water was important, with 55 per cent believing it was not important.

With regard to the question: '*please rate the significance of each of the following barriers to the sustainable and equitable management of*

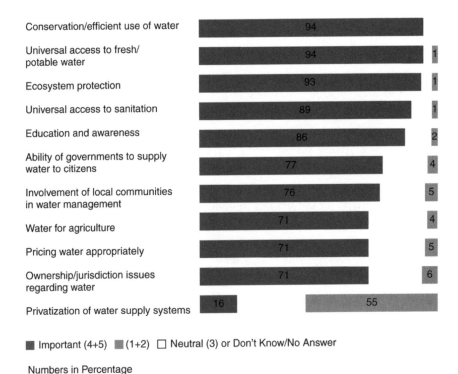

■ Important (4+5) ■ (1+2) □ Neutral (3) or Don't Know/No Answer

Numbers in Percentage

Figure 1.1 *The importance of various issues in the transition to sustainable and equitable management of fresh water*

Source: adapted from SustainAbility and GlobeScan (2010)

fresh water globally', over 70 per cent of respondents rated the following factors as important (ranked 4–5).

- inadequate national/state legislation to protect water;
- lack of awareness/education;
- poverty.

Factors such as inadequate funding/financing, lack of international governance mechanisms and failure to price water at full cost were considered important but only 56–68 per cent of the respondents believed this.

With regard to the question: *'please rate the potential of each of the following policy measures to sustainably alleviate water shortages, both in the short and long term'*, over 80 per cent of respondents believed 'invest in/provide subsidies for water conservation/efficiency improvements' was important. Over 60 per cent believed 'impose water restrictions on users to encourage conservation/efficiency' was important. Less than 33 per cent believed the construction of desalination plants, drawing from local water resources (surface and groundwater) and the importation of water from water-surplus to water-deficit areas was important.

The survey also took a brief look at the linkage between water and energy, with 54 per cent of the respondents believing that *'there are numerous strong linkages that should be considered and integrated into*

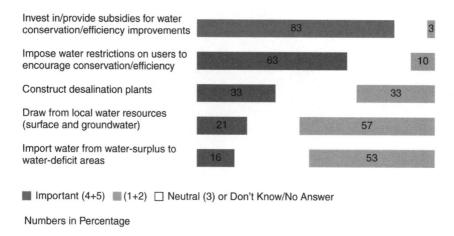

Invest in/provide subsidies for water conservation/efficiency improvements — 83 — 3

Impose water restrictions on users to encourage conservation/efficiency — 63 — 10

Construct desalination plants — 33 — 33

Draw from local water resources (surface and groundwater) — 21 — 57

Import water from water-surplus to water-deficit areas — 16 — 53

■ Important (4+5)   ▨ (1+2)   ☐ Neutral (3) or Don't Know/No Answer

Numbers in Percentage

Figure 1.2 *The potential for each policy measure to sustainably alleviate short- and long-term water shortages*

Source: adapted from SustainAbility and GlobeScan (2010)

policies/strategies'. Less than 3 per cent believed the issues require separate policies or strategies.

With regard to water footprinting (described in greater detail in Chapter 4, Water Accounting), over 78 per cent of respondents believe that it is very important to understand the full life cycle (the entire value chain) water footprints of companies. Less than 8 per cent believe water footprinting to be of lesser importance than carbon footprinting.

In my opinion the most significant conclusion is that *nearly all sectors of the economy will need to 'transform' in response to water shortages.* Over 50 per cent of the survey respondents believe the following sectors will 'need to change their operations or business models as a result of water shortages over the next ten years':

- food/agriculture;
- pulp/paper;
- beverage;
- mining;
- manufacturing;
- chemicals;
- electric utilities;

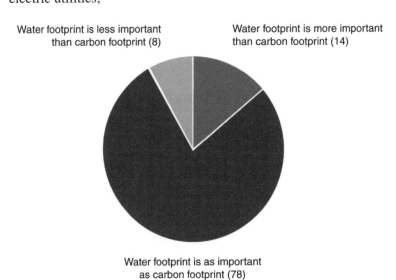

Figure 1.3 *The importance of companies understanding the full life cycle of their water footprint*

Source: adapted from SustainAbility and GlobeScan (2010)

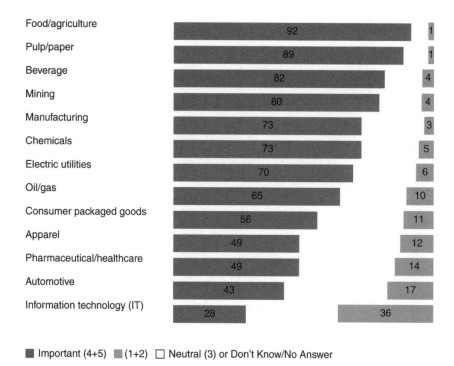

Food/agriculture
Pulp/paper
Beverage
Mining
Manufacturing
Chemicals
Electric utilities
Oil/gas
Consumer packaged goods
Apparel
Pharmaceutical/healthcare
Automotive
Information technology (IT)

■ Important (4+5) ▨ (1+2) ☐ Neutral (3) or Don't Know/No Answer

Numbers in Percentage

Figure 1.4 *The degree to which the sectors need to adapt as a result of water shortages over the next ten years*

Source: adapted from SustainAbility and GlobeScan (2010)

- oil/gas;
- consumer packaged goods.

The IT, automotive, pharmaceutical/healthcare and apparel sectors would also be impacted, according to 28–49 per cent of respondents.

Carbon Disclosure Project Water Disclosure

The case for water disclosure
In November 2009 the Carbon Disclosure Project (CDP) announced the launch of the CDP Water Disclosure questionnaire (more information may be found at: www.cdproject.net/en-US/Programmes/Pages/cdp-water-disclosure.aspx). The CDP Water Disclosure design is similar to the CDP

Carbon questionnaire. As part of the announcement, CDP highlighted the results of a pilot project aimed at better understanding water risk and disclosure in various industry sectors.

Let's examine the CDP Water Disclosure questionnaire rationale first, and then the results of the pilot project questionnaire. Having worked closely with companies in preparing and submitting their CDP Carbon questionnaires, I firmly believe the CDP Water Disclosure questionnaire will be just as successful in driving change in companies reporting on 'resource risks' such as carbon and water.

The rationale for CDP to launch the Water Disclosure questionnaire in 2010 was clear. The goal of the CDP Water Disclosure is to assist institutional investors to understand the financial risks from water-related issues better, and will build upon the success of the CDP Carbon questionnaire. The success of the CDP Carbon questionnaire has not only benefited the investment community, but has resulted in widespread acceptance by private sector companies in measuring and reporting their carbon footprints, along with identifying mitigation measures and business opportunities. Based upon the success of the CDP Carbon questionnaire, it is reasonable to assume that companies will soon accept water footprinting and disclosure as common risk-management practices.

Water scarcity is viewed by CDP as a 'key issue' for the 21st century, with global impacts to the public and private sectors. The rationale for CDP to focus on water risk and disclosure (in addition to carbon) is a recognition that water scarcity will increase due to increased urbanization, increasing population and decreasing water quality. Moreover, for CDP the relationship between climate change and water is very clear. Climate change and associated business risks will impact water scarcity and risks for the private sector.

In launching the CDP Water Disclosure, CDP clearly defined the risks to businesses from water scarcity (in alignment with Morrison and Gleick, 2004):

- physical risks: changes in the quantity or quality of water;
- regulatory risks: current or projected public-policy initiatives such as pricing changes, water rights and use/reuse standards;
- reputational risks: increasing competition between users, typically arising from (actual or perceived) abuse of abstraction rights, or the pollution of groundwater sources, particularly in the developing world.

It is worth noting that concerns regarding brand/reputational issues were a major factor in the success of the CDP Carbon questionnaire, and this issue is covered in greater detail in a subsequent chapter. With increasing value placed on intangible value, and in the absence of a global framework for measuring and reporting on carbon, companies with global, local and national brands responded out of a desire to ensure they protected or built brand/reputational value. Brand/reputational value is shaped by combinations of events, information, media, stakeholder needs, public opinion, NGOs and policies, and all of these are enhanced by increasing stakeholder engagement through the proliferation of social media.

According to CDP, water-risk disclosure will have similar benefits as carbon disclosure, with the primary benefit that companies will develop strategies in response to the questionnaire. If you are asked about your carbon or water risk, and find yourself without an answer, it is time (actually, well past time) to develop a strategy. The operating belief by CDP (which I believe is correct) is that disclosure drives changes in corporate risk reporting and behaviour, along with other related benefits; moreover the experience with the CDP Carbon questionnaire shows that a wide range of other stakeholders also benefit. The latter group includes corporations, investors, regulators, consumers and insurance companies. Disclosure also drives the development of technical protocols such as metrics and target-setting protocols.

Briefly, the benefits consist of:

- Enhancing business awareness and understanding. Typically risks from resource issues have not been well understood or addressed. The CDP process has increased awareness of the issue of carbon and will do the same with water. Many companies are just beginning to understand the impact and implications of having operations or their supply chain in water-stressed areas.
- Developing standards. Although standards, guidelines and protocols for carbon accounting are well developed (supply-chain issues remain, to some degree), they are not mature for water accounting. Water footprinting and accounting practices are nascent at best, and one can expect a rapid movement to standardize practices and protocols over the next couple of years, in response to increased focus on water risk and disclosure.
- Providing relevant information to stakeholders. While primarily investor focused, CDP recognizes that a wide range of stakeholders

use the carbon disclosure information (an example is *Newsweek*'s ranking of the 'Top Green Companies in America'). Rating and ranking schemes will use water-risk information, along with consumers, customers, NGOs, supply-chain companies and regulatory agencies. CDP believes that resource-risk information on carbon and water will ensure better investment decisions, and will direct capital away from risks and towards solutions (new products and services).

- Raising general awareness. Water is not carbon, and water stewardship requires broad-based collaboration among all stakeholders. The disclosure of information is essential for the development of long-term solutions to issues such as watershed management, transboundary water management and virtual water. Information and transparency are the cornerstones for any sound solution to managing water risk.
- Action and dialogue. We have seen that companies take action when they feel pressure to disclose information on carbon. Disclosure results in clear action to measure, reduce and offset as part of an overall strategy. Water disclosure will result in a similar bias for action, as companies seek to set long-term goals, and work towards meeting or exceeding these goals.

The CDP is, in part, basing its predictions on the trajectory of the CDP Water Disclosure on the results of a very modest pilot study. The pilot project was valuable as it provided a sense of how selected industry sectors view water risk and disclosure. The key findings of the pilot project are summarized below:

- 'No surveyed companies in the food and beverage industry responded to the questionnaire.' I share the conclusion with CDP that this is 'surprising'. Although only seven companies in the food and beverage sector were sent questionnaires as part of the pilot, the response remains a surprise. This is in contrast to the paper and packaging sector (nine out of thirteen responses), the manufacturing sector (six out of eight responses), the professional services sector (three out of seven responses), the logistics sector (two out of four responses) and the IT sector (three out of three). My somewhat speculative assumption is that the reason for no responses from the food and beverage sector is that water is such a critical business issue, they were reluctant to participate voluntarily.

- 'Most companies do have information on their direct water usage.' Over 80 per cent of the companies surveyed said they were able to provide data on total water used in their operations, and over 60 per cent could identify which operations were in water-stressed regions. To my mind these are surprisingly high percentages, but if you consider that companies probably view 'direct water footprint' as simply reading the water bill, then it makes sense.
- 'Most companies do not have data on water use or water issues in their supply chain.' In contrast to the last point, most companies do not have data on water use within their supply chain (Tier 1 suppliers) and 87 per cent could not identify which Tier 1 suppliers were operating in water-stressed regions. Moreover, 67 per cent of the companies surveyed did not have data for the total water used in the upstream supply. However, there were many companies that did say they were in the process of investigating water use in their upstream supply chains.
- 'Only half of the respondents see water as a risk for their business and for their supply chain.' 47 per cent of the companies view water as a risk (physical, regulatory or reputational) to their businesses. In addition, 47 per cent of the companies believed water posed a risk to their supply chain.
- 'More than half of the respondents see water as an opportunity.' 60 per cent of the companies surveyed believe water is a business opportunity. The opportunities range from consulting, to new products such as smart water meters.
- 'Many companies have a water management plan, but only for their own plants.' 53 per cent of the companies responded that they have water management plans for their operations (not for their supply chain), and not all companies have targets for water reduction. Employee engagement was identified as a key factor to achieve water-reduction goals.

In summary, the CDP Water Disclosure pilot project provided some good insights into the current state of water-risk awareness and planning. While the sample size was small, it served the purpose of framing the CDP Water Disclosure questionnaire.

In 2010 the initial survey was sent to over 300 of the largest global companies (based upon market capitalization). The general set of initial questions in the CDP Water Disclosure were:

Question W1 Water-related risks and opportunities

- W1a Water-related risks – own operations
  - Regulatory risks: how is your company exposed to regulatory risks related to water in its own operations?
  - Physical risks: how is your company exposed to physical risks related to water in its own operations?
  - Reputational risks: how is your company exposed to reputational risks related to water?
- W1b Water-related risks – your supply chain
  - Regulatory risks: how are the companies in your supply chain exposed to regulatory risk related to water?
  - Physical risks: how are the companies in your supply chain exposed to physical risks related to water?
  - Reputational risks: how are the companies in your supply chain exposed to reputational risks related to water?
- W1c Opportunities
  - How do water-related aspects of climate change present opportunities for your company?

Question W2 Water accounting

- W2a Accounting parameters
  - Reporting boundary: please indicate the category that describes the company, entities or group for which your water usage is reported.
  - Reporting year: please state the start date and end date of the year for which you are reporting water usage.
  - Methodology: please specify the methodology used by your company to calculate water usage.
- W2b Water usage in own operations
  - Are you able to provide data for the total water used in your own operations? If so, please provide it here (in m^3 per year).
  - What is the effect of your water withdrawals and discharges?
- W2c Percentage of operations in water-stressed regions
  - Are you able to identify which of your operations are in water-stressed regions? If so, please report the percentage of your operations which is in these regions.

Question W3 Water management

- W3a Does your company have a water management plan?
- W3b Does the plan address factors outside of directly operated plants? Explain.
- W3c What are the goals of the plan?
- W3d What activities are you considering in the plan?
- W3e Who is responsible for the plan?

Water scarcity and climate change

Nothing will have a greater impact on global water risk to the public and private sector than climate change (climate change is already impacting water availability and water quality globally). A study by Pacific Institute and Ceres in February 2009 (Morrison, Morikawa et al, 2009) clearly identified the impact of climate change on the global business community. The report borrows heavily from that of the Intergovernmental Panel on Climate Change (IPCC) (Solomon et al, 2007). It couples the IPCC analyses with an assessment of the potential water impacts to various industry sectors.

An overview of the impacts of climate change on global water resources is illustrated below in Figure 1.5.

The Ceres and Pacific Institute Report (Morrison, Morikawa et al, 2009) identifies numerous impacts on water quantity and quality from climate change, along with potential implications for businesses. Several key impacts are identified:

- increased water demand for agriculture, primarily due to prolonged and severe droughts;
- increased water demand for hydration of farm animals due to increased temperature;
- increased water needed for industrial cooling due to increased temperature;
- decreased natural water storage capacity from glaciers/snowcap melting, and reduced long-term water availability for about one-sixth of the world's population living in glacier- or snowmelt-fed river basins (areas of China, India, Bangladesh, Pakistan and the western United States);
- increased water scarcity due to changes in precipitation patterns and intensity;

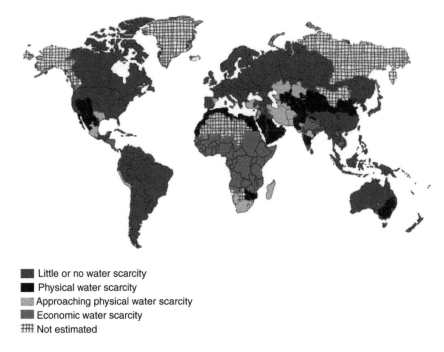

Figure 1.5 *Generalized areas of physical and economic water scarcity*

Source: adapted from International Water Management Institute, http://maps.grida.
no/go/graphic/areas-of-physical-and-economic-water-scarcity

- increased vulnerability of ecosystems due to temperature increases, changes in precipitation patterns, frequent severe weather events and prolonged droughts; this will result in diminished ability of natural systems to filter water (water-quality improvement) and buffering against flooding;
- effects on the capacity and reliability of water-supply infrastructure due to flooding, extreme weather and sea-level rise; most water-treatment plants were not designed to withstand rising sea levels or to accommodate increased concentration (high flow over short periods of time) of snowmelt and precipitation events;
- pressure on non-consumptive water uses such as transportation on inland waterways and fisheries;
- contamination of coastal surface and groundwater from rise in sea level and resultant saltwater intrusion;
- increased water temperatures;

- increased precipitation and flooding, resulting in increased erosion rates and transport of sediments and pollutants;
- increased contribution to environmental health risks, such as the mobilization of pathogens and contaminants.

If one considers the historical growth of water withdrawal by industry sectors, it is reasonable to conclude that climate change will have a very real impact on businesses. Water withdrawal by industry sector is illustrated below in Figure 1.6.

Potential impacts to businesses include:

- higher costs of water;
- regulatory restrictions on water use;
- potential conflicts with communities and other water users;
- decreased availability of water for business use (prioritization of water use);
- operational disruptions and associated financial impacts;
- limitations on future growth and licence to operate;
- increased costs for water treatment;

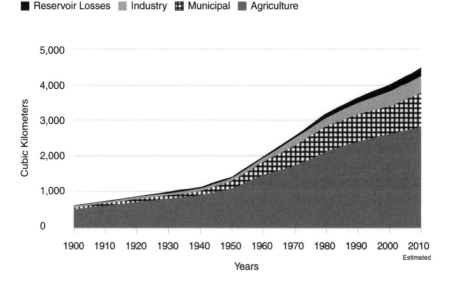

Figure 1.6 *Water withdrawals by industry sector*

Source: adapted from UNESCO, as cited in Knight and Miller-Blakewell (2007)

- increased health costs for employees in impacted areas;
- increased responsibility (and costs) to implement community water infrastructure, and watershed restoration projects, to mitigate reputational risks.

There will also be business opportunities for those companies that can adapt and deliver products and services with less water or no water. Just as 'cleantech' is delivering new energy and low carbon technologies, 'water-tech' will deliver improved water efficiency and treatment technologies. The 'hard approach' to address water scarcity and degradation issues will be coupled with the 'soft approach' to managing water (water stewardship and governance).

Corporate reporting on water risk

A snapshot of how companies perceive their risk from water scarcity and how they communicate this risk and management approach was provided in the 2010 Ceres report (Barton, 2010). The report provided a greater depth of insight on the drivers for companies to develop water strategies and disclosures than was available to date. The CDP pilot project and the Ceres Report clearly illustrate how far companies have to go in understanding the risks from water scarcity and mitigating those risks.

With support from UBS Research and Bloomberg LP, the Ceres Report examined 100 of the largest publicly traded companies (based upon 2008 annual revenue and market capitalization) in the beverage, chemicals, electric power, food, homebuilding, mining, oil and gas, and semiconductors sectors. For the electric power and homebuilding sectors only US companies were evaluated. These sectors were identified as high water-use industries both from direct operations, supply chain and product use (Industry Classification Benchmark codes were used to establish industry categories, and can be found at www.icbenchmark.com).

The Ceres report evaluated how each sector and company disclosed information regarding water use and water risk. Specifically, company disclosure was divided into water accounting, risk assessment, direct operations, supply chain and stakeholder engagement. Each company evaluated was scored using a 100-point scale for the beverage, electric power, food, oil and gas, mining and semiconductor sectors, and a 112-point scale for the chemical and homebuilding sectors (due to an additional category, 'opportunities').

The results of the rankings were:

Table 1.1 *Water disclosure scores: Beverage, electric power, food, mining, oil and gas, and semiconductors (scored on a 1–100-point scale)*

Beverage	
Diageo	43
Anheuser-Busch InBev	34
The Coca-Cola Company	34
SABMiller	30
PepsiCo	29
Heineken	25
Pernod Ricard	18
Brown-Forman	14
Constellation Brands	9
Dr Pepper Snapple	8
Electric Power	
Pinnacle West/Arizona Public Services (APS)	38
American Electric Power (AEP)	36
PG&E	26
Exelon	21
Southern Company	18
Dominion Resources	17
Entergy	16
Xcel Energy	16
Constellation Energy	14
Duke Energy	14
AES Corporation	12
NRG Energy	11
Florida Power & Light Group	8
Food	
Unilever	34
Nestlé	29
Smithfield Foods	25
Danone	20
General Mills	19
Tyson Foods	17
Kellogg	15
Kraft Foods	15
ConAgra	12
Dean Foods	12
Sara Lee	12
Archer Daniels Midland	9

Table 1.1 *(continued)*

Mining	
Xstrata	42
Barrick	38
Rio Tinto	37
Alcoa	35
Anglo American	33
Freeport-McMoRan	31
BHP Billiton	30
Teck	27
Vale	27
Newmont	25
Consol Energy	15
Massey Energy	15
Peabody Energy	8
Oil and Gas	
BP	35
Suncor Energy	27
Total	27
Nexen	26
Royal Dutch Shell	25
Exxon	23
Chevron	16
ConocoPhillips	16
Devon Energy	16
Canadian Natural Resources	12
Chesapeake Energy	7
Range Resources	7
EnCana	4
Semiconductors	
Toshiba	35
Intel	34
Samsung	29
United Microelectronics	27
Taiwan Semiconductors	25
ST Microelectronics	22
Advanced Micro Devices	17
Analog Devices	15
Texas Instruments	15
Infineon Technologies	8
Micron	1

Source: adapted from Barton (2010)

Table 1.2 *Water disclosure scores: Chemicals and home-builders (scored on a 1–112-point scale)*

Chemicals	
Mitsui	33
Sumitomo Chemical	32
PotashCorp	31
DuPont	23
Monsanto	23
Syngenta	22
Dow	21
BASF	20
Reliance Industries	17
Mosaic	15
Praxair	13
PPG Industries	11
Air Liquide	10
Linde	10
Saudi Basic	5
Home-building	
KB Home	15
Pulte	13
Toll Brothers	13
Beazer Homes	11
Lennar	10
Centex	6
D.R. Horton	4
Hovnanian	4
NVR	4
Ryland	4

Source: adapted from Barton (2010)

The key findings of the study along with my observations are:

- Overall disclosure of water risk and water performance was 'surprisingly weak'. The characterization of 'weak' by Ceres is based on how the companies ranked; the highest scoring company, Diageo, scored 43 out of 100 points. The relatively low scores do surprise me, as companies are just beginning to recognize the risk posed by water. Moreover, it has been my experience that companies will only disclose risk publicly after they have a deep understanding of the risk and how to manage it.

- There are 'leading' and 'lagging' sectors. The leading sector was mining, followed by the beverage industry. The home-building sector received the lowest scores. The position of mining was not surprising, because it is critical that this sector must manage water well. The location of mining operations cannot be based upon water availability, and in many cases ore bodies are in arid climates. The beverage sector is acutely aware of the importance of water, not only as a product component in some cases, but also for processing. In contrast, the home-building sector (bear in mind this is the US home-building sector as opposed to the European home-building sector) lags behind, owing to a nearly complete lack of understanding of water scarcity and value.
- Limited disclosure of water risk in financial reporting. The majority of the companies evaluated disclose exposure to water risks in their annual reports. 73 per cent of the companies evaluated report some degree of physical risk from water scarcity. However, Ceres categorizes the disclosure statements as 'vague, boilerplate' language and the companies do not reference specific operations or their supply chains. Only six companies report any water accounting data within their financial filings. Again, this is not surprising: companies will disclose risk only after it is well understood and mitigation measures are established.
- The majority of the companies identify water risk as a physical risk. While physical risk from droughts was identified for the majority of companies, only nine of them identified reputational risk from water, and these were in the beverage, mining and oil and gas sectors. 67 per cent of companies disclosed some level of water-related regulatory risk, with the highest number of companies in the mining, electric power, and oil and gas sectors. 48 per cent report some degree of litigation risk. It is also worth noting that some companies restricted their discussion of water risk to their sustainability reports, and did not include a discussion in their financial reports. In my opinion, the variability of risk profiling by industries reflects the unique sensitivity of each industry sector. For example, the utility sector is highly regulated, and as a result is acutely aware of regulatory risk from water. In contrast the beverage sector is consumer-facing and more sensitive to reputational risks. It is not reasonable to assume that all sectors will perceive water risk in the same manner.
- Few companies provide water performance data at the local level. Approximately two-thirds report total water-use data and only 17 per

cent report data on a regional or local basis. Moreover, few companies identify the number of their facilities located in water-stressed
regions: BP, Diageo, Heineken, Nestlé and SABMiller do make that
identification.

- There is little reporting of water-related policies and management
systems. 24 per cent of companies detail water policies, standards, or
management systems to reduce water-related risks and costs.
- Relatively few reduction targets are established. Not surprisingly, only
21 companies disclose quantifiable targets to reduce water use. Of
these only Diageo, DuPont and Xstrata had water-reduction targets
that were specific to the degree of water stress facing individual operating facilities. 15 companies had specific goals to reduce wastewater
discharge volumes.
- There is little information on water use within supply chains. None
of the companies provided comprehensive data on water performance within their supply chains. However, Danone, SABMiller and
Unilever did provide estimates of the water use embedded in their
supply chains, and 12 companies disclose working with their suppliers
to help them reduce water use or wastewater discharge. Companies in
sectors with a relatively large portion of their water footprint embedded in the supply chain (such as food, beverage and electric power)
did not report that they were engaging their supply chain on water
management.
- Stakeholder engagement is 'weak'. Less than one-third of the companies report engaging and collaborating with local stakeholders to
protect or restore watersheds and ecosystems near their operations.
Surprisingly, only five companies in the mining, and oil and gas sectors disclose engaging or consulting with stakeholders on the water
impacts of siting or expanding operations. This is despite the reputational risk identified by several companies.

Based upon the results of the benchmarking study, Ceres identifies several
recommendations which I believe capture the essence of where companies stand with regard to understanding water-related risks, and how to
mitigate these risks (along with identifying business opportunities):

- Water-risk information should be included in financial filings in order
to communicate to investors that company management understands
and is managing key water risks and opportunities.

- Companies need to develop more detailed risk assessment of water risk both for direct operations and within their supply chain.
- Aggregate water accounting data (water use and treatment) are insufficient for financial filings. In particular, detailed information should be provided for facilities within water-stressed regions.
- There should be disclosure of a water management strategy and supporting systems: essentially, details of the overall corporate water strategy to manage risks, and of the integrated key policies and governance systems in place from the board level to facility level.
- Water-reduction targets should be set (within a corporate water strategy) as a demonstration of the commitment and capacity to managing risk, and the ability to prepare for a more water-constrained future. Targets are more credible with respect to high-risk operations when supported by detailed management plans.
- Water risk in the supply chain must be quantified. Water use embedded in the supply chain accounts for the largest portion of water use for many companies and as a result this must be managed.
- Engagement of critical stakeholders is essential. There must be communication of information on how companies are engaging communities in which they operate, in order to preserve essential water resources, and to maintain a social licence to operate.
- If possible identify and capitalize on business opportunities emerging in a water-stressed world. Investors are increasingly interested in relevant product development and investment goals.

Ceres also recommends the following to investors:

- Engage the companies they own in key water-intensive sectors about how they are assessing and disclosing water risks and related performance information.
- Ask asset managers to evaluate and engage companies on water. Institutional investors should stipulate this to asset managers in requests for proposals, and in annual performance reviews, to ensure that the companies managing their money are giving water, climate and other sustainability risks the attention they deserve.
- Support investor and corporate initiatives to achieve increased water disclosure, including the CDP WP initiative and the United Nations Global Compact's CEO Water Mandate.

Closing Thoughts

Water risk to businesses is real. Companies across several industry sectors have started to take the lead in quantifying their exposure to water risk, and are implementing plans to mitigate these risks. Other companies have identified business opportunities in an emerging water-constrained world.

Those companies that ignore this risk face increasing constraints on their businesses with a resultant financial impact. In subsequent chapters we will explore in greater detail how to effectively manage the challenge of water scarcity and thrive in a water-constrained world.

References

Barton, B. (2010) 'Murky waters? Corporate reporting on water risk', www. ceres.org/Document.Doc?id=547, accessed 5 April 2010

Knight, Z. and Miller-Blakewell, R. (2007) 'Water scarcity: a bigger problem than assumed', Merrill Lynch Equity Strategy Report, 6 December 2007,www. ml.com/media/86941.pdf, accessed 13 September 2010

Morrison, J. and Gleick, P. (2004) 'Freshwater resources: managing the risks facing the private sector', Pacific Institute, www.pacinst.org/reports/business_ risks_of_water/business_risks_of_water.pdf, accessed 5 April 2010

Morrison, J., Morikawa, M., Murphy, M. and Schulte, P. (2009) 'Water scarcity & climate change: growing risks for businesses & investors', Ceres & Pacific Institute, www.pacinst.org/reports/business_water_climate/full_report.pdf, accessed 7 April 2010

The New York Times (2009) 'Clean water act violations: the enforcement record', www.nytimes.com/interactive/2009/09/13/us/0913-water. html?scp=1&sq=clean%20water%20act&st=cse, 13 September 2009, accessed 5 April 2010

Solomon, S., Quin, D., Manning, M., Chen, Z., Marquis, M., Averyt, K. B., Tignor, M. and Miller, H. L. (eds) (2007) *Contribution of Working Group I to the Fourth Assessment Report of the Intergovernmental Panel on Climate Change, 2007*, Cambridge University Press, Cambridge, United Kingdom and New York, NY

SustainAbility and GlobeScan (2010) 'Sustainability survey: pulse poll on water', http://surveys.globescan.com/TSS-water

2

Global Issue with Local Solutions

I cannot change my country ... but I can change my street.

Paulo Coelho

The science

It is important to spend some time discussing the basics of water to highlight why it differs from global environmental issues such as energy and carbon. A fundamental understanding of the science of water will inform solutions to water scarcity and water-quality degradation, and foster innovative technology development and policy changes. Moreover, water is not just an environmental issue, but has significant cultural and social features that are tied closely to its resource aspects.

Most importantly, although water is a global issue, the solutions are translated to the local level and to communities. For a global business this means translating a global water strategy into local actions which address community and stakeholder issues. While carbon is fungible and can be addressed globally equally, water is not fungible. Water issues are always local issues.

Further complicating the challenge of solving global water scarcity and quality problems is the nexus between water and carbon (and energy). Businesses must take into consideration that in water-scarce regions, the goal of reducing carbon emissions may actually be in conflict with reducing water use. As a result numerical reductions in water and carbon may work against each other.

Water is not created or destroyed and essentially operates in a closed loop system. Fundamentally this is why water is not like oil or carbon. A discussion of the hydrologic cycle will illustrate this never-ending system of global water movement, and show why local actions are important in influencing water quantity and quality.

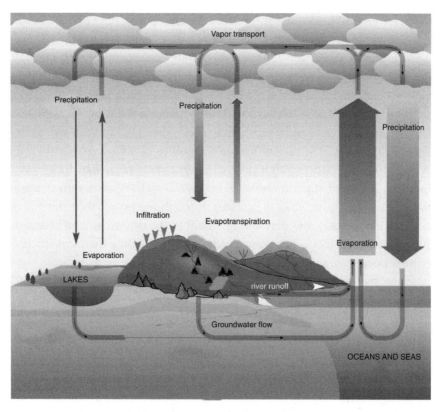

Note: The width of the arrows is approximately proportional to the volumes of transported water.

Figure 2.1 *The general hydrologic cycle*

Source: www.unep.org/dewa/vitalwater/jpg/0102-water-cycle-EN.jpg

As Figure 2.1 shows, the hydrologic cycle begins with the evaporation of water. Water is always in motion, fuelled by the hydrologic cycle. This cycle is driven by the energy of the sun and the force of gravity is its engine (IWR, 1997).

As water vapour rises it cools and condenses to form clouds. Clouds move, and ultimately release water in the form of precipitation. Precipitation, which reaches the ground, can either evaporate back into the atmosphere or may infiltrate the ground to become groundwater. Groundwater either seeps (discharges) into oceans, rivers and streams, or is released back into the atmosphere through plant transpiration. The balance of water that remains on the ground is runoff, which will run into lakes, rivers, streams and ultimately into the ocean.

Water that infiltrates the soil moves through pores, the open spaces in the soil, which can hold large amounts of water. If the pores are well connected (that is, if the soil is permeable) water can readily move through the soil (such as in sand or gravels); and if they are not, water moves slowly (such as in clay).

The water content of the soil will also influence the movement of water. In general, water infiltrates drier soils more quickly than wet soils. Rainfall intensity will also influence the ability of soils to absorb water. A high-intensity storm (high rainfall over a short period of time) may limit the ability of soils to absorb rainwater. If rain (or snowfall) reaches the soil surface faster than it can seep through the pores, then the water pools at the surface, and may run downhill to the nearest stream channel. As a result, high-intensity storms produce more flooding than less intense rainfall does over a longer period of time.

Water that does not infiltrate the soil and instead flows over the land surface is called runoff. Water always takes the path of least resistance, flowing from higher elevations to lower elevations, towards a river, lake or ocean. The concept of a watershed is important in understanding water scarcity and water-quality degradation. Topographic divides (the higher elevations) define watersheds. Understanding the boundaries and interconnection of watersheds is important, as these will control surface water and groundwater flow directions. The direction of surface and groundwater flow will in turn control the movement of contaminants (pollutants) within a watershed. As a result, it is critical to understand the factors that influence the rate and direction of surface water and groundwater flow.

Water that infiltrates soils will migrate downwards until it reaches a depth where all of the pore spaces are filled with water. Simply put, this point of 100 per cent saturation is called the water table (there is a capillary fringe which extends above the water table which is also 100 per cent saturated, but the water is held in place by capillary pressure). The area above the water table is referred to as the unsaturated zone and the area below the water table is the saturated zone.

Although in general the water table mimics the topography of the land, it is not always at the same depth below the land surface. During periods of high precipitation, the water table can rise, and during periods of low precipitation and high evapotranspiration, the water table falls and is found deeper below the surface.

Groundwater in saturated zones is referred to as an aquifer. In aquifers, groundwater flows through the pores of the soil or rock both laterally and vertically. Aquifers can yield significant amounts of water and are either unconfined or confined. The top of an unconfined aquifer is defined by the water table. Confined aquifers are bound on the top by impermeable material, such as clay or shale. Water in a confined aquifer is typically under pressure and can cause the water level in a well to rise above the water table or land surface. If the water rises above the land surface it is referred to as a flowing artesian well. A perched water table occurs when water is held up by a low permeability material (such as a clay) and is separated from a second water table below by an unsaturated zone.

Surface water and groundwater are closely connected. Water moving from an aquifer and entering a stream or lake is called groundwater discharge, and any water entering an aquifer is called recharge. An aquifer can receive recharge from an overlying aquifer, or more commonly from precipitation followed by infiltration. The recharge zone is defined as the area, either at the surface or below the ground, which provides water to an aquifer, and may encompass most of the watershed.

The Concept of Peak Water

Building on our understanding of the hydrologic cycle we will explore the concept of peak water; this helps to explain why water scarcity is ultimately a local issue, and why the era of cheap accessible water is over (or nearly over).

We need to start with the concept of 'peak oil' to frame the concept of peak water. Peak oil is defined as the point in time when the maximum rate of global oil production is reached and the rate of production starts a terminal decline. The concept is based upon the measured production rates of individual oil production wells, aggregated to an entire oil field, and then globally.

The concept of peak oil was developed by M. King Hubbert who was at the time with Shell Oil Company. In 1956 Hubbert used modelling to accurately predict that US oil production would peak between 1965 and 1970. His model (www.hubbertpeak.com/hubbert/1956/1956.pdf) is referred to as the 'Hubbert peak theory' and related models have been used to predict the decline of oil production in other regions of the world.

According to the Hubbert model, the production rate of a *limited resource* will follow a roughly symmetrical logistical distribution curve (sometimes incorrectly compared to a bell-shaped curve) based upon the exploitability of the limited resource and market pressures.

In general, the peak water-concept can illustrate how water demand versus supply can create a water scarcity problem. While water is not created or destroyed on a global scale, local (watershed) constraints can create water shortages and behave like Hubbert's curve. Although oil is a non-renewable resource and water is renewable on a global scale, the production of water on a local (watershed) scale can behave as if it is non-renewable. Therefore, *practically, water can be limited* on a local (watershed) scale, and water stewardship strategies must acknowledge this constraint.

Peak water is helpful in visualizing peak production of fossil ground-water (where withdrawal of water exceeds natural recharge), peak eco-logical water (when ecological disruptions exceed the benefits of new supply projects), potential water production in a watershed, the overall value of water and the increasing human appropriation of water.

An excellent discussion of the concept of peak water is provided by Palaniappan and Gleick (2009). Peak water also helps to frame a 'soft path' approach for water stewardship, one in which conservation and efficiency are used to manage water demand against supply (Brooks, Brandes et al, 2009).

A few comments about the characteristics of water explain how water can behave as a *non-renewable resource on a watershed level*:

- Water demonstrates both renewable and non-renewable characteris-tics, which has implications for applying the concept of peak water. Water is a renewable resource with rapid flows, and the production of water has no effect on recharge rates. However, there are also fixed or isolated supplies of water that can be consumed at rates faster than natural recharge rates (low recharge rates). Non-renewable resources such as oil are stock limited (the volume of oil is consumed faster than it can be replenished), and renewable resources such as water are flow (or rate) limited.
- The consumptive and non-consumptive use of water is an important aspect of the concept of peak water. Consumptive use of water refers to use of water that makes it unavailable for short or intermediate reuse within a watershed (it is important to remember that water is not really consumed, but just recycled, in some cases treated and discharged or used in consumer products). Non-consumptive uses of water include

cooling in industrial and energy production, and water used in washing, flushing or other residential uses, where it can ultimately be collected, treated and reused.

- Water-quality degradation can limit water availability on a local scale, with the result that water behaves as a non-renewable resource. Contaminants introduced into a watershed can limit the availability of water even when contaminated water is treated prior to use.
- Water is not fungible. We can't actually run out of water, and water scarcity really reflects the 'uneven' distribution of water globally. Water cannot be transported globally or regionally to address local (watershed) scarcity. 'There is no fungible stock of water and regional constraints become a legitimate and serious concern' (Palaniappan and Gleick, 2009). When extraction exceeds natural recharge rates the only long-term options are to reduce demand to sustainable levels, move the demand to an area where water is available or shift to increasingly expensive technologies, such as desalination.
- There is no global peak water. Peak water as a concept is only valid on a local (watershed) level when water can behave as a non-renewable resource. Globally, water is a renewable resource but locally it may not be. As such, water stewardship/corporate water strategies must recognize this difference and examine how the concept of peak water can be applied to the local/watershed level.

Palaniappan and Gleick introduce two peak water concepts which have value in understanding how to build a path towards water stewardship; *fossil groundwater* and *peak ecological water*. We will examine both and then look at the scenarios of global water supply and demand.

The easiest peak water concept to understand is the issue of fossil groundwater, where groundwater extraction exceeds natural recharge. Groundwater is essentially mined.

Typically, recharge to groundwater aquifers in watersheds is considered renewable. In this case recharge is equal to or greater than groundwater withdrawal. However, in some watersheds extraction greatly exceeds natural recharge. Here, groundwater has accumulated over thousands of years due to very low precipitation and recharge rates, and is considered to be old or fossil.

These fossil groundwater resources are effectively non-renewable and will behave as a peak water curve. An illustration of the peak water curve for fossil groundwater is provided in Figure 2.2, overleaf.

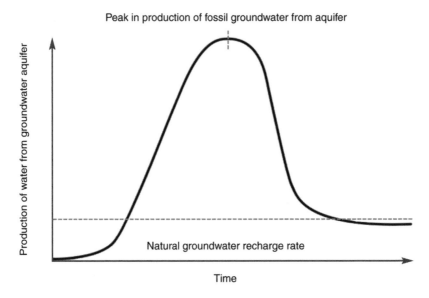

Figure 2.2 *Potential peak water curve for fossil groundwater production*

Source: adapted from Palaniappan and Gleick, (2009)

The dashed line in Figure 2.2 represents the natural groundwater recharge rate. As withdrawals exceed the natural recharge rate the production will continue to increase, but the groundwater is essentially 'mined' from the aquifer. As groundwater continues to be mined the typical solution is to drill deeper groundwater extraction wells as the water table drops deeper below the land surface and/or to increase the number of wells. Neither of these approaches is sustainable and they represent a short-term solution.

Groundwater withdrawal will decline over time until the point when continued extraction is neither economically nor technically feasible (the cost of pumping from great depths is too costly, groundwater becomes too mineralized or too low due to decreased permeability). In some cases extraction could come in line with natural recharge rates but this is rare, as groundwater aquifers are not managed to balance recharge with extraction.

The other peak water concept is peak ecological water. In some locations this is more of a pressing watershed management issue. The reason is that, in a watershed, water is not only used for human water supply, but also has a critical role to play in the ecology of the watershed. Excessive extraction can result in serious and irreversible ecological damage to the biota and habitats.

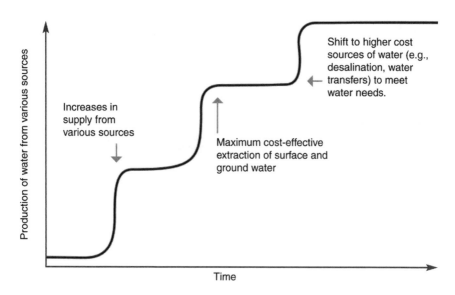

Figure 2.3 *Potential water production in a watershed*

Source: adapted from Palaniappan and Gleick (2009)

The illustration in Figure 2.3 depicts the potential water extraction in a watershed where there is adequate recharge to support groundwater withdrawal. The vertical axis represents increasing water production and the horizontal axis represents time.

As demand for water increases, additional technologies such as dams and reservoirs are built. Once the cost-effective limit of these water sources has been reached, there is a shift to more costly technologies such as desalination, to increase water supply. With every new project to supply water for human consumption comes a decrease in water available for the ecosystem. This decrease in availability results in increased degradation, with an associated impact and cost.

The impact to the ecosystem due to increasing water demands cannot be overstated. Since 1900, approximately 50 per cent of the world's wetlands have disappeared. Since 1970, the number of freshwater species has decreased by 50 per cent, which is more rapid than the decline of species on land or in the sea (Palaniappan and Gleick, 2009).

As Figure 2.4 shows, we can take this concept further and look at the value provided by water versus increasing water withdrawal. The horizontal axis represents the amount of water withdrawn and the vertical axis represents the value of water.

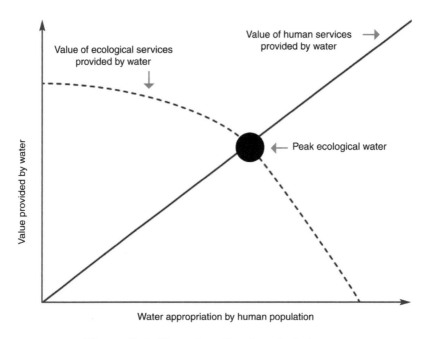

Figure 2.4 *Illustration of peak ecological water*

Source: adapted from Palaniappan and Gleick (2009)

The vertical axis is the 'value provided by water'. Increased water withdrawals by humans result in decreased water available to the ecosystem, and in turn a decrease in the value of water to the ecosystem. At some point (identified by the black circle on the graph) the value of ecological services provided by the water is equal to the value of the human services (drinking water) provided by the water. This point of intersection is considered peak ecological water.

Theoretically, at peak ecological water, society will maximize the ecological and human benefits provided by water. As with any analysis of a finite resource the value increases and then decreases as human appropriation of that resource continues (Figure 2.5).

While these concepts help to explain how competing water demands factor into water use within a watershed, we must be mindful that adjustments in how water is used are constantly shifting. As a result, the point of peak ecological water is subjective, and based on different evaluations of the value of each unit of water in ecosystems, and for humans.

Water is local and the era of cheap water is over; these are the major lessons to be extracted from the concept of peak water. Demands for water

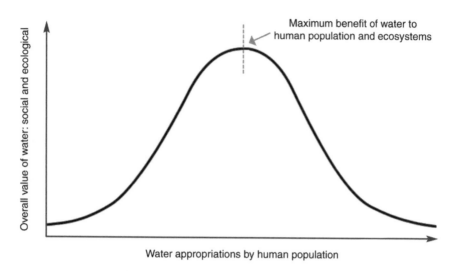

Figure 2.5 *Overall value of water with increasing human appropriation*

Source: adapted from Palaniappan and Gleick (2009)

will continue to increase both from the public and private sectors, which will require creative solutions to water stewardship, at both global and watershed levels.

The end of cheap water means that efforts to find more water will increase, we will look for ways to use water more efficiently, and we will ultimately spend more on water. In fact we are creeping towards a point where the price of water will reflect its real value (more on this topic in subsequent chapters of this book). Most importantly, cheap and readily accessible water can no longer be taken for granted. In most parts of the world, water is not taken for granted and the real shift in valuing water will be in the developed counties.

The Scenarios

Now that we have an understanding of the hydrologic cycle and appreciate that water scarcity is really a local issue, we will examine the projections for water supply versus demand. We will also provide a very brief look at water demands by industry sectors with a more in-depth discussion provided in Chapters 9 to 13.

The investor community is one of the critical stakeholders in recognizing that water is a critical business issue. Two recent reports (J. P. Morgan, 2008; 2030 Water Resources Group, 2009) provide insights on water-scarcity scenarios and potential impacts to the public and private sectors. The 2030 Water Resources Group was formed in 2008 to tackle the issue of advancing 'solutions-driven' programmes to reduce water scarcity. The Group participants consisted of the International Finance Corporation (IFC), McKinsey & Company and an extended business consortium of companies including The Barilla Group, The Coca-Cola Company, Nestlé SA, SABMiller plc, New Holland Agriculture, Standard Chartered Bank and Syngenta AG.

The J. P. Morgan study identified the risks of current and projected water scarcity to businesses and investors. A brief summary is provided below to provide a glimpse of how the investor community views water scarcity and potential impacts:

- Water is increasingly scarce due to population growth, urbanization and the impacts of climate change. Declining water quality further reduces water availability with impacts felt at a local (watershed) level.
- Wall Street is aware of the investment opportunities in traditional water investments such as water-supply infrastructure, wastewater treatment and water demand management. However, there has been less focus on industry sectors and companies that rely on clean water as part of their supply chain and production processes.
- Water-scarcity risks vary between industry sectors and geographic locations due to climatic conditions, water resources and water-use practices. As one might expect, areas such as Northern California in the United States may experience significant water-scarcity pressure due to a reduction in the Sierra Nevada mountain snowpack. In China, where steel production uses more water per unit of production than in the United States or Japan, there will be additional pressure on operations due to inefficiencies.
- The financial impact of water scarcity on specific industry sectors and companies is unknown, as information regarding water use is incomplete. J. P. Morgan believes this will change for the following reasons:
  - Consequences of water-supply shortfalls will lead to increased intervention by the public sector as evidenced by water-use restrictions in the United States (Atlanta, Georgia) and in Australia

(Sydney and Melbourne areas) and resultant changes in the cost structure of water (for example, tiered pricing in Australia).

- Increased potential for business disruption due to water scarcity will result in an increased development of business contingency plans by industries.
- Increased attention to real and perceived behaviour by companies with respect to water use and water discharge, as water becomes more valuable will result in greater sensitivity to how companies are perceived in the marketplace and by consumers.
- Increased disclosure of water-related risks to investors (Barton, 2010) and associated costs from potential changes in water treatment, regulations and potential supply-chain disruptions.

According to J. P. Morgan, the principal factors resulting in 'imbalance' between water supply and demand are:

- Population growth. The current global population is about 6.4 billion and increasing at about 70 million per year with most of the growth in emerging economies. The global population is expected to reach 8.1 billion by 2030 and 8.9 billion by 2050. While growth in countries within the Organisation for Economic Co-operation and Development (OECD) is expected to remain relatively flat, the population of the United States is expected to increase to 370 million by 2030. In general, as population increases so does water withdrawal.
- Urbanization. Greater than half of the global population now lives in cities, and increasing urbanization results in increased industrialization and increased water use.
- Climate change. As previously discussed, climate change will alter hydrologic cycles on both regional and local levels. The long-term and short-term availability of freshwater will be altered, along with changes in water quality (water temperature, dissolved constituents, etc.).

Observations by J. P. Morgan on scenarios for water supply and demand indicate 'worsening trends' and increasing threat to industry sectors and the public. Of particular note is the impact of water scarcity at the local (watershed level). Their conclusions are summarized below:

- Data suggest that as water supply becomes less reliable, certain regions experience worsening trends in water quality. In general, water quality is not declining in developed countries, but there is deterioration in developing countries. In particular fast-paced urbanization, where growth outpaces infrastructure support, leads to increased stress on water quality through releases of untreated sewage and wastes.

- Water-quality issues interact with availability concerns. Water supply and quality are closely connected. Examples include how excessive groundwater pumping can result in saltwater intrusion where salt water is drawn into freshwater aquifers along coastal areas, and where releases of contaminants into groundwater limit the amount of clean groundwater available for potable use.

- Water-quality data are location-specific. Water-quality data such as biological oxygen demand and nitrogen loading reflect the unique aspects of a watershed.

- Businesses face three varieties of water-related risks: physical, regulatory and reputational. Physical risk mostly impacts industry sectors in which water is consumed or evaporated in the production process. A lack of water of adequate quality directly reduces production in the agriculture, beverages and food processing sectors. Regulatory risk is most critical for industry sectors that use or discharge relatively large amounts of water in connection with relatively low-value production processes (such as the energy sector). Finally, reputational risk is tied to increased competition from economic, social and environmental interests. This risk has a significant potential to damage a company's reputation and limit its licence to operate (such as in the food and beverage sectors). Multinational companies operating in developing countries are especially vulnerable to reputation risk from water.

- The three types of risks listed above are closely related and manifest themselves in combination. For example, water scarcity (physical) may lead to the revocation of water licences (regulatory), or to damage to a firm's image and brand (reputation). Physical, regulatory and reputational risks may impact at different points along the value chain and may affect suppliers, production facilities, or users of the product.

- Companies may have significant exposure to water scarcity and water quality even in countries where they do not have production operations. Backward linkages (supply chain) and forward linkages (product use) may create water risks that go unnoticed by management and investors.

- Many industry sectors have a larger water footprint in their supply chain than in their direct production. An excellent example is the food

and beverage sector, which relies upon irrigated agriculture for critical inputs. As a result, water scarcity in key production areas could lead to higher prices for grain, meat and other inputs. Also, aluminium manufacturers in the US North-west experienced the supply-chain impact in 2001, when water shortages led to the curtailment of hydroelectric power supplies, forcing the closure of several aluminium plants.
• Forward linkages can be just as problematic. Consumer products such as washing machines cannot be run without water, and a scarcity of this will impact their use.

Water risk will impact the financial performance of companies in several ways. Financial performance can be impacted through:

• the disruption of production or the supply chain;
• higher costs in the supply chain (especially in the agricultural sector);
• changes in production methods (from improved water efficiency, capital expenditures to change production processes (to improve water efficiency) and to secure, recycle or treat water;
• increased regulatory compliance and increased costs to procure and discharge water; in addition there are impacts to limits of growth and costs to reputation and brand (intangible value).

While the J. P. Morgan report identified general water-related risks to businesses and investors, the 2030 Water Resources Group (2009) took the analysis a major step further, developing a more quantitative analysis of water-scarcity scenarios. The 2030 Group consists of stakeholders who are concerned about water scarcity 'as an increasing business risk, a major economic threat that cannot be ignored, and a global priority that affects human wellbeing'.
    The Group concluded that:

> there is little indication that, left to its own devices, the water sector will come to a sustainable, cost-effective solution to meet the growing water requirements implied by economic and population growth.

This is not an encouraging prognosis for the future, considering the increasing demand for water by both the public and private sectors.
    There are several challenges to understanding the scope of the water-scarcity problem and viable solutions, and a surprising lack of

transparency on fundamental questions. This is not intentional; rather nobody has focused on scarcity in an age of abundant resources. These issues include:

- What will the total demand for water be in coming decades?
- How much supply will be available to meet demand?
- What technical options are available or need to be developed to close the gap between supply and demand?

Just as important are related questions such as:

- Which incentives need to be in place to close this gap?
- What investments need to be made?

The 2030 Group makes the key points that in 'the world of water resources':

- Economic data are insufficient.
- Management is often opaque.
- Stakeholders are insufficiently linked.

The 2030 Group lays out plausible scenarios for water supply, water demand and the 'water gap' on a regional (local) scale. This gap will play a critical role in how businesses address the risk and opportunities. The Group concludes that by 2030, assuming an average growth scenario, and if no efficiency gains are realized, global water requirements will grow from 4500 billion m^3 to 6900 billion m^3. As illustrated in Figure 2.6, this is about 40 per cent above current accessible and reliable supplies.

This 40 per cent gap is really an aggregation of numerous watershed and region-specific shortfalls. For example, about a third of the global population lives in watersheds where this gap will be greater than 50 per cent.

The gap is driven by global economic growth and development. Agriculture makes up the majority of this global water demand, with current use at 3100 billion m^3 or about 71 per cent of total demand. This is expected to increase to 4500 billion m^3 by 2030, which is a slight decline to about 65 per cent of total water demand. Industrial demand is currently 16 per cent with a projected increase to 22 per cent by 2030. Domestic water demand will decrease slightly from 14 per cent to 12 per cent by 2030.

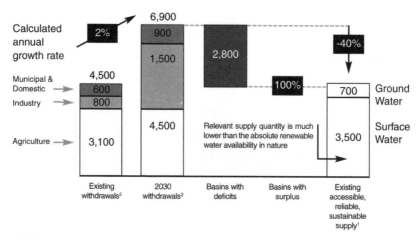

1 Existing supply which can be provided at 90% reliability, based on historical hydrology and infrastructure investments scheduled through 2010; net of environmental requirements.

2 Based on 2010 agricultural production analyses from International Food Policy Research Institute (IFPRI); considers no water productivity gains between 2005-2030.

3 Based on GDP, population projections and agricultural production projections from IFPPI impact-water base case.

Figure 2.6 *Global gap between existing accessible, reliable supply and 2030 water withdrawals (assuming no efficiency gains)*

Source: adapted from 2030 Water Resources Group (2009)

The critical question posed by the 2030 Group is: how will this gap be closed? An examination of the projected gap ('business as usual') and estimated increases in supply and water efficiency is illustrated in Figure 2.7. For example, if we look at historical improvements in water efficiency in agriculture we see only about 1 per cent improvement between 1990 and 2004. A similar rate of improvement was observed in the industrial sector. If these rates of efficiency improvements are projected to 2030, we would only meet about 20 per cent of the 40 per cent gap. If we assume a 20 per cent increase in supply, then 60 per cent of demand would still be unmet.

The assumptions in the projected water-supply increases and water-efficiency improvements should not be assumed. The study did not factor in the impacts of climatic change on individual regions and watersheds where scarcity could become acute. One of the key assumptions is that water demand is based on historical climatic conditions and not projected changes in the climate. Remember that water scarcity is a local issue, and that we can expect great variability in water supply and demand.

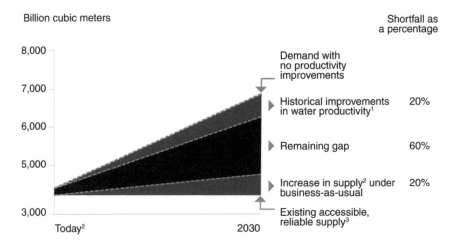

Figure 2.7 *Projected water gap between raw water supply and demand*

Source: adapted from 2030 Water Resources Group (2009)

The economic implications of closing the gap between supply and demand through increased supply or efficiency efforts are significant. A comparison of the economics of supply technologies (desalination and typical groundwater development) and efficiency measures (agricultural and industrial programmes) illustrates the cost-effectiveness of efficiency over supply increases (Figure 2.8). This is not unlike the situation in the energy sector, where energy efficiency is the low-cost approach to alignment of energy supply with demand. Water-efficiency measures can result in a net increase in water availability, and *even net cost savings*, when operating savings of the measure outweigh annualized capital costs (illustrated negative costs).

So what this means is that closing the gap by increasing supply will have a significant economic cost. In some areas of the world this increase in supply will be about US$0.50 versus current costs, which are less than US$0.10/m³, with the highest cost of about 40.50/m³. This comes out to about US$200 billion above current spending, or about four times current spending levels.

Cost of measure (dollars per cubic meter)

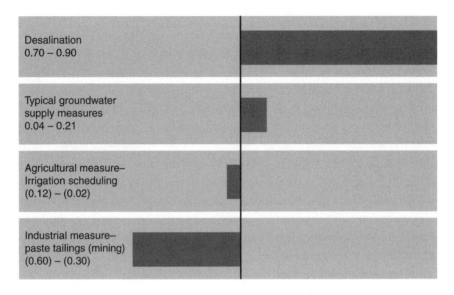

Figure 2.8 *Representative demand- and supply-side measures*

Source: adapted from 2030 Water Resources Group (2009)

Again, the magnitude of the water gap and the economics of how this gap will be closed vary by region, and perhaps even by the watershed. To better understand the variability of water supply versus demand, and the economics of closing this gap, the 2030 Group examined India, China, São Paulo State and South Africa in detail. These areas were selected in part because they represent about 30 per cent of the global GDP, and about 42 per cent of the projected water demand, and they highlight key aspects of water scarcity:

- water competition from multiple users within a watershed;
- agricultural demands for food, feed, fibre and biofuels;
- the energy–water nexus;
- the role of urbanization in water-resource management;
- sustainable growth in arid and semi-arid regions.

The 2030 Group developed a series of *water-marginal cost curves* as part of this study. These are similar to the marginal greenhouse gas cost-abatement curves developed by McKinsey (Enkvist, Nauclér et al, 2007), which are extremely helpful in understanding the cost implications of applying a range of technology solutions to close the gap between supply and demand.

An example of a water-marginal cost curve for India is provided in Figure 2.9, to highlight how to interpret these curves, and to illustrate their value in understanding potential solutions to water scarcity. The water-marginal cost curve compares the technical options to close the water gap with the additional water available. Each of the technical alternatives is represented as a block on the curve. The width of the block represents the amount of additional water that becomes available by adopting the technology, and the height of the block represents its unit cost. A negative unit cost means the payback exceeds the capital cost (as previously mentioned, water-efficiency technologies can result in a net increase in water availability, and *even net cost savings,* when operating savings of the measure outweigh annualized capital costs (a negative unit cost).

The 2030 Group focused on the technical solutions (increasing supply and improving water productivity) in India, São Paulo, China and South Africa, while recognizing that a country could actively reduce withdrawals by changing the economic factors. The opinion of the 2030 Group, which I share, is that a sustainable and cost-effective mix of these solutions would result in a well-managed water industry in these countries. Their analysis indicates that for these regions the solutions would require about

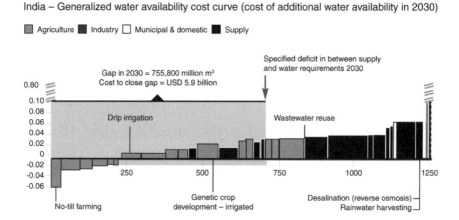

India – Generalized water availability cost curve (cost of additional water availability in 2030)

Figure 2.9 *Water availability cost curve for India*

Source: adapted from 2030 Water Resources Group (2009)

US$19 billion in annual investment until 2030. If these regional analyses are applied globally, the investment to close the gap would need to be about US$50–60 billion, about 75 per cent less than a supply-only solution to close the gap. The bottom line is that water efficiency is critical to closing the gap in a cost-effective manner. Increases in water supply alone will not be enough.

The following conclusions developed by the 2030 Group can be applied to any country, region or perhaps even watershed:

- Agricultural productivity is a fundamental part of the solution to close the water gap. It is critical to focus on this, since the agricultural sector contributes the greatest to global water use, and water efficiency is one of the key low-cost technology solutions. Increasing the 'crop per drop' can be accomplished through an integrated approach of increased drip and sprinkler irrigation, no-till farming, improved drainage, drought-resistant seeds, optimizing fertilizer use, crop stress management, improved best practices (integrated pest management) and innovative crop protection technologies. For example, the 2030 Group analysis of India indicates that low-cost technologies applied in the agricultural sector can close about 80 per cent of the water gap.
- Industrial and municipal productivity is just as critical as agricultural productivity improvements. China provides an excellent example of how efficiency projects in these sectors can provide a positive contribution to closing the water gap. Although agriculture represents about 50 per cent of water use in China, industry represents the fastest-growing sector. Water-efficiency programmes, in particular those incorporating new construction, could close the water gap in China by about 25 per cent, with savings of about US$24 billion.
- Water quality and quantity are linked. The 2030 Group evaluation of São Paulo provides an example of how water quality and water quantity issues and solutions are related (there really is no separation). The recommended approach to closing the water gap in São Paulo is in water efficiency and productivity gains. Water-quality improvements are also a critical aspect of overall water-management issues. Financial benefits to the industrial sector can be obtained from reduced water use, and municipalities can save 300 million m^3 of water through utility leakage reduction. Wastewater reuse for grey water purposes (such as industrial processes and public works uses) can save about 80 million m^3 in 'new water' requirements.

- Most solutions require cross-sector trade-offs. South Africa provides an excellent example of a balanced approach to water stewardship. Cost-effective measures are applied in water supply (water-supply increases can close the water gap by about 50 per cent), agricultural efficiency, productivity improvements (about 30 per cent of the gap), and industrial and domestic solutions (the remaining 20 per cent of the gap). As one would expect, the watersheds dominated by agricultural use rely on agricultural improvements, and industrialized watersheds (Cape Town and Johannesburg) rely on industrial and domestic solutions.

The cost curve used by the 2030 Group is a valuable tool to assist in understanding which technology solutions can close the water gap in the most cost-effective manner within a watershed or region. However, it is clear that technology solutions alone are not enough, and factors such as the ease of technology adoption, policy scenarios and a payback curve need to be considered. Technology solutions need to factor in local conditions and circumstances in order to be successful, and the 2030 Group has refined its thinking and recommendations to take this into account.

First, technology solutions can be classified according to the factors influencing their ease of implementation. Technical solutions may appear feasible, but may encounter barriers such as institutional capacity, policy and cultural barriers, and stakeholder support. An example of how technology implementation challenges can be managed is provided in Figure 2.10.

The value of classifying technologies in this manner is to highlight trade-offs and develop a better understanding of the barriers to technology implementation. This is the first step in moving ahead in closing the water gap.

Scenario planning is another essential tool in understanding the impact of technology decisions on water demand. For example, a question such as 'how would a doubling of ethanol demand impact water use, and what would that do to the water gap?' can be answered.

Finally, the use of a payback curve can be used to quantify the economics of adopting various technologies and solutions (Figure 2.11). With a payback curve, the width of the box represents the amount of water addressed by the technology solution, and is essentially a variation of the cost curve previously described. The payback curve is how long it will take for an investment to have a positive economic benefit.

The quantified analysis using the payback curve, coupled with transparent communication with stakeholders, can help to distinguish between

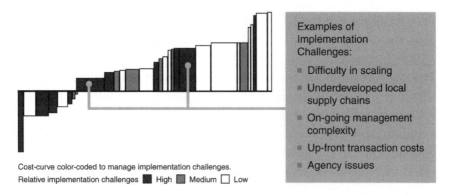

Figure 2.10 *An illustration of managing implementation challenges with the cost curve*

Source: adapted from 2030 Water Resources Group (2009)

technology solutions that can stand on their own and those that may need incentives to promote adoption. The 2030 Group identified payback periods of three years or less (to close about 75 per cent of the water gap in China) to over five years (for about 86 per cent of the technology measures considered for São Paulo).

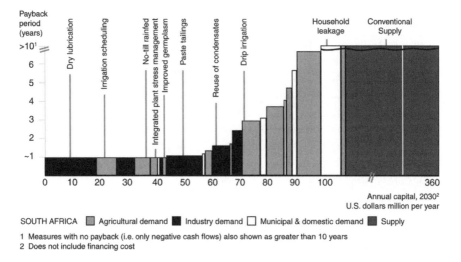

Figure 2.11 *Illustration of end user payback curve*

Source: adapted from 2030 Water Resources Group (2009)

In conclusion, we are fortunate that the science of water is well understood. This, conceptually, will make the solutions to water scarcity relatively straightforward. The challenge is that while water scarcity is a global crisis, the solutions will be local. This means that technology solutions, economics, politics and cultural issues will strongly influence how we address water scarcity and risk.

No one solution will 'fit all'. Instead, global companies will strive to translate a global commitment to water stewardship to the country, region and watershed in which they operate. This will be no small challenge. However, great opportunities to engage with a variety of stakeholders and to connect with communities in a unique way will accompany it. This connection to the watershed and community may well mitigate water risk, and strengthen a company's brand and reputation.

References

2030 Water Resources Group (2009) 'Charting our water future: economic frameworks to inform decision-making', www.mckinsey.com/App_Media/Reports/Water/Charting_Our_Water_Future_Full_Report_001.pdf, accessed 4 October 2010

Barton, B. (2010) 'Murky waters? Corporate reporting on water risk', www.ceres.org/Document.Doc?id=547, accessed 5 April 2010

Brooks, D. B., Brandes, O. M. and Gurman, S. (eds) (2009) *Making the Most of the Water We Have – The Soft Path Approach to Water Management*, Earthscan, London

Enkvist, P.-A., Nauclér, T. and Rosander, J. (2007) 'A cost curve for greenhouse gas reduction', *McKinsey Quarterly*, www.epa.gov/oar/caaac/coaltech/2007_05_mckinsey.pdf, accessed 13 September 2010

IWR (Institute of Water Research) (1997) 'The hydrologic cycle', www.iwr.msu.edu/edmodule/water/cycle.htm, accessed 13 September 2010

J. P. Morgan (2008) 'Watching water: a guide to evaluating corporate risks in a thirsty world', www.soil.ncsu.edu/lockers/Hoover_M/html/wrkshop/Materials_for_on_web/Other_files/Shankar_Artemis_files/JP_Morgan_water_corporate_risks.PDF, accessed 30 June 2010

Palaniappan, M. and Gleick, P. H. (2009) 'Peak water', in P. H. Gleick, H. Cooley, M. J. Cohen, M. Morikawa, J. Morrison and M. Palaniappan (eds) *The World's Water 2008–2009: The Biennial Report on Freshwater Resources*, Island Press, Washington, DC

3

The Disconnect Between Pricing and Value

A cynic is a man who knows the price of everything but the value of nothing.

Oscar Wilde

When thinking about the price of water compared with its value, I am reminded of the 'Tragedy of the commons' by Garrett Hardin (1968). The article tells a story in which multiple individuals, acting independently – and entirely rationally – in their own self-interest, ultimately deplete a shared limited resource, even when it is clear that it is not in anyone's long-term interest for this to occur.

Hardin crafts a hypothetical story set in mediaeval Europe, in which herders share a common parcel of land (the commons) to graze their livestock. All the herders, acting in their own self-interest, continually add livestock to the land and ultimately exceed its carrying capacity. Each individual herder receives all of the benefits from an additional cow, while the entire commons is damaged, impacting everyone. While individually this is a rational economic decision, it is a death sentence for the commons.

The message from Hardin is simple: a vital resource can be depleted out of the actions of self-interested individuals who have access to a shared resource. He also argued that humans have an inherently destructive relationship with the environment and as a result commonly over-exploit natural (common) resources, and felt that we need to recognize that natural resources are 'the commons' and they require management. Hardin could have just as easily used water as an example of a shared resource, instead of the commons.

Lux Research (2008) makes the case that water is a resource available to everyone but owned by no one. They correctly point out that water is not priced according to value because of 'ownership by no one in particular' coupled with 'availability to everyone'. This creates an 'economic disincentive for stewardship'.

This is the 'disconnect between the pricing and value' of water. Although the topic of water pricing is too large to cover in one chapter, I will touch on the main issues and the relevance of water pricing and value for businesses.

The Problem – Water Pricing

What is wrong when the price of water in arid Phoenix, Arizona, is lower than in Boston, Massachusetts (Walton, 2010)? Phoenix gets about 8 inches of rain a year and Boston over 42 inches of rain per year. A family of four in Phoenix using 150 gallons per person per day pays an average of US$59.84 a month. In contrast the bill would be US$99.72 in Boston. For perspective, the average price for cable TV in the United States (in 2008) was US$60.00 per month (Richtel, 2008).

The discrepancy between the value of water and pricing of water is not new – one need look no further than Adam Smith. In a passage in *An Inquiry into the Nature and Causes of the Wealth of Nations: A Selected Edition* (Smith, 1776, Book I, Chapter 4) he describes the paradox of value between water and diamonds:

> *The word Value, it is to be observed, has two different meanings, and sometimes expresses the utility of some particular object, and sometimes the power of purchasing other goods which the possession of that object conveys. The one may be called 'value in use'; the other, 'value in exchange'. The things which have the greatest value in use have frequently little or no value in exchange; and, on the contrary, those which have the greatest value in exchange have frequently little or no value in use. Nothing is more useful than water; but it will purchase scarce anything; scarce anything can be had in exchange for it. A diamond, on the contrary, has scarce any value in use; but a very great quantity of other goods may frequently be had in exchange for it.*

To bring the discussion into the present, the European Union (EU) has tackled the issue of water pricing and value. The EU Water Framework

Directive states that water is not 'a commercial product like any other but, rather, a heritage which must be protected, defended and treated as such' (OECD, 2009). The EU Policy Directive goes on to state that water policy must focus on the allocation of water resources among competing users and its protection against excessive deterioration. As a result this has led to the concept of an integrated approach to water resources management that acknowledges the need to coordinate and allocate water among competing users. Inherent in this approach is the recognition of the natural capital of water and related ecosystems, wetlands and marshes.

The implementation of water policy and the allocation requires capital. Water management capital consists of generally three components:

- Financial or supply costs. These are directly associated with supplying water and sanitation services to users, and consist of operation and maintenance costs, and capital costs for infrastructure.
- Economic costs. These comprise supply costs, and the opportunity costs which reflect the scarcity value of the resource, the costs of depriving a potential user and the economic externalities. The economic externalities consist of two elements: positive externalities, such as the groundwater recharge benefits from irrigation or water reuse; and negative externalities, such as the upstream diversion of water or the release of pollutants downstream within an irrigation system.
- Full costs. These are the sum of the supply and economic costs, plus externalities such as costs to public health and ecosystems (for example the costs from the contamination of water from agricultural runoff).

There is then the question of who pays these costs? It comes down to very few options – taxes, tariffs and transfer of funds from international donors or from private charities. Water investment projects are potentially viewed as suffering from high risk and low financial returns, coupled with the political context and controversy which typically accompanies them (for example, the Chinese south-to-north water transportation project (EcoSeed, 2010).

In 2008, *The Economist* opened a debate on water and pricing, which to a large degree captures the spectrum of issues on valuing water and pricing (Environmental Economics, 2008). The debate was opened with two opposing views from Stephen J. Hoffmann (Managing Director of

WaterTech Capital, and co-founder of Palisades Water Index Associates) and Dr Vandana Shiva (Director of Research Foundation for Science, Technology and Natural Resource Policy). Mr Hoffmann argued that water needs to be priced according to actual value to address the 'severe spatial and temporal imbalances in the supply of and demand for water' in order to resolve global water challenges. Further, he stated that the connection between sustainability and water will permeate 'virtually' every aspect of water-resource management in the 21st century – sustainability will influence regulations, water policy initiatives and technologies. Despite the critical nature of water, its price remains artificially low (an artefact of the time when supply exceeded demand, and when contamination did not have as large an impact).

Hoffman rightfully pointed out that that the starting point for sustainability is efficiency. A market-driven price is the way to increase water efficiency. Economics will be a major factor in ensuring that resources are allocated in a manner to leave future generations no worse off than ourselves. According to Hoffmann, the 'pricing of water must go beyond the mechanical and political aspects to the basic factors that affect the relationships between producers and consumers, and that are implicit in the rate structure'. Efficiency cannot be achieved without the proper signals included in market prices. Resource economics requires the convergence of two key principles: equimarginal value in use, and marginal cost pricing. For example, additional water can be made available by expending additional resources to deliver the water at a given marginal cost.

Hoffman argued that additional water should be made available to customers as long as they can pay the incremental or marginal costs incurred. Moreover, the price should be made equal for all customers in a given class (categories of users). Between classes, the price of water should differ, and the difference is the marginal cost in providing water to the different classes.

To paraphrase Hoffman:

1   Water rates should be designed to fully recover the costs of providing water, by charging customers in accordance with how they contribute to the costs. Water rates that charge customers in accordance with the cost of service would be efficient from the economic point of view – the price of a unit of water would be equal to the cost of the resources used to obtain and deliver that water. Pricing would be equitable, in that no customer would be required to subsidize any other customer.

2   Scarcity, spatial and temporal characteristics of water must be reflected in a pricing mechanism, as water is like any other economic good for which there is supply and demand.
3   Market pricing is essential to allow for the efficient allocation of water. This recognizes that market prices convey information regarding incentives, efficiency and allocation considerations.
4   The pricing of water based on its actual market value is also critical in resolving issues associated with its allocation among competing beneficial uses. The signals and incentives contained in pricing water at its market value enable water recycling, reuse and conservation, which are key to achieving sustainable water use. The failure to price water at its market value is the key reason for the presence of issues about water quality and quantity.

The opposing view was presented by Dr Vandana Shiva, whose bottom-line position was:

> *the idea that the management and distribution of and access to a scarce and vital resource like water can be left to the market – and that the market can assign a reliable price reflecting the real value of water – is both absurd and irresponsible.*

Moreover, Dr Shiva maintained that the 'commoditization' of water shifts the focus from the water cycle to water markets. The water cycle includes ecosystems that a commodity does not. His key points were:

1   There is a need to focus on water cycles rather than on water markets, on human rights to water rather than profits to be made from commoditizing a scarce resource – the disciplines of ecology and hydrology need to guide efforts at conservation.
2   Privatization and commodification of water threaten to accelerate the processes that lead to the growing crisis of drought, desertification and water famines.
3   The assumption that water markets will overcome the water crisis is 'fallacious and malicious' as water markets cannot reduce water use and conserve water. Higher water prices do not reduce water consumption. Instead they increase consumption by those who can afford water and deprive the poor of an essential need.
4   Water pricing and water trade cannot increase water supplies.

5   Non-sustainable water use and technologies 'which violate the limits and the integrity of the water cycle are creating a water crisis'.
6   Market-based water pricing cannot respect the ecological limits inherent in the hydrologic cycle, nor value water as the basis of life. 'The real value of water is assigned by culture, which treats water as sacred; it is also assigned by rules of social equity and justice which recognize that everyone has a human right to water.'

Finally, Dr Shiva argued that water markets take water from where it is needed to where there is purchasing power for water as a commodity. Managing a scarce and precious resource such as water requires conservation, equity and the recognition that as the basis of life, *water is priceless.*

Human right to water, and businesses

One of the key aspects of Dr Shiva's position on water pricing and value is tied to the human right to water – *water is priceless.* This is a critical issue for global businesses. In General Comment 15 on the right to water (WHO, 2003), the UN states that 'The human right to water entitles everyone to sufficient, safe, acceptable, physically accessible and affordable water for personal and domestic uses.'

The 1977 United Nations Water Conference in Mar del Plata, Argentina, established the concept of basic water requirements to meet fundamental human needs. This was reiterated at the 1992 Earth Summit in Rio de Janeiro, Brazil. General Comment 15 on the right to water, adopted in November 2002 by the Committee on Economic, Social and Cultural Rights (CESCR), sets the criteria for the full enjoyment of the right to water.

However, in 2008 the UN General Assembly stopped short of declaring water as a human right, although the CESCR states a human right to water in Articles 11 and 12 of the International Covenant on Economic, Social and Cultural Rights (WHO, 2007). This includes an obligation to prevent corporate third parties from infringing on the right to water by 'polluting and inequitably extracting from water resources'.

The CEO Water Mandate has weighed-in on this topic with a discussion paper on water and human rights (Tripathi and Morrison, 2009), itself based upon the publication 'Draft business, human rights, and the right to water: challenges, dilemmas and opportunities roundtable consultative report' (Institute for Human Rights and Business, 2009).

The authors of the CEO Water Mandate discussion paper support the belief that water is a human right and they explore its implications for businesses. The paper specifically poses the question of what adoption of the 'corporate responsibility to respect' principle would look like with respect to water. The authors argue that a rights-based approach means that access to water for public use should be prioritized over other water uses such as agriculture and industry, to maintain sufficient water supply for domestic use.

A rights-based approach to water means that priority would be provided to those stakeholders who do not have access to water, and would require that individuals and communities have access to 'information, justice and participation in decision-making processes concerning water-related issues'. It is also argued that access to free water is a legal entitlement for all humans, and as a result should be prioritized over other uses, including agricultural and industrial. Moreover, the trading of water as a commodity, or considering the delivery of water as a service, would be subordinate to providing water to all people. The authors feel that business should operate on the basis that access to safe drinking water is a human right.

Sustainable water pricing

Can water be priced according to its value while still acknowledging the human right to water? This is the challenge of sustainable water pricing, which will require a systems-based approach and the integration of factors such as equity in water availability and affordability (Beecher and Shanaghan, 2001).

Beecher and Shanaghan maintain that sustainable water management requires both appropriate price signals and a balance between other policy goals such as affordability and equity among stakeholders. Moreover, they recommend that a sustainable water price is one that will:

- reflect true costs and induce efficient water production and consumption;
- promote optimization or the achievement of least-cost solutions to providing water service;
- achieve equity in terms of incorporating cost-sharing practices as needed, to enhance affordability;
- enhance the long-term viability of the water utility.

They also raise an important point – in establishing sustainable water pricing, the size of the system is important. The larger water systems (as dictated by the boundaries of the water service area and utility) are more likely to achieve optimal pricing solutions, as they can spread the cost of service in an equitable manner for the customer base. Moreover, they maintain that sustainable water pricing may require an 'evolution from the somewhat rigid doctrine that guides pricing today', such as marginal-cost pricing principles.

The Real Value of Water for Business

The price of water for a business is not typically a significant line item in a profit and loss statement. However, the value of water to a business far exceeds its actual price.

What is the real value of water from a business perspective? I believe *the real value of water resides in issues such as business continuity, licence to operate, reputation/brand and as a driver of innovation.* Further, I would argue that currently the real value of water for a business mostly resides with intangibles (licence to operate, reputation/brand value and innovation), as long as the price of water is an insignificant operating cost.

Business intangibles (AllBusiness.com, 2010a) are the total value of a business minus the total value of its net tangible assets. Intangible value consists of aspects of a business such as patents, trademarks and goodwill. Goodwill represents factors that include a business name and reputation, and customer relations (AllBusiness.com, 2010b). Issues such as reputation, brand and stakeholder relations are currently essential aspects of the value of a business, and in particular those of companies considered sustainability leaders (see Chapters 9 to 13 for snapshots of companies committed to sustainability and water stewardship).

The intangible value of a business is, in general, increasingly an aspect of the total value of a business. Moreover, intangible value can drive business performance. An excellent analysis of intangible business value is seen in *Invisible Advantage* by Jonathan Low and Pam Cohen Kalafut (2002). The thesis of the book is that intangibles are transforming how businesses are run, manage employees, design and sell products, and interact with customers. These intangibles include reputation/brand value and innovation. Since this book was published in 2002 the value of sustainability in building intangible value has only become more important.

How a business manages its resources, including water use, will impact the intangible value of the company. This has never been more critical to the success of a business, as globalization has increased, and businesses are competing for scarce resources in developed and developing countries.

Business continuity

Chapters 1 and 2 showed that water scarcity can represent a physical risk to a business. Essentially this means that a business operation can be disrupted if there is no water to run production processes, for product ingredients and as a component of supply chains. Moreover, a business is disrupted if water is not available for consumers to use the products manufactured by a company.

Water scarcity, which disrupts a business, can be quantified in economic terms. It is the economic value lost – the difference between what happened, and what would have happened but for the disruption. While the concept is simple, the calculations can be complex.

How does a business minimize the risk of disruption and ensure continuity? If water is a key component of your upstream or downstream value chain and/or used in the manufacturing processes and product ingredients, then it is critical that water is managed in a manner to ensure business continuity in the event that it is not available or supplies are interrupted.

Licence to operate

Licence to operate has become a critical business risk which has to be managed, and is no longer a matter of business licences and permits. Licence to operate can be given and withdrawn by a variety of stakeholders important to a business. Nowhere has this been more important and visible than in developing economies in Africa and India. Global food and beverage companies know all too well the risk of not engaging stakeholders on critical resource issues such as water. The emerging issue of the human right to water will only make the competition for water more acute. This competition, in turn, increases the risk to a company's licence to operate unless water stewardship is a key aspect of business strategy, governance and operations for both direct and indirect water use.

Reputation and brand value

There is much discussion of reputation and brand value these days as the notion of a 'green' brand has entered our lexicon. A *brand is a promise*, and a relevant and distinctive promise helps to build a brand. A corporate *reputation is built by fulfilling that promise* to stakeholders. Simply put, *a company owns its brand, but stakeholders own its reputation* (Reputation Institute, 2010). If a company breaks a promise to stakeholders, its reputation, and in turn its brand, are damaged. A promise such as operating in a sustainable manner with respect to water use has the ability to enhance reputation and brand value.

Before we look at the brand value of water we need to step back briefly and discuss the connection between sustainability and brand value. Brand value is a key component of a company's market capitalization (Interbrand, 2010), and global brands develop a strong relationship with their customers to increase purchasing over time. The brand creates value by generating demand, reducing risk and building future revenue (Environmental Leader, 2008). According to Interbrand, a sustainability programme that is consistent with a brand's positioning will create value for a company by creating greater brand value. Simply put, sustainability can drive brand value and in turn generate increased buying of products and services. Examples include General Electric (GE) with their ecomagination[SM] initiative (a recognized strong green brand) and Toyota with the Prius.

How companies rank as a green brand is increasingly important, and is reflected in numerous annual surveys such as the Cohn & Wolfe, Landor Associates annual study (2010). Their findings illustrate that water stewardship is increasingly a key component of brand value:

- The majority of consumers (over 60 per cent) in all countries want to buy from environmentally responsible companies.
- Consumers say environmental consciousness is an important corporate priority – ranking behind good value, trustworthiness and caring about customers.
- Consumers expect green companies to engage in a broad set of actions, particularly reducing toxics, recycling and *managing water*.

Innovation value

A final thought on the real business value of water: sustainability is a driver for innovation and water scarcity will drive innovation in new products and services (more on this topic in Chapter 6). Two places to start in developing an understanding of how sustainability drives innovation and the creative destruction of industries are the papers by Nidumolu, Prahalad et al (2009) and Hart and Milstein (1999). These will provide the basis for understanding how companies such as GE, Syngenta and The Water Initiative are building innovative businesses to solve water-scarcity challenges, and why an organization such as ImagineH2O is focused on promoting water innovation in the water industry (discussed in greater detail in Chapter 6).

In conclusion, the price of water for your business is almost irrelevant. The real reason to build a credible water stewardship programme is that it will build both tangible and intangible value. Moreover, stakeholders are watching and will weigh in on your performance.

References

AllBusiness.com (2010a) 'Business glossary', www.allbusiness.com/glossaries/intangible-value/4943887-1.html, accessed 30 June 2010

AllBusiness.com (2010b) 'Business glossary', www.allbusiness.com/glossaries/goodwill/4942319-1.html, accessed 30 June 2010

Beecher, J. A. and Shanaghan, P. E. (2001) 'Sustainable water pricing', https://waterportal.sandia.gov/literature/economicsofwater/sustainable.pdf, accessed 30 June 2010

Cohn & Wolfe, Landor Associates (2010) 'Global media deck: 2010 ImagePower® green brands survey', www.cohnwolfe.com/sites/default/files/whitepapers/2010_GreenBrands_Global.pdf, accessed

EcoSeed (2010) 'Diverting water: China reroutes supply from south to north', www.ecoseed.org/en/general-green-news/green-topics/water-technologies/7153-Diverting-water-China-reroutes-supply-from-south-to-north, accessed 30 June 2010

Environmental Economics (2008) 'A water pricing debate at *The Economist*', www.env-econ.net/2008/09/a-water-pricing.html, 30 September 2008, accessed 30 June 2010

Environmental Leader (2008) 'Sustainability and its impact on brand value', www.environmentalleader.com/2008/09/28/sustainability-and-its-impact-on-brand-value, accessed 30 June 2010

Hardin, G. (1968) 'Tragedy of the commons', *Science*, vol. 162, no 3859, pp1243–48

Hart, S L. and Milstein, M. B. (1999) 'Global sustainability and the creative destruction of industries', *Sloan Management Review*, vol 41, no 1, www.ce.cmu.edu/~gdrg/readings/2006/09/26/Hart_GlobalSustainabilityAndTheCreativeDestructionOfIndustries.pdf, accessed 30 June 2010

Institute for Human Rights and Business (2009) 'Business, human rights, and the right to water: challenges, dilemmas and opportunities roundtable consultative report', draft report, www.institutehrb.org/reports.html, accessed 30 June 2010

Interbrand (2010) www.interbrand.com, accessed 14 September 2010

Low, J. and Kalafut, P. C. (2002) *Invisible Advantage*, Perseus Books Group, Cambridge, MA

Lux Research Water Intelligence (2008) 'Water: evolution & outlook of the "hydrocosm"', Lux Research Inc., http://www2.luxresearchinc.com/water_hydrocosm_download, accessed 30 June 2010

Nidumolu, R., Prahalad, C. K. and Rangaswami, M. R. (2009) 'Why sustainability is now the key driver of innovation', *Harvard Business Review,* http://hbr.org/2009/09/why-sustainability-is-now-the-key-driver-of-innovation/ar/1, accessed 30 June 2010

OECD (Organisation for Economic Co-Operation and Development) (2009) 'Managing water for all: an OCED perspective on pricing and financing', www.oecd.org/document/16/0,3343,en_2649_34285_42289488_1_1_1_1,00.html, accessed 30 June 2010

Reputation Institute (2010) 'About advice', www.reputationinstitute.com/advisory-services, accessed 30 June 2010

Richtel, M. (2008) 'Cable prices keep rising, and customers keep paying', *The New York Times*, www.nytimes.com/2008/05/24/technology/24cable.html, accessed 30 June 2010

Smith, A. (1776) *An Inquiry into the Nature and Causes of the Wealth of Nations*, 2008 edition, Oxford University Press, Oxford

Tripathi, S. and Morrison, J. (2009) 'The CEO Water Mandate discussion paper, water and human rights: exploring the roles and responsibilities of business', www.unglobalcompact.org/docs/issues_doc/Environment/ceo_water_mandate/Business_Water_and_Human_Rights_Discussion_Paper.pdf, accessed 30 June 2010

Walton, B. (2010) 'The price of water: a comparison of water rates, usage in 30 US cities', www.circleofblue.org/waternews/2010/world/the-price-of-water-a-comparison-of-water-rates-usage-in-30-u-s-cities, accessed 30 June 2010

WHO (2003) 'Right to water', www.who.int/water_sanitation_health/rightowater/en, accessed 30 June 2010

WHO (2007) 'Health and human rights: international covenant on economic, social and cultural rights', www.who.int/hhr/Economic_social_cultural.pdf, accessed 30 June 2010

4

Water Accounting:
Water Footprint and Virtual Water

Ecological Footprint is not about 'how bad things are'. It is about humanity's continuing dependence on Nature and what we can do to secure Earth's capacity to support a human existence for all in the future.

Mathis Wackernagel and William Rees

What is a water footprint and why would a country or a company calculate one? As examples, we will look initially at Spain and SABMiller later in this chapter to understand the value of water footprinting and also its relationship to virtual water. Water footprinting is essentially water accounting, and is similar in concept to the greenhouse gas (GHG) protocol established by the World Business Council for Sustainable Development (WBCSD) and Water Resources Institute (WRI) (GGPI, 2010), for carbon accounting.

Spain is the most arid country in Europe and the largest per capita consumer of water in the world followed by the United States and Italy (Chapagain and Hoekstra, 2004). Recently, Spain performed an evaluation of the water footprint of the country in response to the European Union (EU) Water Framework Directive (WFD) 2000/60/EC (Europa, 2010). Spain was the first country that included the water footprint analysis into governmental policy-making in the context of the WFD (Aldaya et al, 2009).

The rationale for determining the water footprint of Spain was to develop a transparent and multidisciplinary framework to guide and optimize water-policy decisions. It was believed that water scarcity in Spain is more the result of weak water governance than of physical scarcity of water – essentially, a water management problem (Garrido et al, 2010).

The water footprint evaluation used the consumption-based methodology of water use (Hoekstra and Chapagain, 2008). This methodology is defined as the total volume of fresh water that is used to produce the goods and services consumed by the individual or community.

The water footprint was also used to evaluate virtual water-flow imports and exports. Water footprint and virtual water are closely linked concepts (Allan, 1997). Virtual water is essentially the volume of water used in the manufacturing of a product and represents the amount of *water embedded in traded products*. Or, put another way, it is how much water a country imports and exports in the form of water embedded in products. It is discussed in more detail later in this chapter.

Aldaya et al concluded that water scarcity in Spain is due primarily to poor management of water in the agricultural sector (agricultural water use for irrigation is approximately 80 per cent of total water use), namely:

> *practices such as flood self-sufficiency, the still imperfect World Trade Organization (WTO) regulations, the absence of appropriate economic instruments for water management, national policies that promote irrigated agriculture to contribute to regional stability and agricultural commodity prices.*

In addition, it was calculated that Spain is a net virtual water 'importer' of agricultural products, and a net virtual water 'exporter' of livestock products.

The authors concluded that Spanish farmers are moving from a policy of 'more crops and jobs per drop' towards one of 'more cash and nature per drop'. In addition, the authors conclude that there is enough water to supply the Spanish agricultural sector, but efficient allocation and management of this resource is required. Action by the Spanish government is required to address the water management problem.

It is likely that these conclusions could have been developed only from the performance of the water-footprinting effort – an evaluation that was clearly valuable to inform future Spanish water policy and agricultural practices.

What is a Water Footprint?

Water footprinting is essentially water accounting, and is similar in concept to the GHG protocol established by WBCSD and WRI for carbon accounting (GGPI, 2010). However, water accounting is nowhere near the level of standardization achieved by carbon accounting. That being said, methodologies and tools for water footprinting are emerging, and these are being used by companies to calculate enterprise-wide and product water footprints.

In April 2010, a report from the Pacific Institute and the Institute for Environmental Research and Education was released by the CEO Water Mandate (Morrison and Schulte, 2010). Entitled *Corporate Water Accounting: An Analysis of Methods and Tools for Measuring Water Use and Its Impact*, this report is part of the United Nations Environment Programme (UNEP) Water Footprint, Neutrality and Efficiency umbrella project, designed to 'encourage convergence and compatibility among water accounting methods and management tools'. This is an excellent resource for those wanting a detailed overview of the current tools and methodologies.

The CEO Water Mandate report focuses on four primary methods and tools in use today:

- Water Footprint Network's 'water footprint';
- life-cycle assessment;
- WBCSD's Global Water Tool;
- GEMI's Water Sustainability Tool.

The tools are all somewhat different, ranging from calculating water footprints to strategic water-risk mapping. They can be used alone, or in parallel, to provide a broader perspective on water risk (the WBCSD and GEMI tools have been used side by side by several companies).

While not discussed in the CEO Water Mandate report, there are also emerging methodologies such as the 'Water risk tool' (developed by General Electric, World Resources Institute and Goldman Sachs), and non-open-source methodologies such as the 'Corporate water gauge' (Center for Sustainable Innovation, 2009).

The CEO Water Mandate report identified the following needs:

- Current methods are a good start for measuring water use and impacts, but they are inadequate for benchmarking.
- Water accounting methods would benefit from harmonization and increased field testing.
- There should be a broad consensus on the concept of 'water footprinting'.

- The local contexts in which the companies operate (particularly social dimensions such as accessibility and affordability of water resources) need to be better measured and characterized.
- More consistent ways to measure and communicate water-related information across industry sectors and regions should be developed.
- Water risks and impacts across the full supply chain need to be systematically assessed.
- Efforts should be coordinated among companies so that their relationship with water resources and sustainable water management can be measured better and put into context.

The WBCSD and International Union for Conservation of Nature (IUCN) also evaluated water-footprinting tools and private sector initiatives in a March 2010 report, 'Water for business: initiatives guiding sustainable water management in the private sector'. The report summarizes 16 initiatives and tools, developed as part of private and public sector initiatives, with a goal of helping companies identify which initiatives and approaches are best suited to meet their specific needs. The report provides a matrix summarizing the initiatives and tools, factsheets, a glossary of terms and references.

Brief summaries of six water-footprinting tools follow.

Water Footprint Network (WFN)

The Water Footprint Network (www.waterfootprint.org) developed a methodology that is being increasingly adopted, in particular by the beverage industry. This is summarized in the 2009 online report 'Water footprint manual', and in *The Water Footprint Assessment Manual* (Hoekstra, Chapagain et al, 2011).

The WFN methodology is based upon the 'water footprint' concept developed by Hoekstra in 2002 (see Hoekstra, 2003), being an indicator of both direct and indirect fresh water use. The water footprint of a product is the volume of freshwater used to produce the product, measured over the full supply chain. The methodology quantifies water consumption by source and polluted volumes by type of pollution; all components of a total water footprint are specified geographically and temporally. The differences between water types (blue, green and grey) are illustrated in Figure 4.1. The blue water footprint refers to consumption of blue water resources (surface and ground water) along the supply chain of a product (as illustrated in Figure 4.2).

The methodology defines consumption as:

> *loss of water from the available ground-surface water body in a catchment area, which happens when water evaporates, returns to another catchment area or the sea or is incorporated into a product.*

The green water footprint refers to:

> *consumption of green water resources (rainwater stored in the soil as soil moisture)*

and the grey water footprint:

> *refers to pollution and is defined as the volume of freshwater that is required to assimilate the load of pollutants based on existing ambient water quality standards.*

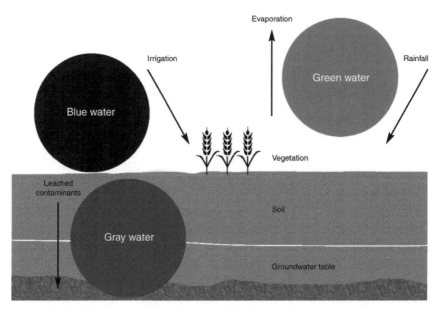

Figure 4.1 *Definitions of blue, grey and green water*

Source: adapted from SABMiller and WWF UK (2009)

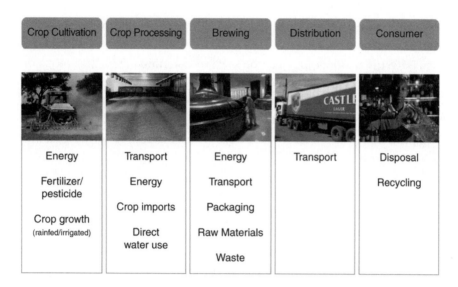

Figure 4.2 *Generalized value chain for water footprinting for a beverage product*

Source: adapted from SABMiller and WWF UK (2009)

The WFN methodology is fundamentally different from the traditional definition of water use in the following ways:

- It is not restricted to blue water use, but also includes green and grey water.
- It is not restricted to direct water use, but also includes indirect water use.
- It does not include blue water use if this water is returned to where it came from.

As a result, the WFN methodology provides a broader evaluation of direct and indirect water use. It is a volumetric measure of net water consumption and pollution, and not a measure of the severity of the local environmental impact of water consumption and pollution. The methodology also provides specific information on how water is used for various purposes.

As with carbon accounting, it is critical to set water boundaries for a water footprint. The boundary setting must also consider the following questions: will the boundaries focus on environmental, social and/or economic aspects or sustainability, and will these be at local, basin and/or global level?

The WFN methodology can be used to determine the water footprint of a business (enterprise-wide) or products. As previously discussed and illustrated in Figure 4.2, the water footprint of a business is defined as the total volume of direct and indirect water use. The term 'business water footprint' is the same as 'corporate water footprint' or 'organizational water footprint'.

In addition to the operational and supply-chain water footprint, a business may like to distinguish an 'end-use water footprint' of its product. This refers to the water consumption and pollution by consumers when using the product, such as the wastewater generated from the use of household soaps, for example. Typically, the end-use water footprint of a product is not considered as part of the business water footprint or the product water footprint, but part of the consumer's water footprint. Although not part of a product's water footprint, companies may consider calculating this externality (this issue is considered further in the discussion of leadership and reporting in Chapter 7 of this book).

The WFN methodology can also be used to measure the water footprint of products. Another way to look at this is to consider that the 'water footprint of a business' is equal to the 'sum of the water footprints of the business output products'. The 'supply-chain water footprint of a business' is equal to the 'sum of the water footprints of the business input products' (SABMiller and WWF UK, 2009).

Calculating a business water footprint or calculating the water footprint of the major product(s) produced by a business is about the same thing, but the focus is different. In the calculation of a business water footprint there is a strong focus on making the distinction between an operational (direct) and supply-chain (indirect) water footprint. This is highly relevant from a policy perspective, because a business has direct control over its operational water footprint, and indirect influence on its supply-chain water footprint.

When calculating a product water footprint there is no distinction between direct and indirect inputs; one simply considers the water footprints for all relevant processes within the production system. It is possible to calculate a hybrid between a product and a business water footprint account by focusing on the calculation of the water footprint of a particular product – for example, by looking at just one of many products produced by a business – but making explicit which part of the product's water footprint occurs in the business's own operations and which part in the business's supply chain.

An excellent example of how the WFN methodology was used to calculate the water footprint of a product is a 2009 study performed by SABMiller and WWF. Many consumer goods businesses, including SABMiller, have undertaken detailed carbon footprints of specific products such as beer, carbonated soft drinks, fruit juices and potato chips. In the case of SABMiller the water footprints of beers produced in the Czech Republic and South Africa were calculated and the water use was compared along the value chain for each. Another example of the assessment of the water footprint of a product, sugar from sugar beet, can be found in Hoekstra, Chapagain et al (2011).

The SABMiller and WWF report raises a number of questions which are relevant to the current discussion on the merits of environmental footprinting of consumer products and labelling. These questions include:

- What can a water footprint tell us about the impact on natural ecosystems of manufacturing and consuming a product?
- What is the principal value of a footprint exercise? To understand value chains better, to reduce business risk, or to improve transparency?
- If a footprint sends a clear message regarding environmental damage or risk, what practically can be done about it, and who is responsible? And how much influence do consumers, manufacturers or campaign groups have?
- What are the key variables in a footprint figure and how often do they change?
- What does this mean for the provision of reliable data for different purposes?

For SABMiller, water footprinting was a valuable exercise, characterized as having 'measure to manage' value. Moreover, this evaluation advanced water-footprinting methodology and SABMiller recommends avoiding the pitfalls that became apparent in the emergence of carbon accounting methodology by rallying around the WFN approach.

The evaluation performed by SABMiller was valuable in building awareness of water used in the value chain to produce its products. The company cautions that consumer labelling at this time would be counterproductive, and at worst 'misleading', due to the complexity in quantifying water footprints.

International Standards Organization (ISO) 14046

ISO (www.iso.org) is also working on developing a standard for water footprinting, ISO 14046. This is based upon the life-cycle analysis (LCA) approach and is currently entitled 'Water footprint – requirements and guidelines'.

The standard will address principles, requirements and guidelines for a water footprint metric of products, process and organizations. It will also include the different types of water sources (groundwater and surface water), any water releases (grey water) and how local environmental and socio-economic conditions should be factored. For example, the ISO standard would clarify the distinction between process water and consumptive uses of water. Humbert (2009) provides information regarding the development of the ISO standard.

World Business Council for Sustainable Development (WBCSD) Global Water Tool

WBCSD's Global Water Tool was released at the 2007 Stockholm World Water Week, updated in 2009 and again in 2010 (www.wbcsd.org). The tool is available publically and is designed to assist companies in mapping their water use and determining risks to their supply chains and operations. The tool helps answer key questions such as:

* Where are your water risks?
* How many of your sites are in extremely water-scarce areas? Which sites are at greatest risk? How will that look in the future?
* How many of your employees live in countries that lack access to improved water and sanitation?
* How many of your suppliers are in water-scarce areas now? How many will there be in 2025?

The output of the tool allows the following:

- comparison of a company's water use (direct and supply chain) with water supply and treatment availability on a watershed scale;
- calculation of water consumption and efficiency;
- clarification of relative water risks to enable prioritized action, including more detailed assessment of water risk within the watershed;
- creation of key water Global Reporting Initiative (GRI) indicators, inventories, risk and performance metrics and geographic mapping;
- information for use in engagement and communication with key stakeholders on water issues.

Global Environmental Management Initiative (GEMI)

GEMI's Water Sustainability Work Group developed a tool to help companies to understand their water use (www.gemi.org/resources/ConnectingTheDrops.pdf). The GEMI Water Sustainability Tool is designed to provide the evaluation necessary to support the development of a water strategy and provides a roadmap for companies to:

- conduct a systematic assessment of their relationship to water;
- identify specific opportunities and risks associated with this relationship;
- assess the business case for action;
- tailor a water strategy that addresses specific needs and circumstances of the organization;
- ensure that water-related opportunities and risks are tracked and managed effectively into the future using a continual improvement framework.

The Water Sustainability Tool is organized according to a series of modules. For each stage in the value chain, the users examine how water flows through their business and value chain. The tool builds upon data from environmental management systems, to assist in a better understanding of direct and indirect water use (Figure 4.3).

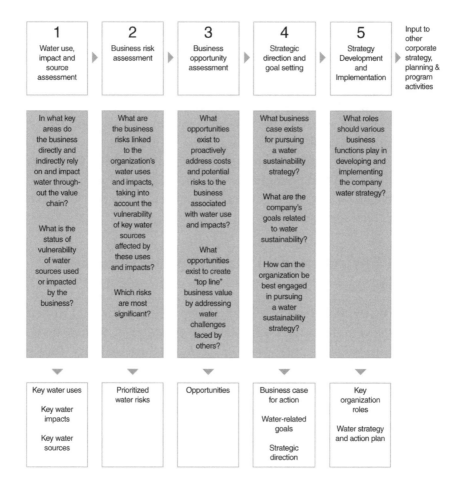

Figure 4.3 *GEMI Water Sustainability Tool modules*

Source: adapted from The GEMI Water Sustainability Tool, www.gemi.org/resources/ ConnectingTheDrops.pdf

The tool comprises the following modules:

- Module 1: Water use, impact and source assessment;
- Module 2: Business risk assessment;
- Module 3: Business opportunity assessment;
- Module 4: Strategic direction and goal setting;
- Module 5: Strategy development and implementation.

Water Initiative (General Electric, Water Resources Institute and Goldman Sachs)

The World Resources Institute (WRI), General Electric (GE) and Goldman Sachs collectively launched a Water Initiative to quantify the corporate risk and opportunities facing companies and their investors. The goal of the initiative is to develop a water index as a standardized approach to identify and mitigate water-related corporate risk, through the aggregation of approximately 20 weighted factors capturing water availability, regulations, water quality and reputational issues.

The water index will be designed so that companies and investors can determine various aspects of water risk transparently. The water index will use publicly available information regarding physical scarcity of water and water quality, coupled with regulatory setting, social factors and reputational issues.

GE, WRI and Goldman Sachs believe the water index will allow each of the companies to provide more robust analysis of water risk and opportunities to their clients. Current water-risk tools do not factor regulatory and reputational water risk, and as a result can only assess physical water risk to a company's operations and supply chains.

Corporate Water Gauge – Center for Sustainable Innovation

The Center for Sustainable Innovation (2009) developed a Corporate Water Gauge designed to measure the sustainability of a company's water use (there are costs associated with using the tool). It is based upon the ecological sustainability of a company's water use and is focused on the watershed, is technology-enabled, using GIS, and calculates the 'rate of use of water against the rate of renewable water supply'.

The Corporate Water Gauge consists of the following five steps:

1 Profile facilities using inflow/outflow analysis.
2 Determine watershed(s) in which facilities have impact.
3 Determine net renewable water supplies in watershed(s) of interest, and allocate proportionate share to facilities.
4 Determine net water use by facilities in watershed(s) of interest.
5 Populate Corporate Water Gauge™ quotient with data developed in steps 1–4 above, and compute sustainability scores accordingly.

According to the Center for Sustainable Innovation, these tools have the following advantages over other water-footprinting tools:

- They measure sustainability performance with local context taken fully into account.
- They assess water use in terms of local renewable water-resource levels, which are allocated to a facility in per capita terms and/or as a function of economic factors.
- They make it possible to score sustainability at a local, regional, national, global and enterprise-wide level, with local contexts taken fully into account.
- They make use of advanced GIS tools in combination with site-specific datasets.
- They result in measures that are more fully compliant with GRI (i.e. include 'sustainability context').

My current experience is that, in general, the WFN approach is being adopted by the beverage sector industry (with input from the Beverage Industry Environmental Roundtable – www.bieroundtable.com), with the WBCSD Water Tool and the GEMI Water Sustainability Tool being used across diverse industry sectors such as IT and consumer products goods. In addition, some companies are running both the WBCSD and GEMI tools concurrently, to gain a broader perspective of potential water risk.

Water Footprinting, Virtual Water and Water Offsets

As previously discussed in relation to the evaluation performed by Spain, the concept of a water footprint is closely linked to, but not the same as the concept of virtual water first developed by Professor John Anthony Allan (1997). This 1997 paper first presented the concept of virtual water and applied it to Middle Eastern economies and the transfer of water in agricultural products. Virtual water is defined as the volume of water required to produce a product within the context of trade. The genesis of the concept helps to explain its value. Professor Allan developed this concept to conceptualize water scarcity in the Middle East, where high imports of virtual water in food help to alleviate water-scarce resources within these countries. He was awarded the Stockholm Water Prize in 2008 for the development of the concept.

Professor Allan believes that by understanding the movement of virtual water, international trade can be used to save water if a water-intensive commodity is traded from an area where it is produced with high water productivity (with a resultant low water footprint) to an area with lower water productivity (and a corresponding high water footprint). At a national or regional level, a nation can preserve its domestic water resources by importing products instead of producing them domestically. As previously discussed, this is relevant to arid or semi-arid countries with scarce water resources such as Spain. For global businesses the implication is that they are potentially participating in the movement of virtual water through the production and global distribution of products.

While the virtual water concept helps to focus discussions on water use and efficiency, it has been criticized. Possible shortcomings in the concept are:

- It assumes that all water is of equal value.
- It assumes that if water was available from a high-use activity it would be available for a less water-intensive activity.
- It fails as an indicator of environmental impact; see, for example, Frontier Economics (2008).

Taking water footprinting and virtual water further, private and public entities have explored the concept of water neutrality through the use of water offsets. This is where the 'carbon world' meets the 'water world'. However, the concept of an offset used as a means to achieve carbon neutrality does not translate well to water. The reason is that water is local, and reducing water use in one part of the world does not mitigate water scarcity elsewhere.

However, like the concept of virtual water, water offsets are worth exploring and may have merit as part of a global, regional or local water stewardship strategy. In 2007, several organizations met to discuss the topic of water neutrality. The group, comprising representatives from Twente University, World Wide Fund for Nature (WWF), The Coca-Cola Company, WBCSD, Water Neutral (www.waterneutral.org), Emvelo Group and UNESCO-IHE Institute of Water Education published 'Water neutrality – a concept paper' (Gerbens-Leenes, Hoekster et al, 2007).

This provides a summary of thinking on the topic of water offsets and some of the challenges in applying an offset framework to water. Another overview which advances the topic of water neutrality and water offsets was published by Hoekstra (2008).

Most recently the Bonneville Environmental Foundation has established a water offset programme, selling the credits as 'BEF Water Restoration Certificates™' (WRCs); they plan to trade the credits just like carbon offsets (www.b-e-f.org/newsroom/archive/081809). Customers who have invested in the WRCs by mid-2010 include the Bullitt Foundation, the Natural Resources Defense Council (NRDC) and WhiteWave Foods Company. It remains to be seen if this model is adopted, but nevertheless it is an interesting market-based initiative in developing a water-offset market.

What This Means for Business

Water-footprinting methodology and the concepts of virtual water and water offsets/neutrality are evolving rapidly. While widely accepted methodologies have yet to be developed, there is merit in companies measuring their water footprints and considering the implications of virtual water and the potential for water neutrality through offsetting. The value is in developing a better understanding of water use and the potential to improve water efficiency. Moreover, as water stewardship requires pro-active stakeholder engagement at the watershed scale, companies need to know how they are using water and be aware of options to improve water management. Enterprise-wide and product water footprinting is a start.

References

Allan, J. A. (1997) 'Virtual water: a long term solution for water-short Middle Eastern economies?', *SOAS Water Issues Study Group*, Occasional Papers, www.soas.ac.uk/waterissues/papers/file38347.pdf, accessed 30 June 2010

Aldaya, M. M., Garrido, A., Llamas, M. R., Varzla-Ortega, C., Novo, P. and Casado, R. R. (2009) 'Water footprint and virtual water trade in Spain', *Natural Resource Managment and Policy*, vol 35, www.waterfootprint.org/Reports/Aldaya-el-al-2010-WaterFootprint:Spain.pdf

Center for Sustainable Innovation (2009) 'Corporate water gauge™', www. sustainableinnovation.org/Corporate-Water-Gauge.pdf, accessed 14 September 2010

Chapagain, A. K. and Hoekstra, A. Y. (2004) 'Water footprints of nations, Volume 1: Main report', *Value of Water Research Series*, no 16

Europa (2010) 'The EU Water Framework Directive: integrated river basin management for Europe', October 2000, Directive 2000/60/EC, http://europa. eu/legislation_summaries/agriculture/environment/l28002b_en.htm, accessed 30 June 2010

Frontier Economics (2008) 'The concept of "virtual water": a critical review', report for the Victorian Department of Primary Industries, www.dpi.vic.gov. au/DPI/nrenfa.nsf/LinkView/A1F945CE4D56F40ACA257412002310642 B72296A5108C4FFCA25734F0009F96F/$file/Virtual%20Water%20-%20 for%20release%20-%20STC%2008-03-07.pdf, accessed 30 June 2010

Garrido, A., Llamas, M. R., Varela-Ortega, C., Novo, P., Rodríguez, C. and Aldaya, M. M. (2010) *Water Footprint and Virtual Water Trade in Spain: Policy Implications*, Springer Science & Business Media LLC, New York, NY

Gerbens-Leenes, W., Hoekster, A., Holland, R., Koch, G., Moss, J., Ndebele, P., Orr, S., Ronteltap, M. and de Ruyter van Stevenink, E. (2007). 'Water neutrality: a concept paper', www.indiaresource.org/campaigns/coke/2008/ Waterneutrality.pdf, accessed 30 June 2010

GGPI (Greenhouse Gas Protocol Initiative) (2010) 'About', www.ghgprotocol. org, accessed 14 September 2010

Hoekstra, A. Y. (ed.) (2003) 'Virtual water trade: proceedings of the international expert meeting on virtual water trade', *Value of Water Research Report Series*, no 12

Hoekstra, A. Y. (2008) 'Water neutral: reducing and offsetting the impacts of water footprints', *Value of Water Research Report Series*, no 28

Hoekstra, A. Y. and Chapagain, A. K. (2008) *Globalization of Water: Sharing the Planet's Freshwater Resources*, Blackwell Publishing, Oxford

Hoekstra, A. Y., Chapagain, A. K., Aldaya, M. M. and Mekonnen, M. M. (2011) *The Water Footprint Assessment Manual*, Earthscan, London, forthcoming

Humbert, S. (2009) 'ISO standard on water footprint: principles, requirements and guidance', www.unep.fr/scp/water/documents/Presentations/ISO%20 Activities%20on%20Water%20Accounting%20(Sebastien%20Humbert).pdf, accessed 14 September 2010

Morrison, J. and Schulte, P. (2010) *Corporate Water Accounting: An Analysis of Methods and Tools for Measuring Water Use and Its Impacts*. The CEO Water Mandate, Pacific Institute, Oakland, CA

SABMiller and WWF UK (2009) *Water Footprinting: Identifying & Addressing Water Risks in the Value Chain*, SABMiller, Woking, UK; WWF-UK, Godalming, UK

Wackernagel, M, and Rees, W. (1996) *Our Ecological Footprint: Reducing Human Impact on the Earth*, New Society Publishers, Gabriola Island, BC

WBCSD and IUCN (2010) 'Water for business: Initiatives guiding sustainable water management in the private sector', WBCST/IUCN Report, Version 2, March 2010, www.wbcsd.org/docroot/3wlfdj0ssdskcjwibbku/wbcsd_water_for_business_web.pdf

5

Partnerships and Stakeholders

Never doubt that a small group of thoughtful, concerned citizens can change the world. Indeed it is the only thing that ever has.

Margaret Mead

In 2009 Molson Coors announced a strategic collaboration with Circle of Blue (a non-profit affiliate of the Pacific Institute) as part of the company's long-term commitment to the protection of global fresh water. Their first initiative was the launch of an independent survey of public awareness and concern about freshwater issues in 25 countries around the world. The independent survey was performed by GlobeScan (www.globsescan.com) and the results were presented at the Stockholm Water Week in August 2009.

One of the reasons Molson Coors undertook this collaboration with Circle of Blue (one of several strategic relationships it has developed as part of its global water stewardship programme) was to develop the underlying research needed to provide leadership on retaining and restoring freshwater resources (Molson Coors, 2009).

This is just one of many strategic partnerships undertaken by multinational companies to better understand how to develop and implement water stewardship strategies.

Later in this book, profiles of global companies such as Campbell, Coca-Cola, Diageo, Ford, Intel, MillerCoors, Nestlé Waters and SABMiller, to name a few, highlight the value of partnerships with local, regional and global non-governmental organizations (NGOs) in becoming water stewardship leaders. Partnerships with global, regional and local NGOs and other key stakeholders are now part of any corporate water stewardship programme. The importance of partnerships with NGOs and communities in effectively building and executing a successful water stewardship programme cannot be overemphasized.

Why Partnerships are Critical

The need for truly collaborative partnerships is driven by a number of factors. Neither the public nor private sector alone can solve global issues, such as climate change and water scarcity. As a result, companies are increasingly forging new types of partnerships, and rethinking relationships with traditional stakeholders.

Leading companies must be able to take on externalities such as water (Meyer and Kirby, 2010). Externalities are defined as the side-effects (negative impacts) or the spillover effects (positive impacts) of a business operation; an example would be how a consumer disposes of a product after use (a negative side-effect, as this creates waste). Moreover, leadership now demands a transparent engagement with stakeholders that includes establishing priorities and setting measurable goals and actions.

Mapping and Engaging Stakeholders

In the book *Green to Gold* (2006), Daniel C. Esty and Andrew S. Winston show how the 'waverider' companies (green leaders) recognize that a stakeholder strategy is an essential component to their overall sustainability programmes. They identify brainstorming; grading and scoring key stakeholders; stakeholder engagement evaluation; compatibility assessment; due diligence on potential partners; and determination of partnership strategy as key elements of the process.

The stakeholder process outlined by Esty and Winston is based upon the research of Savage, Nix et al (1991). This outlines a process for identifying key stakeholder groups, and highlights the advantages of proactive engagement of stakeholders important to a business. An illustration of the stakeholder matrix from Savage et al is provided in Figure 5.1.

Savage, Nix et al identify four types of stakeholders and provide recommended actions for engagement:

- Type 1: the supportive stakeholder *involve* –
- Type 2: the marginal stakeholder *monitor* –
- Type 3: the non-supportive stakeholder *defend* –
- Type 4: the mixed-blessing stakeholder *collaborate* –

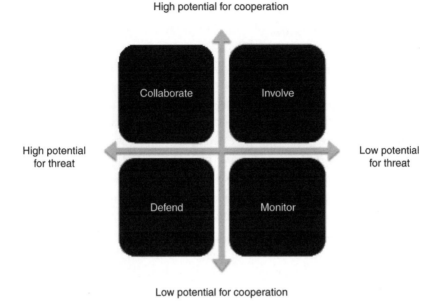

High potential for cooperation

High potential
for threat

Low potential
for threat

Collaborate   Involve

Defend   Monitor

Low potential for cooperation

Figure 5.1 *Stakeholder engagement mapping*

Source: adapted from Savage, Nix et al (1991)

The categories of stakeholders and ways to engage them are self-explanatory. For example, for 'supportive stakeholders' a company would want to actively involve them in planning and implementing a water strategy, in an effort to increase the success of the programme. Conversely, for a 'non-supportive' stakeholder who fundamentally is not interested in constructive collaboration, a company's only option may be to defend its position.

Stakeholders include investors, employees, local communities, regional, national and global NGOs and intergovernmental organizations (IGOs). In Chapters 1 and 2, we discussed the importance of investors as critical stakeholders in driving corporate water strategies. In the following sections we will see that employees and NGOs play an essential role in developing and implementing a corporate water strategy.

Employees

As stakeholders, employees are critical in building and implementing a corporate water strategy. They will be the ones who will not only develop and implement a water strategy, but who will also help communicate a company's success and performance to other stakeholders. The importance of employees cannot be underestimated.

In May 2010 Ogilvy Public Relations Worldwide (Ogilvy PR) surveyed 1000 American adults to measure awareness of water sustainability and conservation issues and assess consumers' willingness to take personal actions in conserving water. As experts in building brands and reputation management, Ogilvy PR was interested in learning how much consumers actually *understand* about water and how seriously they take the issue. The survey also explored perceptions of whom consumers trust the most when it comes to getting information on a company's water use and sustainability strategy. The results of the Ogilvy PR survey are summarized in Figures 5.2 to 5.4.

According to Michael Law, Ogilvy PR's managing director for the West Coast of the United States, the results show that Americans generally have a very low 'water IQ,' meaning that while most acknowledge that there is a freshwater shortage and say they pay attention to what companies are doing regarding the environment, many are either unwilling or don't understand the concept of taking personal action to solve the problem. Interestingly, the survey found that consumers place the burden of responsibility for water conservation and stewardship squarely on the

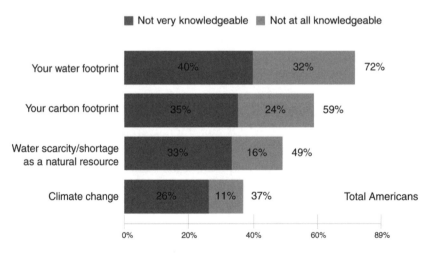

Figure 5.2 *Water footprints: a survey of 1000 American adults*

Source: courtesy of Michael Law, managing director for Ogilvy PR, 2010

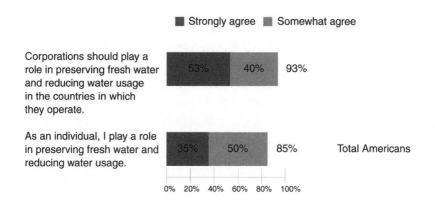

Figure 5.3 *Reducing freshwater usage: a survey of 1000 American adults*

Source: courtesy of Michael Law, managing director for Ogilvy PR, 2010

business community. As a result, brands are increasingly expected to communicate with stakeholders about their own water use or they risk damage to their commercial reputation.

Law remarks:

> *Research shows us that, at a minimum, companies should be accurately measuring or taking stock of their water footprint and beginning to evaluate their vulnerabilities around water. Anything less is irresponsible reputation management.*

Law believes that the conversation with communities and consumers about many environmental issues, including water scarcity and conservation, is not being translated into terms and concepts that the American public can easily understand. As a result, consumers turn their attention to other more pressing daily concerns. He feels that:

> *Complexity begets complacency. The key to consumer engagement is delivering simple, relevant, personal messages tailored to the local community where your stakeholders live and work.*

As an example of how poor communications surrounding key issues can result in complacent consumer response, Law cites the public discourse on climate change. Once just a complicated scientific issue, only vaguely understood by the general public, global warming has been transformed into a polarizing political debate with multiple factions arguing over its existence instead of having rational, productive conversations about what can be done to address it. Of even more concern, fewer Americans today believe the underlying science supporting the hypothesis that human activity affects climate change. Law believes that the public discussion about water and water conservation must not go the same way.

Law believes that we have the opportunity to learn from the climate debate, and apply that knowledge to the water crisis, before it spirals into a murky and politicized issue that few people truly understand. I agree with this view: we are in a position to frame the discussion on water clearly and simply to the public and other stakeholders, including employees.

Law recommends that as a first step, businesses and brands should change the way they are talking about water. So where does a company begin to shift the tone of the conversation? The answer is inside its own walls. Employees are a brand's best storytellers. If your employees are engaged in the water conversation, you know your message is resonating and you can be assured that those employees are talking to their families and friends about it.

Not only are your employees your greatest ambassadors, they are also some of the most trusted sources of information about your company. Consumers are sceptical about information coming from corporations. Nevertheless, when asked who they trust to provide information about a company's water-use strategy, the same percentage of people who said they would trust the mainstream media said they would also trust the company's employees.

Beth Haiken, senior vice president for Ogilvy PR and expert in employee engagement feels that:

> *Getting the message right from the beginning with your own employees is critical to establishing credibility and communicating with all stakeholder groups. Meaningful and relevant employee communications around an issue like water sustainability can set your company apart as an environmental leader and a responsible corporate citizen, not to mention a great place to work.*

Law and Haiken maintain that if green equity is important to your brand – and in today's environmentally conscious world it absolutely should be – water needs to be a priority. As companies and brands navigate

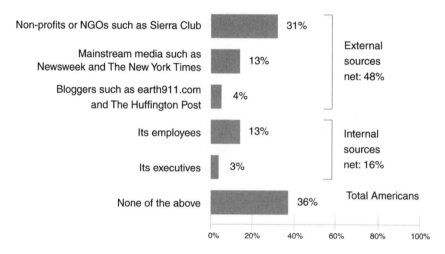

Figure 5.4 *Responsible corporate water use: a survey of 1000 American adults*

Source: courtesy of Michael Law, managing director for Ogilvy PR, 2010

the challenges of communicating about water sustainability, simplifying and localizing the conversation, and activating employees, are critical steps to maximizing the 'water IQ' of your stakeholders and minimizing reputational risk.

Non-governmental Organizations

There are numerous regional and global NGOs either partially or completely focused on water issues. A limited list of well-known global NGOs is provided below, with a brief summary of their missions and programmes. This list is by no means meant to be exhaustive. Instead, it is meant to illustrate the breadth and depth of potential partners for companies to engage with, in building a water strategy.

Specific examples of how global companies are working collaboratively with these and other NGOs is provided in the company profiles. Typically, companies are working with a range of NGOs at local, regional and global levels, to build a broad base of collaboration and broaden our expertise and knowledge in addressing water risks.

The Nature Conservancy (www.nature.org)

Since the founding of this US non-profit organization in 1951, more than 119 million acres of land and 5000 miles of rivers worldwide, from grasslands to coral reefs, have been protected. The Nature Conservancy operates internationally, including in all 50 US states and in more than 30 countries, using a collaborative, science-based approach. By employing over 700 scientists who can research and supply data in a fully transparent setting, the organization is well equipped to partner with small communities of all kinds, businesses, government, other non-profit organizations and more. The Nature Conservancy relies heavily on healthy relationships with these entities, and works to see that 'pragmatic solutions to conservation challenges' are met.

The Nature Conservancy's mission is to 'protect ecologically important lands and water for nature and people'. Not only is fresh water a priority for this organization, but safe drinking water drives much of the freshwater conservation efforts. These focus on protecting surrounding watershed and riparian land, maintaining healthy river flow levels, and promoting efficient water use. The Nature Conservancy does this through focusing on how to reduce the negative impacts to bodies of fresh water from climate change and human action. Areas of focus are public policy pertaining to deforestation; protection and restoration of freshwater ecosystems, floodplains and wetlands; water-supply system design; basin-wide water management strategies; water infrastructure management; and removing physical barriers to fish and other aquatic life that prevent necessary migratory movement. Currently The Nature Conservancy has over 600 water sites around the world.

Project WET (www.projectwet.org)

In 1984 the North Dakota State Water Commission set Project WET, or Water Education for Teachers, into play. Focused on educating the general public about water issues, the programme trained teachers and informal educators about water resources and management. Since that time the wildly successful single-state programme has become the Project WET Foundation, serving communities, teachers, parents, corporations, governments and educational facilities such as zoos, aquariums and museums, in all 50 US states and around the world (for example, in Costa Rica, Fiji, Hungary and Vietnam).

With a mission to 'reach children, parents, educators and communities of the world with water education', Project WET is open and accessible to anyone wishing to educate or find educational tools related to water. The organization's core beliefs, driving its efforts, are that water connects us all and should be available for all users, it should be managed sustainably and personal responsibility should be taken for water resources. Project WET puts this into action by publishing water-resource materials in several languages, providing training workshops for educators on topics such as watersheds, water quality and water conservation, organizing community water events and building a worldwide network of water educators, resource professionals and scientists. To date, Project WET has more than 100 coordinators and 3000 facilitators in 42 countries on five continents.

WWF – World Wide Fund for Nature (formerly the World Wildlife Fund) (www.wwf.org)

The WWF was founded in 1961 as the World Wildlife Fund, with a mission that focused on the preservation of specific animal species. In the 1980s the organization embraced a more holistic vision of conserving the environment, recognizing that all things are interconnected. It then became the World Wide Fund for Nature, and started expanding its work to include aspects of nature that are integral for survival, such as water.

The Global Freshwater Program focuses on six key areas: water stewardship, water security, freshwater habitat protection, freshwater ecosystem services, climate change adaption and water governance. The main focus is to secure water for people and nature, and the main tactic is collaboration with a diverse set of partners. WWF teams up with governments, development agencies, businesses, international conventions and other non-profit organizations to provide effective water management tools, such as integrated river basin management, community-based watershed management plans and agricultural successes with the top three water-intensive crops: cotton, sugar and rice.

The Global Water Program is a known leader in wetland conservation and other areas such as water security and stewardship. At the centre of WWF's freshwater work is development: education and implementation surrounding water footprints. It is the organization's view that 'humanity's water footprint has exceeded sustainable levels in several areas around the world', and promoting this information is a priority.

Global Water (www.globalwater.org)

In 1982 Dr Peter Bourne and former United States Ambassador John McDonald created Global Water with the underlying beliefs that humanitarian relief efforts in developing countries were ideal in times of crisis but not sustainable outside of those situations, and that the 'lack of access to safe drinking water is the primary cause of hunger, disease and poverty throughout the developing world'. Practices such as handing out bottled water are key when a community is in the midst of something unusual, such as a natural disaster or a famine, and Global Water wanted to see other practices used for communities stuck in an unsustainable water situation every day, or on the verge of a water crisis. The organization works to bring permanent safe drinking water supplies to the millions of people without it, by using sustainable, self-sufficient means.

Global Water does this by accessing, purifying and distributing new sources of safe water in rural villages, building bathroom facilities for dignified, safe waste disposal and building hand-washing facilities for rural schools. The main programme, Rural Outreach Water Supply, follows a regimen of seeking out local non-profit organizations also active in water projects and advocacy, providing funding, technical equipment and expertise on mutually beneficial projects, and assembling emergency response teams where necessary.

Water.org (http://water.org)

In 2009 Matt Damon's H2O Africa Foundation merged with Gary White's WaterPartners to form Water.org, an organization focused on 'creating accessible, safe water supplies in developing countries'. Water.org uses funding from donors around the world to invest in community-level water supply projects where safe drinking water is either non-existent or extremely hard to come by. The main focus for Water.org is the local community's involvement, and projects move through a number of clear stages:

• Selection of local partners to assist with the project. This step is taken seriously, and each potential partner is evaluated with great care and detail. Not only must the partner be equipped with the necessary expertise, resources and structure, but there must be a way to ensure women are involved in the entire process, as women are often the ones saddled with the burden of finding clean water for the entire family.

- Ensuring the people of the community are the owners of the project. From electing their own local water committee to ongoing project maintenance, the community leads the way.
- Use of appropriate technology, ensuring that whatever tools and techniques used are available and understood locally.
- Sound education and integration of projects. This ensures that water is handled safely as well as being made available.
- The WaterCredit Initiative, the first loan programme of its kind, accessible only to the local communities partnering with Water.org.

Charity: Water (www.charitywater.org)

Founder Scott Harrison left a fast-paced, well-paid life in New York City to rekindle his soul through charity work in Africa. The experience was life-changing, and in 2006 he started Charity: Water to bring 'clean and safe drinking water to people in developing nations'. In just three and a half years, this non-profit organization has created over 2500 sustainable projects around the world, by partnering with local organizations that understand their own community's needs and the best way to achieve them.

Charity: Water's approach is to engage the public, both in developed countries where donations can be gathered, and in developing countries where the water projects need to take place. The organization then acts as a bridge between the two worlds, providing funding and support to locally based project partners, and bringing to donors the stories of communities changed by clean drinking water and better sanitation.

Stating that 100 per cent of every dollar raised through public donations is delivered directly to projects on the ground, Charity: Water encourages donations in several ways. The website provides tools for individual fundraising campaigns for wells, school-based programmes to support schools located in water-poor areas, a store where you can purchase Charity: Water paraphernalia to support the organization as a whole, and straightforward opportunities to donate. The organization's website also shows each water project using Google Maps and GPS coordinates, which allows donors to see exactly where their money has been spent.

Water for People (www.waterforpeople.org)

Two former American Water Works Association officers and a colleague put their efforts into creating an organization dedicated to 'building a world where all people have access to safe drinking water and sanitation, and where no one suffers or dies from a water- or sanitation-related disease'. Currently working in 11 countries, Water for People was formed in 1991, and to date it has supported hundreds of thousands of successful water projects in 40 countries.

Water for People operates on a localized system. It establishes deep relationships with local governments, businesses, organizations and people to understand the water issues and resources at hand. Each country has its own Water for People coordinator who connects the funding and support of the organization with worthy projects in areas with the most need. Water for People uses a dedicated, well-trained group of volunteers known as the World Water Corps to monitor work in the field. The Corps keeps the lines of communication open, and brings a great amount of integrity to the work Water for People is so dedicated to doing. Other areas where Water for People stands out include its desire to constantly learn about water issues on a micro-level, its ability to encourage locally based businesses in water-poor communities, and the development of a new data monitoring project to allow for continual monitoring and public broadcasting of its projects.

United Nations Children's Fund (www.unicef.org)

Founded in 1946 by the United Nations in an effort to meet the emergency needs of children in post-war Europe and China, UNICEF was given a broader mandate in 1950 to address the long-term needs of children and women in developing countries everywhere. It is precisely these two groups of people that are often burdened with finding water for their families and all that entails, making clean water issues a priority for UNICEF.

Working in more than 90 countries on issues of water, sanitation and hygiene – the WASH programme – UNICEF is working for:

> *children's rights to survival and development through promotion of the sector and support to national programmes that increase equitable and sustainable access to, and use of, safe water and basic sanitation services, and promote improved hygiene.*

The organization does this using a human rights-based approach in partnership with the communities it touches. In addition to the WASH issues, UNICEF focuses on the environment and dealing with emergency situations, and is also tuned-in to the need to keep women and girls at the forefront, helping to keep girls in school as active students and away from the responsibility of finding clean water and cleaning bathrooms both at school and at home.

WaterAid (www.wateraid.org)

Founded as a charitable trust of the United Kingdom's water industry in 1981, WaterAid is now an international leader in bringing clean water to the places that need it most. With a mission to 'transform lives by improving access to safe water, hygiene and sanitation in the world's poorest communities', WaterAid is dedicated to exposing the connection between poverty and the lack of clean water and sufficient sanitation. With global member offices in the UK, the United States, Sweden and Australia, the organization has a global presence with regional support.

A current goal is to see that 25 million people have access to safe water and improved hygiene and sanitation by 2015, and that the organization's legislative work affects another 100 million. These goals will be achieved using the time-tested approaches of partnership, integrated projects, community participation and advocacy. WaterAid is also leading the way with integral studies, such as its recent effort to explore sustainability and equity aspects of community-led sanitation initiatives, which expose the various social barriers that stand in the way of safe water, hygiene and sanitation for everyone.

Active:Water (www.activewater.org)

After creating and completing the Earth Expedition, Daren Wendell founded Active:Water in 2008 to inform the world about the need for safe drinking water and to create long-lasting projects in communities where safe drinking water is an issue. The organization does this by 'creating a vocal platform built from athletic quests that attract overwhelming interest and media exposure'. The attention gained is then used to fuel inspiration and direct action towards water projects around the world. Called Team Active:Water, individuals can use the organization's website to find an athletic event in which they want to participate, and then work with the organization to establish fundraising tools and techniques to raise money for Active:Water's cause.

Active:Water has a holistic approach, seeking to go deep rather than wide with its drinking water projects. The organization takes on only a few at a time, dedicating a number of years to each one. Currently the fledging organization is focused on making change in Zambia, and has plans for a project in Latin America in the near future. With each project comes meaningful and carefully selected partnerships with the local community and other organizations who support the same holistic approach. Active:Water also believes that every person who is inspired by this model should participate. As such, they embrace grass-roots fundraising efforts beyond athletic events from cake sales to public speaking, even encouraging people to submit their own unique fundraising ideas.

Columbia Water Center (http://water.columbia.edu)

A part of the Earth Institute at Columbia University, the Water Center was founded in 2008 to 'creatively tackle the issue of global water scarcity through innovations in technology, public policy and private action'. Its academic base gives the organization the unique ability to lead 'intellectual inquiry' into why there is a global shortage of clean, safe drinking water, and what to do about it.

With studies and projects taking place around the world, The Water Center is currently focusing much of its energy on the largest user of water worldwide: agriculture, in both the public and private sectors. The organization is also well suited to bring people together around this most pressing of issues, and is currently seeking funding for the Global Roundtable on Water (GROW). GROW will allow leading forces to work together to create 'efficient, global and holistic strategies to resolve the current problems of water scarcity'. The organization is also working on projects related to water and development, climate, security, conflicts and cooperation.

Worldwide Water Foundation (www.wwwf.org)

An international non-profit organization dedicated to 'serving the world's developing countries by providing a solution to water-related problems', the Worldwide Water Foundation takes the unique approach of travelling by water to its destinations around the world. Travelling by ship allows the staff to bring all the equipment and goods necessary for drilling wells, and additional goods for humanitarian aid.

The organization has three areas of focus: to supply clean drinking water through well-drilling and water-resource projects; to consolidate and transport humanitarian goods to developing nations; and to assist other humanitarian efforts with well-drilling, water-resource projects and shipping of equipment and containers. Recently the Worldwide Water Foundation partnered with another organization to supply 130 water wells to indigenous people who live along the Amazon River in Brazil, and is expanding its fleet of ships to accommodate more water-resource projects.

Global Water Foundation (www.globalwaterfoundation.org)

Started by former professional tennis champion Johan Kriek, and water and sanitation expert Minnie Hildebrand in 2006, the Global Water Foundation is a charitable trust that supports humanitarian efforts 'with the ultimate goal of providing safe, healthy drinking water and adequate sanitation in areas where it is not available or where accessibility and supply have been compromised'.

As a trust, Global Water Foundation provides financial support in the form of grants to communities around the world. The type of projects funded are local incentives, new and existing local projects, replication projects and local entrepreneurial endeavours. Funding in these areas is strictly limited to projects in water and sanitation. Both of the organization's founders hail from South Africa, and consequently the main focus at present is on African countries, although some projects are taking place elsewhere. The Global Water Foundation also works with other current and former tennis players to raise money and awareness for water issues.

Water Missions International (www.watermissions.org)

A non-profit Christian organization grounded in engineering, Water Missions International (WMI) works around the world to bring safe, clean drinking water and sanitary conditions to communities in developing countries and disaster areas. With a vision 'that no person should perish for want of safe drinking water or an opportunity to hear the "Living Water" message', WMI has projects in 40 countries on three continents.

WMI starts its response to the global water crisis by employing 'engineering with compassion'. Dedicated to using available, appropriate technologies, the WMI engineering team designs systems that work for each location. The two most commonly used designs are The Living Water™ Treatment System and the Sanitary Pit Latrine. WMI also works with each community many months before the water project starts, helping to ready the people for a constant supply of clean drinking water. Once the water is there, education about health and hygiene continues. In disaster situations, both man-made and otherwise, the organization employs The Living Water™ Treatment System. Since 1998, WMI has helped deliver water in more than 20 countries where such disasters have occurred. All of this is done in the name of Jesus Christ and delivering the Living Water message.

International Union for Conservation of Nature (IUCN) (www.iucn.org)

The IUCN established the Water Programme in 1985 and has been working globally to protect and conserve water resources, primarily in the Middle East, Africa and Central and South America. The programme addresses issues such as integrated water-resource management, environmental flows, water economics and watershed ecosystems, as well as riverbank rehabilitation, and the effects of climate change on global water supply and distribution.

The goals of the IUCN Water Programme are to promote, influence and 'catalyse' sustainable use and sharing of water and protect ecosystems. The objectives of the programme are:

- development and implementation of a focused Union-wide water programme;
- establishment of an active network of members, commissions, individuals and institutions to implement the programme;
- influencing global debate and decisions on conservation and sustainable use of water resources;
- establishment of partnerships through the implementation of joint activities on water conservation.

UNESCO International Hydrological Programme (IHP) (www.unesco.org)

IHP is UNESCO's international scientific cooperative programme for water research, water resources management, education and capacity-building. It is also the only broad-based science programme within the UN organization.

The primary objectives of the IHP are to:

- facilitate cooperation of member states in increasing their knowledge of hydrological issues and increase capacity to better manage water resources;
- develop techniques, methodologies and approaches to better define hydrological conditions;
- improve water management, locally and globally;
- act as a catalyst to stimulate cooperation and dialogue in water science and management;
- assess the sustainable development of vulnerable water resources;
- serve as a platform for increasing awareness of global water issues.

World Water Council (WWC) (www.worldwatercouncil.org)

An international multi-stakeholder platform, established in 1996 by water specialists and international organizations with the intent to address global water issues. Its mission is:

> *to promote awareness, build political commitment and trigger action on critical water issues at all levels, including the highest decision-making level, to facilitate the efficient conservation, protection, development, planning, management and use of water in all its dimensions on an environmentally sustainable basis for the benefit of all life on earth.*

The Council provides a platform and framework to promote debates and an exchange of experience and ideas regarding the management of water resources across a wide range of stakeholders. Moreover, the Council catalyses initiatives and activities within the context of the World Water Forum.

Funding of the Council's activities and the World Water Forum is provided through membership fees and additional support from the host city of Marseilles, France. Specific projects and programmes are financed through donations and grants from governments, international organizations and NGOs.

Global Water Partnership (GWP) (www.gwp.org)

The Global Water Partnership's mission is to support the sustainable development and management of water resources; it promotes an integrated approach to managing the world's water resources.

The guiding principles of the organization are based upon the Dublin and Rio statements (1992); the Millennium Development Goals which arose from the Millennium Assembly in 2000; and the World Summit on Sustainable Development Plan of Action (2002). The Partnership expanded on these principles to promote the 'equitable and efficient management and sustainable use of water'. The principles of the Partnership are that:

- Fresh water is a finite and vulnerable resource, essential to sustain life, development and the environment.
- Water development and management should be based on a participatory approach involving users, planners and policy-makers at all levels.
- Women play a central part in the provision, management and safeguarding of water.
- Water is a public good and has a social and economic value in all its competing uses.

Integrated water resources management is emphasized, and as a result there is recognition that:

> water is an integral part of the ecosystem, a natural resource, and a social and economic good, whose quantity and quality determine the nature of its utilization.

International Water Management Institute (IWMI) (www.iwmi.cgiar.org)

The IWMI is focused on solving water and land management challenges faced by poor communities in the developing world. The IWMI contributes towards achieving the UN Millennium Development Goals (MDGs) to reduce poverty, hunger and to create a sustainable environment.

The IWMI primarily focuses on research, with the agenda organized around water availability and access; productive water use; water quality, health and environment; and water and society. It also develops research on the:

> assessment of land and water productivity and their relationship to poverty, identification of interventions that improve productivity as well as access to and sustainability of natural resources, assessment of the impacts of interventions on productivity, livelihoods, health and environmental sustainability.

IWMI efforts are collaborative, and it partners with a variety of public policy organizations, development agencies, individual farmers and private sector organizations.

blood:water mission (www.bloodwatermission.com)

Founded by the award-winning band Jars of Clay, blood:water mission started its journey by funding a late-stage AIDS hospice in Africa, where the organization quickly learned that clean water and HIV/AIDS are linked. In 2005 blood:water mission started the 1000 Wells Project, aimed at getting enough funding to supply clean drinking water and sanitation to 1000 communities in sub-Saharan Africa. Since then the organization has partnered with over 800 communities and brought clean water and sanitation to over half a million people, growing its 1000 Wells Project into a programme that supports overall healthy communities by also funding health clinics, community health workers and support groups.

blood:water mission believes in empowering the sub-Saharan communities it touches. To this end the organization works to draw out the people-power already in existence in these communities, and promotes 'a journey of self-discovery, giving communities a platform for understanding their own capabilities, assets and most importantly self-worth'. Partnerships are another backbone of the organization. Working hand in hand with local organizations, blood:water mission grows the partnership through its own model of CREATE: collaboration, relationships, empowerment, accountability and technical excellence. The organization then supplies funding and guidance for full-scale programmes called iWASH: Integrated Water, Sanitation and Hygiene. These programmes focus on education, community behaviour change, and sound practices relating to clean water and sanitation habits, as well as building and implementing a water infrastructure appropriate to the area.

References

Esty, D. C. and Winston, A. S. (2006) *Green to Gold: How Smart Companies Use Environmental Strategy to Innovate, Create Value, and Build Competitive Advantage*, Yale University Press, New Haven, CT

Meyer, C. and Kirby, J. (2010) 'Leadership in the age of transparency', *Harvard Business Review*, www.verizonbusiness.com/resources/reports/rp_harvard_business_leadership_transparency_en_xg.pdf, April 2010, accessed 15 September 2010

Molson Coors (2009) 'Molson Coors and Circle of Blue to partner in water sustainability research and public engagement', www.molsoncoors.com/newsroom/press-releases/2009/45-2009/608-molson-coors-and-circle-of-blue-to-partner-in-water-sustainability-research-and-public-engagement, accessed 30 June 2010

Savage, G. T., Nix, T. W., Whitehead, C. J. and Blair, J. D. (1991) 'Strategies for assessing and managing organizational stakeholders', *Academy of Management Executive*, vol 5, no 2, www.scribd.com/doc/31595252/International-Business-Research, accessed 15 September 2010

6

Water Technology

In the middle of every difficulty lies opportunity.

Albert Einstein

In June 2010, the United Kingdom's first desalination plant opened (Jowit, 2010). The facility, located in East London's Beckton, was built by Thames Water to address the water shortages faced by London and south-east England in 2005 and 2006. The £250 million desalination plant is designed to deliver about 140 million litres of fresh water for up to approximately 400,000 homes from the treatment of water from the sea and River Thames. The plant is novel in that it will run on biofuels, such as cooking oil and waste fat, in an effort to limit its overall impact on the environment through reduced greenhouse gas emissions.

This desalination plant was not without controversy. Thames Water maintained that current water resources were not able to keep up with predicted water demand in London and, as a result, they were tapping into the resource of the River Thames. The opponents, including former London Mayor Ken Livingstone, argued the plant was a waste of money, as it failed to address the real problem in London: leakage from the city's water-distribution network, which dates back to the Victorian period. It was also argued that the plant would increase greenhouse gas emissions.

The key opposing argument was that supplying extra water instead of deploying water metering and water efficiency would perpetuate the waste of water. The opposition finally conceded that, while the plant is more energy-efficient, it remains a carbon-intensive solution to addressing water scarcity.

The arguments for and against the Thames desalination plant highlight the inherent problems with how the public sector currently 'solves' water-scarcity problems. It also provides context for what needs to change, potential technologies to move the water industry into the 21st century, and options for industries to choose whether to manage water-scarcity risk or to invest in water technologies.

Overview of the Current Water Industry

What does the water industry need? Innovation. Not just innovation in technologies, but innovative pricing, partnerships and building entrepreneurship. Although the water industry has been characterized as slow to change, it is, in fact, changing.

An overview of the US water industry sets the stage for a discussion of what potential technology solutions will move the public and private sectors into 21st-century water stewardship. The US industry is sophisticated and mature but can benefit from new thinking on diversification of water sources and water reuse.

US water sector/infrastructure

The US water-supply infrastructure is centralized and consists of dams, reservoirs, groundwater well fields, pumping stations, aqueducts for water distribution, water-treatment plants and water towers. In the United States, about 14.5 per cent of the population has its own source of water, typically groundwater wells (USEPA, 2002a; US Geological Survey, 2005). The water-distribution system consists of approximately 1.8 million miles of water pipes (USEPA, 2002b). This centralized system also consists of 1.2 million miles of sewers (both sanitary and combined), pumping stations and more than 16,000 publicly owned wastewater-treatment plants (USEPA, 1999).

In the United States, publicly owned wastewater-treatment plants service approximately 190 million people and treat about 32.1 billion gallons per day. More than 9000 facilities provide secondary treatment; 4400 facilities provide advanced treatment; and 2000 facilities do not discharge (USEPA, 1999).

US water supply

Water in the United States is supplied primarily from surface water and/or groundwater. More than 90 per cent of public water systems there receive water from groundwater (USEPA, 2009b, 2010a). Some of the largest cities in the country (Boston, New York City, San Francisco and Portland) do not need to treat their surface water sources beyond disinfection, because their water sources are located in the upper reaches of protected watersheds and meet regulatory requirements (Committee to Review the New York City Watershed Management Strategy and National Research Council, 2000). For example, New York City's water supply is fed by the 2000 square mile (5200km²) watershed in the Catskill Mountains, which is one of the largest protected wilderness areas in the United States (New York City Department of Environmental Protection, 2005). Several major US cities, such as Phoenix and Los Angeles, are required to treat surface water prior to use.

Of the major US cities that are supplied primarily by groundwater, Miami obtains its drinking water primarily from the Biscayne Aquifer. Faced with increasing water demand, Miami-Dade County is considering the use of reclaimed water to help preserve the Biscayne Aquifer (MiamiDade.gov, 2010). Some cities, such as Houston, source both from groundwater and surface water. Approximately 71 per cent of the supply for Houston comes from the Trinity River into Lake Livingston, and from the San Jacinto River into Lake Conroe and Lake Houston. Deep underground wells provide the remaining 29 per cent of the city's water supply (City of Houston, 2010).

US water utilities

In 2007, there were about 52,000 community public water systems in the United States, which were either publicly owned, cooperatives or privately owned. Approximately 4000 systems provide water in locations with more than 10,000 residents, and the remaining 50,000 systems provide water in locations with fewer than 10,000 people (USEPA, 2009a).

US regulators

Regulation of water and sanitation service providers in the United States (including rate setting) is usually the responsibility of agencies such as public utility commissions (PUCs) at the state level, which are organized in the National Association of Regulatory Utility Commissioners. However, while all investor-owned utilities are subject to tariff regulation, only a few public utilities are subject to the same regulation. Only 12 states have laws restricting pricing practices by public water and sanitation utilities (Whittington and Boland, 2001). Environmental and drinking-water-quality regulation is the responsibility of state departments of health or environment and the US Environmental Protection Agency (USEPA) (The National Academies' Water Information Center, 2009).

US water use

It is not surprising that per capita water use in the United States is high when compared with other developed economies, being more than four times as high as in England (150 litres per person per day; Environment Agency, 2008) and five times as high as in Germany (126 litres per person per day) (ATT, BDEW et al, 2008).

Public water supply in the United States used 43 billion gallons (163 million m^3) per day in 2000, serving 242 million people, which is about 21 per cent of total water use in the same year (US Census Bureau, 2010;US Geological Survey, 2005). Residential (home) water use accounts for 66 per cent of publicly supplied water in the United States (USEPA, 2002b), with the remainder used by offices, public buildings, businesses and industry that do not have their own water sources.

Total water use was 161 gallons (608 litres) per capita per day from 1996 to 1998: 58 per cent is used outdoors for such things as gardening and swimming pools, corresponding to 101 gallons (382 litres) per capita per day; and 42 per cent is used indoors, corresponding to 60 gallons (226 litres) (Mayer, DeOreo et al, 1999). As amazing as it sounds, the arid US West has some of the highest per capita residential water use in the US, primarily due to landscape irrigation.

Only a very small share of public water supply is used for drinking. An estimated 56 per cent of Americans drink tap water, and an additional 37 per cent drink filtered tap water (USEPA, 2003). In addition, estimates of water losses in the United States are about 18 per cent of treated municipal water and approximately 40 per cent of municipal leakage in other developed economies (Lux Research Water Intelligence, 2008).

A New Way of Thinking

What does this overview tell us? The US water industry is complex and inefficient: water-supply sources are essentially limited to surface water and/or groundwater, water treatment is centralized and extensive distribution systems move water to points of use.

This is in the process of changing; with this change comes business opportunities.

Fortunately, there is movement towards a sustainable water infrastructure in the United States. Recently, the USEPA announced their 'Sustainable Infrastructure Initiative' (2010b), which has the goal of changing how the United States 'views, values, manages and invests in its water infrastructure'. The key elements of the initiative are focused on better management practices, efficient water use, full-cost pricing of water and a watershed approach. In summary, the programme is designed to address:

- Improved water management. Utilities are encouraged to adopt asset-management and environmental-management systems, along with consolidation and public/private partnerships.
- Full-cost pricing. This is promoted to assist utilities in capturing the actual costs of operating water systems and as an incentive to promote water-use efficiency.
- Water efficiency. Market incentives are created to promote the efficient use of water, along with the USEPA 'Water Sense' programme (www.epa.gov/watersense).
- Watershed management. The programme develops a broad view of water management to include the watershed. This goes well beyond a typical concern for water utilities in the United States.

The US Sustainable Infrastructure Initiative reflects elements identified in the Lux Research Water Intelligence report (2008). This excellent report lays out what is needed to transform how the public and private sectors manage water. In a world of increasing water scarcity, the status quo is no longer an option.

The central thesis of the Lux Research report is that the world currently 'hunts water' and will need to move to a framework of 'water cultivation'. Water is a classic 'tragedy of the commons' (Hardin, 1968).

Ownership by 'no one in particular', coupled with 'availability to everyone', creates an economic disincentive for stewardship. The current framework is characterized by:

- inefficiency: highly inefficient use of water from leakage and irrigation;
- disposability: a view of water as a single-use, disposable resource;
- homogeneous sources of supply: basically surface water and groundwater as water sources.

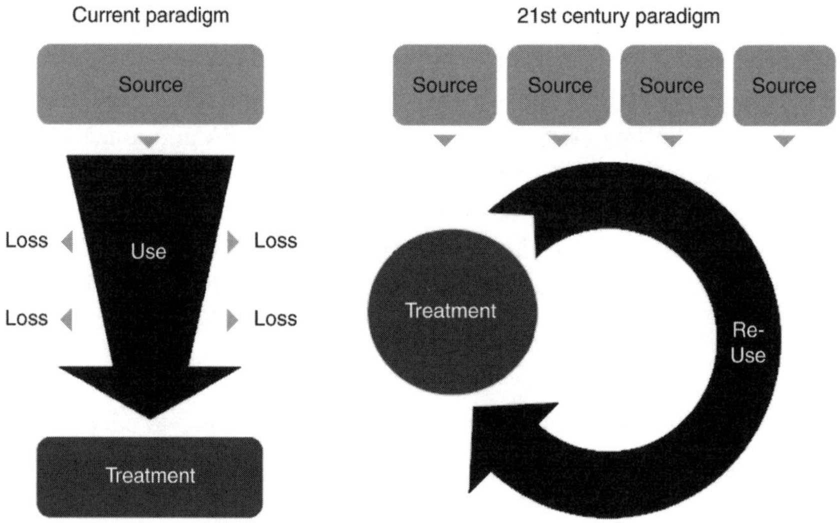

Figure 6.1 *Generalized view of current and 21st-century water frameworks*

Source: adapted from Lux Research Water Intelligence (2008)

What is needed is a new way to manage scarce water resources, and a water-cultivation mindset. This new mindset is illustrated in Figure 6.1, and see also Chapter 14.

The key elements of this new water framework are:

- efficiency: moving to maximize the economic output per unit of water;
- water-supply diversification: moving beyond surface water and groundwater as the only sources of water;
- reuse: treating water as a renewable and durable resource.

There is no shortage of technology opportunities within each of these key elements. Examples include:

- Efficiency:
  - repair of leaking infrastructure: cost-effective repair or replacement;
  - precision agriculture: moving to water-efficient agricultural water use, including adoption of drought-resistant crops;
  - mitigation of evaporation: movement to underground water storage and technologies to reduce water evaporation;

- water-efficient residential and industrial equipment: adoption of simple technologies, such as water-efficient toilets, washers and other household appliances.
- Water-supply diversification:
  - desalination: cost-effective conversion of salt water to fresh water;
  - groundwater exploration and extraction: exploration and sustainable development of groundwater aquifers, including deep aquifer extraction using innovative drilling techniques such as horizontal drilling (adopted from the oil and gas industry);
  - rainwater capture: adoption of simple rainwater-capture systems and corresponding changes in public policy and laws (for example, US western water law of prior appropriation);
  - long-distance water transport: development of cost-effective distribution systems to move water from water-rich to water-scarce areas;
  - water-vapour collection: technologies to capture and concentrate water vapour.
- Reuse:
  - simple reuse: adopting technologies to reuse water onsite with little to no treatment required, such as the reuse of greywater for flushing toilets or irrigation;
  - onsite reuse: treating water to the quality when it first arrived onsite; point-of-use water recycling technologies;
  - offsite reuse: development of cost-effective centralized water-recycling systems, essentially a closed-loop system.

Figure 6.2 shows a generalized view of water-reuse scenarios.

What Are the 'Water-Tech' Opportunities?

There will be no shortage of opportunities for entrepreneurs and established companies to develop innovative technologies to address water scarcity. The overall landscape for the water industry and technology categories is illustrated in Figure 6.3.

Opportunities within the water industry (new technologies and new business models) have been evaluated by Lux Research and McKinsey (Lux Research Water Intelligence summaries, October 2008; McKinsey & Company, December 2009). According to Lux Research, the challenge

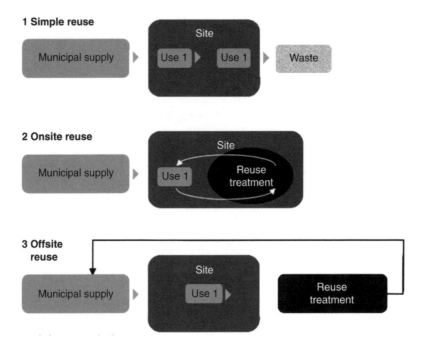

Figure 6.2 *Generalized view of water-reuse scenarios*

Source: adapted from Lux Research Water Intelligence (2008)

with the water sector is that markets are 'highly fragmented, each technology depends on each other, and adoption cycles are long'.

The 2008 Lux Research report, 'Water cultivation: the path to profit in meeting water needs' has some interesting findings:

- Global water-industry revenues were estimated at US$522 billion in 2007, with a rough breakdown of: US$385 billion in services, US$64 billion in equipment, US$9 billion in chemicals and US$62 billion in bottled water. An estimated 14 per cent of the revenue was in growth technologies and business models, of which about US$3.3 billion is in desalination technologies.
- Revenue is estimated to increase to about US$961 billion in 2020, as growth segments such as zero liquid discharge, ultraviolet (UV) disinfection, drip irrigation, and metering and monitoring emerge as viable technologies.
- Investors are increasingly moving to water technologies with about US$1.2 billion in venture-capital funding since 1998, and 59 per cent

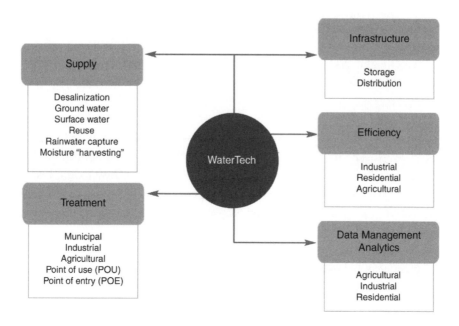

Figure 6.3 *The generalized 'water-tech' opportunities landscape*

Source: William Sarni

invested in the two years prior to the Lux Research report. In the past ten years, there were 506 mergers and acquisitions worth US$176 billion, and 39 initial public offerings have raised US$4.8 billion.

Currently identified technology and business-model opportunities include the following:

- sesalination advances, such as hybrid reverse osmosis, forward osmosis and freeze crystallization;
- infrastructure integrity, including trenchless drilling, in situ rehabilitation, infrastructure assessment and remote monitoring;
- innovative disinfection techniques, such as cavitation and high-energy irradiation for treatment of endocrine-disruptive substances;
- waste-management approaches, including zero liquid discharge, wastewater mining and brine disposal;
- water/energy technologies, such as pressure recovery, microbial fuel cells and sludge gasification;
- crop technologies, such as drought-resistant crops and crop-protection chemicals;

- data management to drive water efficiency in industrial, residential and agricultural uses;
- water rights and transportation, from private water districts and rights-management exchanges, to water exploration and long-distance transport models.

There are too many innovative water technologies to summarize (to track rapid developments, visit Lux Research www.luxresearch.com and Global Water Intelligence www.globalwaterintel.com), but a few examples of innovative water technologies and companies are provided below and discussed in the following section to get a sense of what water innovation looks like:

- NanOasis (www.nanoasisinc.com): desalination;
- NanoH2O (www.nanoh2o.com): desalination;
- Aquascience (www.aquasciences.com): atmospheric water capture and purification technologies;
- HydroPoint Data Systems, Inc. (www.weathertrak.com): water-efficient landscape watering;
- Fruition Sciences (www.fruitionsciences.com): precision agriculture;
- Rainwater HOG (http://rainwaterhog.com): rainwater capture;
- Water Smart Software (www.watersmartsoftware.com): water conservation software.

Water Innovation as a Business Opportunity

Several companies, including GE and Syngenta, have committed to developing innovative water technologies and practices; building innovative business models coupled with technologies ('The Water Initiative') and building innovation capacity in the marketplace (ImagineH2O). These innovators are highlighted below.

GE: More than imagining the future

For more than 100 years, GE has been an important part of what is known worldwide as American ingenuity. From engines and power generation to financing and medical imaging, GE has experience as varied as the entities it supports. That's why the unveiling of 'ecomagination^{SM}' in 2004, and with it GE's greener side, was no surprise. Not just another environmental advertising campaign, ecomagination^{SM} actively works towards solving global problems related to environmental sustainability challenges.

Ecomagination's initial focus was energy and greenhouse-gas reduction, but after a few years GE recognized that water scarcity represents a global challenge for both the public and private sectors. It was time for the company to emphasize this both internally and externally, so GE's water-related goal was announced in 2008: a 20 per cent reduction of all freshwater consumption, using a six-year baseline established from 2006–2012 (recently amended to 2006–2015) and a 25 per cent reduction. It's a massive undertaking, and GE is now actively gathering data and working through the details of how to reduce water company-wide, in 100 countries, with more than 300,000 employees.

This new goal has given GE employees a new level of awareness. Internally, they are beginning to understand their own water footprint and are moving towards reducing water use. Externally, with one foot in the municipal sector and the other in industry, GE is helping to lead the way in solving water-related issues through water reduction, water reuse and water technologies.

New water, less water

As a worldwide presence with 50,000 customers, GE is keenly aware of pressing global environmental issues. It has only been in recent years that water, both in quality and quantity, has come to the forefront. 'This is the first time global demand for water exceeds the supply', says Jeff Fulgham, chief sustainability officer at GE Water. 'In many parts of the world where they have not had scarcity issues before, there is a real struggle to get enough water to meet their needs.' GE is answering this cry for help by working with customers in all sectors of business to identify two things: sources of 'new water' and ways to reduce consumption.

New water: water reuse

Many entities have strived for water reduction using a water footprint as their guide. While this process reveals the quantity of water used to create a product or service, it falls short of looking at the entire water picture. The hidden costs of energy used to move that water, water treatment and even quality assurance are essential to understanding the bigger role water has to play and where reductions can be made. As director of environmental health and safety for corporate GE, Mark Stoler, says, it is not simply about looking at the cost of water and figuring out a return on investment based on that price – there are many other costs.

GE strives to internalize these externalities at its own facilities and in those of its customers. Internally, this allows GE to use its own water-saving technologies and practices, which makes them more meaningful when offered externally. By using its 2500-member engineer sales team as problem-solving engineers liaising with customers, Fulgham says:

> *[They can] look holistically at the entire site and develop ways to optimize the overall use of water from inlet to outlet, taking into account all incoming water sources, water and energy efficiency and wastewater reduction and reuse.*

GE says the most common areas for water reuse in an industrial plant include using alternative sources of water for supply, such as treated municipal wastewater; collecting and reusing utility water, such as cooling-tower blowdown; and capturing, treating and reusing the plant discharge. The common theme is closing loops – changing linear processes into cyclical ones that either support the process itself, or work in other businesses (the latter is commonly called 'industrial ecology').

When examining the source of water, GE looks to create 'beneficial water reuse'. Fulgham says: 'We work with our customers to examine less expensive, more sustainable sources of water.' Instead of allowing reclaimed water to be used for things such as irrigation and landscape, the company pushes for higher-value uses, such as cooling or boiler feeder-water applications. It's a shift in thinking – one of highlighting the resource readily available right onsite and deciding the best use for it. Outside of this rethinking of water onsite, GE looks to technologies such as desalination to create new sources of water.

In the utility sector, GE engineers help make the existing processes the most efficient they can be, thereby saving water and money. Whether achieving the highest recovery rates out of a membrane or a cooling tower, it's about reducing consumption and closing process loops.

Water discharge is an area where GE is able to lend a hand on several fronts. Many of its customers are direct-discharge entities that must meet regulations for clean water. Other customers are challenged by what to do with contaminated water produced while cleaning air in wet-scrubber systems. Fulgham explains:

> *Air problems are being addressed, but it's often shifting that con-taminant into a water stream. We can separate out metals, such as arsenic, selenium and mercury, and other contaminants, and allow that water to be discharged back into the environment without any problem.*

Viewing water discharge in this way has also poised GE to help in places where water quality is poor at either end of the process. 'We are looking at ways to pull useful, reusable material out of what, today, is looked at as a waste stream', Fulgham says. This turns a liability into an asset. In emerging markets, where industrial growth is often moving faster than regulation, the incoming water can be very low quality, and it takes a concerted effort to get that water up to par. As the water leaves the facility, the plant is expected to meet ever more stringent discharge guidelines. In the water-intensive extractive industries of unconventional gas and oil, Fulgham says GE technology can convert the wastewater produced into pure water, and, through a series of concentration, purification and drying processes, the resulting solids can be used as something else, such as an industrial salt or a chlor-alkali feedstock.

Less water: reduce consumption

Part and parcel of GE's brand of water reuse is a way to reduce the amount of water needed in any given process. While the idea of closing loops doesn't preclude the notion that less water is needed, it does mean that water is used in a larger variety of ways, which reduces the overall amount of water required.

Perhaps nowhere is this more obvious than where water meets energy. As Fulgham points out, 'It takes a large amount of energy to make water, and it takes a large amount of water to make energy.' When you can reduce one, you reduce the other. An example of this inter-relationship is Pennant Hills Golf Course in Australia, where ongoing drought and watering restrictions posed a continuous threat to the sustainability of the business. GE's water-reuse solution was to tap into a municipal sewer line and withdraw wastewater as the source of a new, drought-proof water supply for the golf club. In addition to providing a sustainable supply of

170,000 gallons of irrigation water per day, the municipality's energy consumption is reduced, as it no longer needs to pump and treat this wastewater stream – a true win–win result. According to Fulgham, 'GE is always looking at these interplays between water and power, and finding new opportunities for savings.'

Drawing the connection between water and other essentials, such as power, is also important in validating the examination of water issues. While we may know that water is essential for life, the water-pricing structure does not always reflect this level of importance. Fulgham agrees that the low cost of water in many parts of the world, relative to its value, is the main issue preventing behaviour change. Where cost savings from reducing water consumption are obvious, the gap is bridged more easily. GE's efforts to bring these issues to light in a positive way, such as working with the US Congress on a bill for an investment tax credit for industrial water reuse, are helping to create a clearer picture of just how much water affects everything around it, and the absolute need to conserve it, even if this results in higher prices.

Water technology: products and partnerships

GE is a company as well known for products as it is for services, and it is using technology to change the way people view and use water. GE is also working closely with international entities to help fill the gap in water-analysis tools by creating some of its own.

From the popular ultra-filtration product ZeeWeed, to energy-efficient desalination plants, the menu of water-related technologies is impressive. Perhaps even more telling is that GE is using its own technology, such as ultrasonic flow sensors and reverse-osmosis systems in its own facilities, as it works to understand and ultimately achieve its 25 per cent reduction goal.

Mark Stoler says:

> We've been utilizing our own product internally to get a better idea within our own facilities where our water flows are coming from and how much flow there is. We've identified a number of big projects at facilities, which I think will be very good demonstration projects for GE water technology.

GE is also partnering with Goldman Sachs and the World Resource Institute to develop a water-risk index. While many similar tools are available, they focus mainly on water availability. Fulgham explains:

> *We wanted to look beyond availability to water quality, social and*
> *political issues at the local level, regulatory effects and overall be-*
> *haviours around water. We look at this as a 'water opportunity' tool.*

Goldman Sachs, on the other hand, is very interested in using this tool to
look at long-term investment risk. The company wants to be sure it can
provide customers with an accurate assessment of how sustainable water
supplies might be 5–10 years from now in any given area. This comple-
ments GE's desire to encourage customers to think long term about water,
and the timing is right. 'I've been in this space for 28 years, and I've never
seen as much interest in long-term sustainability around water as there is
today', Fulgham says.

To meet this need, the new water-indexing tool has recently completed
its pilot in China's Yellow River Basin. 'It's an area with heightened
interest and a lot of water challenges', Fulgham says. 'It's booming from
a growth standpoint. If we can get data there, we can probably get it anywhere.' Fulgham wants the tool to be available for use by the public by the
end of 2011. 'It isn't something we're going to hide behind the curtain', he
says. 'It's something we want to put out there for anyone to use.'

While GE plans to use the tool itself and with its customers, it does not
want to push anyone away from a successful tool they are currently using.
In addition to assessing water risk, there is a multistep process to reducing
water consumption and increasing water reuse, and GE feels its strength is
in guiding the latter part of the process. Fulgham says:

> *If a customer has adopted the World Business Council for Sustainable*
> *Development's water tool or GEMI, that covers step one of the pro-*
> *cess. I'd like to see us continue to steps two, three, four and so on.*

Still, he concedes that their water-risk index is meant to fill a lot of gaps
that exist with other water-indexing tools, such as local regulatory government and attitudes about water in a localized region.

ecomagination[SM]

The GE ecomagination[SM] initiative has been a clear success in demonstrating that sustainability can drive innovation in the energy sector. Now
GE is at the forefront of creating new business opportunities in the water
sector and deploying integrated approaches to reducing energy use, water
use and carbon emissions.

Syngenta: sowing the seeds

Agriculture has been part of human existence for thousands of years, leaving in its path civilizations that have both flourished and disappeared. Water has always been at the core of these historic success and failures, even in our modern day, where water is often taken for granted. In 2000 Syngenta was formed, a new agribusiness which also has water at its core, giving it a decidedly different flavour from other agribusinesses.

With more than 25,000 employees working in more than 90 countries, Syngenta has a global view of water issues and a deep understanding that, while water is a global resource, it's still a very local problem. According to Robert Berendes, Syngenta's head of business development, it is a keen knowledge of this fact that guides Syngenta, driving a business model that relies on a marriage of technology, commercial awareness, alliances and leadership. While Syngenta has a robust global water strategy that includes reducing its own water use, it recognizes that the bigger contribution in addressing global water issues is getting the global agricultural sector – from the tiny family farm to the largest commercial grower – to use water more efficiently.

Four strategies: a complete package

Syngenta takes a 'crop per drop' view. 'We're developing integrated programmes of products that improve water consumption and efficiency across the board', Berendes says. This has given Syngenta what Berendes calls the 'broadest toolbox in the industry' to create meaningful change in agriculture around the world:

> *If you want to tackle agricultural problems, you have to apply all different elements of the toolbox. If you really want to come to a breakthrough, it's foolish to assume a single silver bullet is going to get you there.*

Technology

Technology is the one area most people think about when considering the agribusiness sector, and is certainly an important tool when looking to fix water issues. At Syngenta, technology reaches beyond working with genetically modified crops and creating better herbicides, though those are two areas in which Syngenta does work. In fact, they currently offer crop-protection technology for wheat that reduces water needs by 25 per cent and yields 10 per cent more per crop. 'We'll work on genetically modified solutions', Berendes says, 'but we don't believe those solutions, on their own, will be sufficiently effective.' To that end, the company has dedicated research and development resources to create non-genetically modified crops, such as a corn bred through natural processes to be drought-tolerant. Scheduled for release in 2011, it saves 10 to 15 per cent of the water of standard corn and has a 20 per cent higher yield.

One of the biggest technological advancements for Syngenta is not in altering the crop at seed, but its product Invinsa™, which is applied to the crop after planting to prevent withering and death from drought, while obtaining a 10 per cent water saving. Invinsa™ is composed of an ethylene-blocking chemical called 1-methylcyclopropene (1-MCP). This blocks the release of ethylene, a process required for the maturing of the plant, which can be triggered early by water deprivation and other environmental stress factors.

Syngenta tested the use of Invinsa™ in a gaseous form inside greenhouses. Berendes says:

> *You can't do that in an open field. Our technology development of Invinsa™ has been able to put the gas into granules, which can be applied in an open field. Through the interaction with water, the chemical is slowly released, having the same effect on the plant as the gas in the greenhouse.*

Commercial: making the technology accessible

Syngenta may be developing important water-saving and crop-saving technologies, but it would all be for nothing if these products seemed inaccessible to the end user. In the world of agribusiness, this happens more often than one might think. According to Berendes, the information available to farmers allowing them to compare technologies, chemicals and seeds with monetary savings and water management is not well organized or well presented:

> *That leads to confusion, and confusion leads people away from adopting technology – despite the fact it's shown to have a real effect in the field ... [Syngenta works] ... in both the technology-innovation side and the commercial side to put agronomic solutions together for the grower, making sure they see the benefit [of the combined resources available to them].*

Part of the confusion growers feel is due to the global nature of agri-business. 'The solutions for Australia look different from those for the southern United States, which look different from southern India, which look different from those in Vietnam', Berendes explains. This means Syngenta has adopted 'very local economy logic', making sure to get the right message to the right audience.

A piece of this approach is assessing just what people mean when they say 'water issue', and then acting on that localized concern. Berendes says:

> *People use one [term] but actually mean other things by it. Some people mean heat spells, others mean drought tolerance, and still others may mean simple water reduction under normal circumstances.*

One of the ways Syngenta addresses this is to commit to partnerships and relationships with government, non-governmental organizations (NGOs) and other companies.

Alliances: breaking down barriers

A major strength of Syngenta is in its willingness and desire to engage multiple stakeholders. This is, without a doubt, a differentiating factor that serves the company well. Since its inception, Syngenta has managed to work with many different entities, always in the name of breaking down barriers, to achieve agricultural milestones that reduce water use and increase crop yield around the world.

According to Berendes, when Syngenta looks to partner with another business, they're not seeking to create an alliance with a competitor. 'It's more about companies down the food chain and other influential companies in various situations', such as finding like-minded businesses with complementary skill sets to seeds, crops and water.

So far, Syngenta has partnered with those in drip-irrigation technologies, water awareness and crop breeding, to name a few areas of interest. With each of these partnerships comes new interconnected products and ideas, as well as breakthrough technologies such as Invinsa™. The partnership with the drip-irrigation sector, for example, has led to the possibility of developing seeds bred to thrive specifically with the use of drip irrigation, creating both economic development and water-wise crops. It has also led to examination of common practices, such as flooding rice paddy fields for weed control, and provoked discussion about possible new approaches that use a combination of efforts such as drip irrigation and herbicide to effectively grow rice using far less water. 'Engaging with others collectively and being known as a company that can come up with credible solutions is an important element to success', Berendes says.

Thought leadership

The first three strategies really culminate under the fourth of leadership. It is here Syngenta takes its role in the global water game very seriously, joining forces and pushing boundaries to spread the word that global water resources are fast approaching – if not already facing – a major crisis. 'Water is such an instrumental, base requirement; there is nothing more basic. Whenever people have issues with water, it immediately leads to that crisis situation', Berendes says.

He feels that it is the enormous role agriculture plays in the water picture globally that pushes Syngenta to stretch its reach into places such as the World Economic Forum (WEF) (www.weforum.org), an 'independent international organization committed to improving the state of the world by engaging leaders in partnerships to shape global, regional and industry agendas'. In collaboration with the WEF and other leading corporations such as Nestlé, Coca-Cola and SABMiller, and the international management consulting firm McKinsey & Company, Syngenta helped to create the water report, 'Charting our water future: economic frameworks to inform decision-making' (2030 Water Resources Group, 2009). The report 'provides greater clarity on the scale of the water challenge and how it can begin to be met in an affordable and sustainable manner'.

One of the key aspects of the report underscores Syngenta's belief that, while water is a global issue, it needs to be dealt with in a very local manner. This makes the report an especially useful tool for governments and NGOs that work with the agricultural sector. Berendes says most of the measures identified in the report for farmers are extremely cost-effective, and are often cost-free to the farmer. By using situations in hot-spot areas around the world as case studies, the report was able to develop a framework to solve water problems anywhere in the world. According to Berendes, the report takes a daunting issue such as water and helps people to see how it is possible to start dealing with it in a cost-efficient way.

Valuing water

As Syngenta moves forward with its four water strategies, it is helping the world recognize the very value of water. With tools such as 'Charting our water future' and strong economic-development partnerships, Syngenta has the ability to educate governments around the globe about the varied connections among water, agriculture and local economies.

One of the areas where this becomes challenging is with regard to water pricing. According to Berendes, pricing structures should vary depending on the availability of water and the success of the local economy. In areas where the markets are developed and thriving, a higher price on water would be 'an enabler of driving technology', because the additional benefits of saving water and money would be highly quantifiable. However, in places where the market is developing, using some form of government subsidy to enforce the right kind of water behaviour would be of long-term benefit. 'If you just put the burden through with a price on the farmers in an unprotected way, it creates a very tough situation', he explains.

Syngenta believes subsidies, when used thoughtfully, are a tool in that ever-important toolbox. 'If you want to encourage water-efficiency behaviour in developing markets where water is scarce but practically free, incentives via subsidies might be a smart way', Berendes says.

He also says government can and should have a larger role in creating water-saving standards for farmers through regulatory frameworks. In order to do that, publicly funded research and development dollars need to be more available: 'Public spending for agriculture has gone from 17 per cent in the 1950s to about 3 per cent recently.' This puts the brunt of the research and development squarely on the shoulders of business. Syngenta believes a partnership between government and business would be a far stronger approach.

Water as a critical global issue

It's Syngenta's view that water is the most important issue of our time; Berendes says that:

> *The base facts are clear, the issue is well-defined, and the upcoming gap has been identified. The biggest issues and, thus, improvements have also been identified. It is now time to move into action, and Syngenta is a company that can lead us there by example.*

The Water Initiative: the point is now

Based on studies, surveys, conversation and just plain common sense, water is *the* issue to which people worldwide should be devoting more time and energy. While many corporations are looking at ways to reduce process-related water consumption or create products to consume less water down the value chain, The Water Initiative (TWI) is moving straight to what is called 'point of drinking' (POD) technology and solutions. TWI Chairman Kevin McGovern says:

> *There's so much dialogue, and studies about unclean water issues, and so little funding and other resources dedicated to innovations and deployment of solutions ... contaminated-water issues affect us today; so many other issues garnering far more support are tomorrow's issues.*

TWI believes the global focus needs to shift away from second-tier needs such as oil and power generation, when the most basic of all needs is not being met. Currently focused on deploying solutions in Mexico, TWI hopes to employ 10,000 local people and provide safe, clean drinking water to one million homes in Latin America. It will then move on to other areas in need, through a process that involves stimulating the local economy, as it lowers the rate of death due to water-borne disease.

Global issue, local solutions/diagnostics

The global consensus about water is that each region, and even localities within those regions, have water issues specific to their geographic and social climates. A localized approach to solving water issues makes the most sense. TWI has taken this view and internalized it, creating a business model that focuses deeply in any given region and works with local change agents to spread the word and sell their products. It's a marriage of water awareness, technology, social networking and business generation. By approaching water issues in this manner, TWI is creating more than just new technology.

Water awareness

This is the beginning of the TWI multistep process, and something any water-solutions company ought to have: an understanding of water and the local issues surrounding it. According to the TWI website (www. thewaterinitiative.com):

> *Many 'made in USA' technological solutions have been introduced to low-income markets, but have failed to gain traction because they do not address the communities' unmet needs and are perceived as foreign.*

To avoid this, the first thing TWI does is make a comprehensive regional assessment that includes understanding the water supply, contaminants and their sources, infrastructure and community needs. To aid in this process, the company is creating a front-end software programme that will include current water technologies. Used as a field diagnostic, this programme will be able to process the aforementioned factors against the list of technologies, and suggest an optimal solution or combination of solutions for any given area.

Having chosen Latin America, an area of the world where pathogens (bacteria and viruses), as well as both arsenic and fluoride, regularly contaminate water, TWI is immediately learning how to combat all these common issues in the global drinking-water supply. Not only does this deepen the company's water awareness from the beginning, but it also gives unique insight that allows TWI to create comprehensive, cutting-edge, meaningful technology that addresses all issues with one device.

Technology/development

The ability to create 'tailored solutions to the local market' is manifested both in new technology and a reliable process that can be applied around the world. WATERCURA®, possibly the gem in TWI's array of meaningful products, is the latest in the young company's product list.

One of the WATERCURA® products is an arsenic-removal system, designed to be installed in the home, that removes the common carcinogen to World Health Organization-approved safety standards, and disposes of it through a means that meets the USEPA's Toxicity Characteristic Leaching Procedure. It also provides pathogen, chlorine (bad taste) and pipe-particle removal, treats 1000 gallons of water for continuous availability and relies on gravity flow. Even in countries such as the United States, where water quality is perceived to be high, arsenic is present and detectable in more than 30 states at concentrations that exceed acceptable USEPA standards.

TWI uses four technological steps to create safe drinking water on a municipal or facility level in Mexico, where it has worked since 2007 – a process it calls 'point of drinking technology'. First the water is pre-filtered, removing particulates of at least 5 microns in size. Next, chemicals such as arsenic, fluoride, mercury, nitrates, nitrites and lead are all removed. TWI is careful to use different absorption material based on the chemical profile revealed in the initial local water assessment. The process then improves the colour and odour of the water by removing tannins or chlorine. The last step disinfects the water.

'Unclean water – and resultant waterborne diseases – is the No. 1 public health issue in the world today', McGovern explains. Adding a disinfectant stage allows for a 'measure of assurance'. Water is then stored, tested and available for sale. TWI is also examining additional options, such as heating, cooling or even flavouring the water upon exit from the system.

Social networking and business generation

While TWI conducts a water analysis and co-creates technology for its target market, the company focuses on community immersion. With a sound understanding of local issues, TWI works with a 'carefully selected representative' or groups of locals to co-create the products for market. Accomplished by mobilizing the 'bottom of the pyramid' (BoP) population through forming and supporting local businesses focused on the water technology at hand, TWI calls this its:

> BoP Protocol, [which is] co-creation – the integration of the capabilities of the local community and the sponsoring company (in this case TWI) to develop a business that neither alone could develop and that addresses the community's expressed needs.

Partnering with local citizens in this fashion not only fortifies the local economy, but it's also a sound investment for TWI. As many governments and corporations focus on the 'ToP' or 'top of the income pyramid' for apparently available dollars, TWI has found that, in fact, the buying power and influence of the bottom pyramid segment is substantial – to the tune of 5 trillion dollars a year, globally. According to the company, 'Indeed, while per capita incomes may be low at the BoP, taken as a whole, there is substantial purchasing power.'

Once these local relationships are formed and businesses are thriving, TWI looks again to social networks for business expansion, both within the region and to neighbouring areas also in need. The goal is to create new local companies in all areas where water issues occur, thereby placing the health of the local water supply, citizenry and a section of the local economy squarely in the hands of the local people. 'Entrepreneurial engagement is essential to implement sustainable unclean water solutions', McGovern says.

In addition, upgraded versions of WATERCURA® will be marketed to middle-class markets and home developers to generate increased cash flow for TWI's sustainability initiatives.

Future movement

Mexico has proved an exemplary place for the company to start, as it provides strong political support, grant money and a population facing many of the same issues as others in need of clean, safe drinking water. From here, The Water Initiative plans to bring its process to Africa, China and other countries where the need is great.

Imagine H20: seizing the opportunity

In an era where corporations have an increasing responsibility to citizens around the world and are stepping up their corporate social responsibility actions and reports, it's surprising that so much of the important action on water issues comes from the already-strapped non-profit sector. Instead of seeing this challenge as yet another fault in 'the system', Imagine H2O is seizing the opportunity. A non-profit organization started in 2007 by a unique and powerful group from Harvard Business School, Imagine H2O (www.imagineH2O.org/about/ourstory.php) is entirely focused on what it calls 'the water opportunity'. By offering competitions, cash prizes, business incubation and a water-resources network, Imagine H2O is hoping to create real impact on all water-related issues around the world.

Inspire, incubate, interconnect

The founders of Imagine H2O were seeking answers to global water questions that no one could provide:

- What does the water market look like in dollars?
- What problems need to be solved?
- Which of those offer the best commercial opportunities?
- With whom should we connect for help, advice and partnership?

It became obvious to them that, in order to find these answers, they would need to mobilize people around the world who were willing to investigate water problems and find viable, commercially sustainable solutions to these problems. If there were competitions that awarded large cash prizes, those people would come forward; and if the contestants were offered more than simple cash prizes and trophies – if they were given real sustenance, such as business incubation – then local economies would be strengthened, while the global water crisis is being solved.

The shrewd group of leaders from the energy, water and non-profit sectors decided against creating a venture-capitalist business to fund this vision. Instead, they opted for the creation of a non-profit organization, armed with the knowledge that non-profit organizations are in a unique position to unite stakeholders from across all sectors: government, business and the people. Appropriately, Imagine H2O also seeks to create an 'ecosystem' of water innovators and resources from around the world to support the new business ventures.

One of the main differences between Imagine H2O and other nonprofit organizations is its foundation: it was started by entrepreneurs and has business development at its core. According to Imagine H2O, the water market for products and services is valued at US$500 billion and is one of the largest industries in the world. Herein is 'the water opportunity'. With a mission to 'inspire and empower people to solve water problems' and a vision to 'turn water problems into opportunities', the fledgling non-profit organization has a fresh approach to tackling water issues.

Inspire

Citing historic competitions such as the Orteig Prize, which prompted the success and innovation of Charles Lindberg, Imagine H2O believes nothing can motivate and generate creative thinking quite like good old-fashioned competition. A proven tactic in sectors across business, offering a competition appeals to those with an entrepreneurial spirit. It can be enough to nudge a burgeoning idea into reality, and, when it comes to solving the global water crisis, it can be a lifeline into communities where water issues are great and financial support is not. Imagine H2O wants to 'harness the power of competition, capitalism and entrepreneurship, instead of relying on philanthropy and policy-based solutions' in the developing and developed world (www.imagineH2O.org/about/ourmodel.php).

Open to anyone and everyone around the world, the Imagine H2O annual competitions change focus each year and aim to support as many viable business ideas as they can. The non-profit organization also sees the value of competition outside the business arena. In the future, there will be competitions in the areas of science, youth innovation and policy. These are all areas where Imagine H2O wants to help 'turn great ideas into real-world solutions that ensure available clean water and sanitation' around the world.

Incubate

One of the ways the Imagine H2O model stands out is in its commitment to incubating businesses along with its competitions. As an organization founded and fuelled by the energy of entrepreneurs, Imagine H2O operates with a clear vision: the large struggle for water is a large business opportunity. By keeping the focus of each competition solely on water and ensuring that well-developed countries are not excluded as potential users of the new products and services being presented, Imagine H2O has been able to attract a wide range of contestants.

The winners are not only given cash prizes but are also supported with in-kind services in the areas of accounting and law, and given resources and contacts in other areas that can be hard for a new business to obtain. But Imagine H2O doesn't believe supporting only the winners will create real change around the world quickly enough, as time to put effective measures in place is running short. The non-profit organization provides seminars, workshops, business feedback, networking and team-building opportunities, and guidance to every single contestant.

So far the competitions have helped to make water savings from businesses in the areas of irrigation, rainwater storage, water-based software programs and others.

Interconnect

Perhaps the most vital aspect of Imagine H2O is the organization's drive to create and provide 'an ecosystem of stakeholders to the next great water innovations' (www.imagineH2O.org/about). An ecosystem implies dynamic, interconnected relationships, not static operations. With this as the model, Imagine H2O uses its non-profit status to position itself in the middle of this intricate web of business resources, helping guide both business and resource as they look for appropriate connections. Water is a global issue with very local implications. As the thread that weaves Imagine H2O's web of interconnectivity together, it is, in more ways than one, an underpinning to its success.

References

2030 Water Resources Group (2009) 'Charting our water future: economic frameworks to inform decision-making', www.mckinsey.com/App_Media/Reports/Water/Charting_Our_Water_Future_Full_Report_001.pdf, accessed 4 October 2010

ATT (Association of Drinking Water from Reservoirs), BDEW (German Association of Energy and Water Industries), DBVW (German Alliance of Water Management Associations), DVGW (German Technical and Scientific Association for Gas and Water), DWA (German Association for Water, Wastewater and Waste) and VKU (Association of Local Utilities) (2008)*Profile of the German Water Industry 2008*, wvgw Wirtschafts- und Verlagsgesellschaft Gas und Wasser mbH, Bonn

City of Houston (2010) 'Drinking water operations', Department of Public Works and Engineering, Public Utilities Division, www.publicworks.houstontx.gov/utilities/drinkingwater.html, accessed 30 June 2010

Committee to Review the New York City Watershed Management Strategy and National Research Council (2000) *Watershed Management for Potable Water Supply: Assessing the New York City Strategy*, National Academies Press, Washington, DC

Environment Agency (2008) *Water Resources in England and Wales: Current State and Future Pressures*, http://publications.environment-agency.gov.uk/pdf/GEHO1208BPAS-e-e.pdf, December 2008, accessed 30 June 2010

Hardin, G. (1968) 'Tragedy of the commons', *Science*, vol 162, no 3859, pp1243–1248

Jowit, J. (2010) 'Thames Water opens first large-scale desalination plant in UK', *The Guardian*, 2 June, www.guardian.co.uk/environment/2010/jun/02/thames-water-desalination-plant, accessed 3 November 2010

Lux Research Inc. (2008) Press Release: 'Water cultivation: The path to profit in meeting water needs', Nov. 13, 2008, www.luxresearchinc.com/press/release_water_SMr_11_13_08.pdf

Lux Research Water Intelligence (2008) 'Water: evolution & outlook of the hydrocosm', Lux Research, http://www2.luxresearchinc.com/water_hydrocosm_download, accessed 30 June 2010

Mayer, P. W., DeOreo, W. B., Opitz, E., Kiefer, J., Davis, W., Dziegielewski, B. and Nelson J. O. (1999) *Residential End Uses of Water*, American Water Works Association Research Foundation, Denver, CO

McKinsey & Company (2009) 'The business opportunity in water conservation', *McKinsey Quarterly*, no. 1

MiamiDade.gov (2010) 'Reclaimed water', www.metro-dade.com/wasd/water_reclaim.asp, accessed 30 June 2010

The National Academies' Water Information Center (2009) 'Drinking water basics', http://water.nationalacademies.org/basics_part_5.shtml, accessed 30 June 2010

New York City Department of Environmental Protection (2005) 'New York City 2005 drinking water supply and quality report', www.nyc.gov/html/dep/pdf/wsstat05.pdf, accessed 30 June 2010

US Census Bureau (2010) 'Table 354. US Water withdrawals per day by end use: 1940 to 2000', http://tiny.cc/j826l, accessed 30 June 2010

USEPA (United States Environmental Protection Agency) (1999) 'Drinking water state revolving fund (DWSRF): frequent questions', www.epa.gov/owm/cwfinance/cwsrf/cwsrf.pdf, May 1999, accessed 30 June 2010

USEPA (2002a) 'Drinking water from household wells', www.epa.gov/privatewells/pdfs/household_wells.pdf, January 2002, accessed 30 June 2010

USEPA (2002b) 'Community water system survey 2000', www.epa.gov/ogwdw000/consumer/pdf/cwss_2000_volume_i.pdf, December 2002, accessed 30 June 2010

USEPA (2003) 'Analysis and findings of the Gallup Organization's drinking water customer satisfaction survey', www.epa.gov/safewater/ccr/pdfs/tools_survey_gallup_customersatification2003.pdf, August 2003, accessed 30 June 2010

USEPA (2009a) 'FACTOIDS: drinking water and ground water statistics for 2009', www.epa.gov/safewater/databases/pdfs/data_factoids_2009.pdf, November 2009, accessed 30 June 2010

USEPA (2009b) 'Water on tap: what you need to know', www.epa.gov/safewater/wot/pdfs/book_waterontap_full.pdf, December 2009, accessed 30 June 2010

USEPA (2010a) 'New York City watershed: filtration avoidance', www.epa.gov/region02/water/nycshed/filtad.htm, accessed 30 June 2010

USEPA (2010b) 'Sustainable Infrastructure Initiative', http://epa.gov/waterinfrastructure, accessed 20 September 2010

US Geological Survey (2005) 'Estimated use of water in the United States in 2000: domestic supply', http://pubs.usgs.gov/circ/2004/circ1268/htdocs/text-do.html, accessed 30 June 2010

Whittington, D. and Boland, J. (2001) 'Reflections on water pricing and tariff design', http://web.mit.edu/urbanupgrading/waterandsanitation/resources/powerpoint/DaleWhittingtonMumbaiApril3.ppt, April 2001, accessed 30 June 2010

7

Reporting, Disclosure
and Leadership

If your actions inspire others to dream more, learn more, do more and become more, you are a leader.

John Quincy Adams

Voluntary Reporting is No Longer Voluntary

More and more global companies are reporting on environmental and social sustainability performance within voluntary reporting frameworks such as the Carbon Disclosure Project (CDP, www.cdproject.net/en-US/Pages/HomePage.aspx), the Water Disclosure Project (WDP, www.cdproject.net/en-US/Programmes/Pages/cdp-water-disclosure.aspx) and the Global Reporting Initiative (GRI, www.globalreporting.org). Companies are also making public commitments to partnerships such as the UN Global Compact and the CEO Water Mandate (www.unglobalcompact.org).

Companies are increasingly committing to global sustainability goals such as the Millennium Development Goals (MDGs) (www.un.org/millenniumgoals). They do this for a variety of reasons, including the perceived value of engaging with stakeholders (including NGOs) and investor groups, and of demonstrating global leadership on critical business issues. Several companies have now committed to being leaders in addressing global water issues, and as a result have engaged with a variety of global initiatives.

Investors are one of the key stakeholder groups focused on water reporting and disclosure, having realized that water, like carbon, can represent a material risk for companies. However, water performance reporting and disclosure is lagging behind carbon reporting, and can handicap rigorous investment analysis. There is a need for a more robust understanding of how to measure water use, water risk and exposure, together with greater transparency. Several investor-led initiatives such as the CDP Water Disclosure Project are driving increased water reporting and disclosure.

Leadership also goes beyond reporting. A recent article in the *Harvard Business Review* (Meyer and Kirby, 2010) effectively makes the case that the key to becoming a corporate leader is to take responsibility for externalities – essentially internalizing externalities such as water use, across your entire value chain. Companies will be recognized as leaders if they understand that water stewardship requires collaboration among a wide range of stakeholders. Moreover, these leaders will strongly influence both upstream (supply chain) and downstream (consumers) water use.

Global Commitments and Leadership

Public commitments and transparent reporting drive sustainability performance. An excellent example of how public reporting improved environmental performance is the US Environmental Protection Agency (USEPA) Toxic Release Inventory (TRI, www.epa.gov/tri). The USEPA enacted the Emergency Planning and Community Right to Know Act (EPCRA) in 1986 with the purpose of informing communities of chemical hazards in their areas. EPCRA also requires the USEPA and US states to collect annual data on releases and transfers of certain toxic chemicals from industrial facilities, and to make the data available to the public in the TRI. The USEPA compiles the TRI data submitted by regulated facilities each year and makes the data available through several web-based tools. USEPA considers the programme a success in reducing chemical use and transport.

Currently there are several global water initiatives, which can harness the power of global companies in addressing the challenge of water scarcity.

UN Global Compact

The UN Global Compact was established in 2000 and is a policy platform and framework for companies committed to sustainability. The compact was established to promote the alignment of business operations and strategies with ten principles of human rights, labour, environment and anti-corruption. The objectives of the compact are to promote the following:

- adoption of the Global Compact principles in business activities around the world; and
- catalyse actions in support of broader UN goals, including the Millennium Development Goals (MDGs).

Three of the ten principles of the UN Global Compact are to:

- support a precautionary approach to environmental challenges;
- undertake initiatives to promote greater environmental responsibility;
- encourage the development and diffusion of environmentally friendly technologies.

Millennium Development Goals

The Millennium Development Goals (MDGs) were established in 2001 and consist of eight development goals approved by 192 UN member states and 23 international organizations. They are considered by the UN to be the most broadly supported and comprehensive global development goals. The goals provide quantitative targets to address global issues such as income poverty, hunger, maternal and child mortality, disease, inadequate shelter, gender inequality, environmental degradation and the development of a Global Partnership for Development.

The MDGs set a target of 2015 to reduce world poverty by half. Consisting of 21 quantified targets using 60 indicators, the goals are:

1 Eradicate extreme poverty and hunger.
2 Achieve universal primary education.
3 Promote gender equality and empower women.
4 Reduce child mortality.
5 Improve maternal health.
6 Combat HIV/AIDS, malaria and other diseases.
7 Ensure environmental sustainability.
8 Develop a global partnership for development.

Goal 7 is focused on environmental sustainability and consists of the following sub-goals:

- Target 7a: Integrate the principles of sustainable development into country policies and programmes.
- Target 7b: Reduce biodiversity loss, achieving, by 2010, a significant reduction in the rate of loss.

The 7a and 7b indicators consist of:

- 7.1 proportion of land area covered by forest;
- 7.2 CO_2 emissions, total, per capita and per US$1 GDP;
- 7.3 consumption of ozone-depleting substances;
- 7.4 proportion of fish stocks within safe biological limits;
- 7.5 proportion of total water resources used;
- 7.6 proportion of terrestrial and marine areas protected;
- 7.7 proportion of species threatened with extinction.

Target 7c is:

> *Reduce by half the proportion of people without sustainable access to safe drinking water and basic sanitation.*

The following indicators apply:

- 7.8 proportion of population using an improved drinking-water source;
- 7.9 proportion of population using an improved sanitation facility.

CEO Water Mandate

The CEO Water Mandate (www.unglobalcompact.org/issues/Environment/CEO_Water_Mandate) is an initiative of the UN Global Compact and is designed to work with private sector companies to address their impacts on water resources. The goal is to:

> *make a positive impact with respect to the emerging global water crisis by mobilizing a critical mass of business leaders to advance water sustainability solutions – in partnership with the United Nations, civil society organizations, governments and other stakeholders.*

Participants in the CEO Water Mandate are working to contribute to the success of the UN Global Compact and the MDGs.

Quoting directly from the CEO Water Mandate, companies pledge to the following actions:

- Direct operations:
  - Conduct a comprehensive water-use assessment to understand the extent to which the company uses water in the direct production of goods and services.
  - Set targets for our operations related to water conservation and wastewater treatment, framed in a corporate cleaner production and consumption strategy.
  - Seek to invest in and use new technologies to achieve these goals.
  - Raise awareness of water sustainability within corporate culture.
  - Include water sustainability considerations in business decision-making, due diligence, and production processes.
- Supply chain and watershed management:
  - Encourage suppliers to improve their water conservation, quality monitoring, wastewater treatment and recycling practices.
  - Build capacities to analyse and respond to watershed risk.
  - Encourage and facilitate suppliers in conducting assessments of water usage and impacts.
  - Share water sustainability practices – established and emerging – with suppliers.
  - Encourage major suppliers to report regularly on progress achieved related to goals.
- Collective action:
  - Build closer ties with civil society organizations, especially at the regional and local levels.
  - Work with national, regional and local governments and public authorities to address water sustainability issues and policies, as well as with relevant international institutions – e.g. the UNEP Global Programme of Action.
  - Encourage development and use of new technologies, including efficient irrigation methods, new plant varieties, drought resistance, water efficiency and salt tolerance.
  - Be actively involved in the UN Global Compact's Country Networks.

- – Support the work of existing water initiatives involving the private sector (e.g. the Global Water Challenge; UNICEF's Water, Environment and Sanitation Program; IFRC Water and Sanitation Program; the World Economic Forum Water Initiative) and collaborate with other relevant UN bodies and intergovernmental organizations (e.g. the World Health Organization, the Organisation for Economic Co-operation and Development and the World Bank Group).
- • Public policy:
  - – Contribute inputs and recommendations in the formulation of government regulation and in the creation of market mechanisms in ways that drive the water sustainability agenda.
  - – Exercise 'business statesmanship' by being advocates for water sustainability in global and local policy discussions, clearly presenting the role and responsibility of the private sector in supporting integrated water-resource management.
  - – Partner with governments, businesses, civil society and other stakeholders – for example specialized institutes such as the Stockholm International Water Institute, UNEP Collaborating Centre on Water and Environment, and UNESCO's Institute for Water Education – to advance the body of knowledge, intelligence and tools.
  - – Join and/or support special policy-oriented bodies and associated frameworks – e.g. UNEP's Water Policy and Strategy; United Nations Development Programme (UNDP)'s Water Governance Programme.
- • Community engagement:
  - – Endeavour to understand the water and sanitation challenges in the communities where we operate and how our businesses impact those challenges.
  - – Be active members of the local community, and encourage or provide support to local government, groups and initiatives seeking to advance the water and sanitation agendas.
  - – Undertake water-resource education and awareness campaigns in partnership with local stakeholders.
  - – Work with public authorities and their agents to support – when appropriate – the development of adequate water infrastructure, including water and sanitation delivery systems.

- Transparency:
  - Include a description of actions and investments undertaken in relation to the CEO Water Mandate in our annual Communications on Progress for the UN Global Compact, making reference to relevant performance indicators such as the water indicators found in the GRI Guidelines.
  - Publish and share our water strategies (including targets and results as well as areas for improvement) in relevant corporate reports, using – where appropriate – the water indicators found in the GRI Guidelines.
  - Be transparent in dealings and conversations with governments and other public authorities on water issues.

The CEO Water Mandate has comprehensive commitments to water stewardship and leadership. For those companies that not only commit to the mandate but follow through with these commitments they can become true water stewardship leaders. Performance against these commitments can be demonstrated through robust and transparent water reporting and disclosure.

Water Reporting and Disclosure

Reporting on water risk and opportunity is weak at best and is nowhere near the sophistication of current carbon reporting. However, this is changing rapidly with the launch of the CDP Water Disclosure programme and the benchmarking report by Ceres (Barton, 2010).

An overview of the current state of water reporting and disclosure were provided by the Ceres report and by the CEO Water Mandate. The latter provides a critical assessment of how global companies are reporting water performance when compared to the CEO Water Mandate commitments (an additional perspective on water reporting and disclosure from Ceres is provided later in this chapter).

The Pacific Institute report (Morrison and Schulte, 2009) examined the water reporting of 110 companies. It concluded that the majority (a slim majority of only 62 per cent) adhered to one of the three factors used by the Pacific Institute to evaluate water reporting, and the approaches adopted by the 110 companies to determine water performance were considered inadequate. The three factors for water reporting considered by the Pacific Institute were:

- providing a description of a systematic materiality assessment process;
- engaging stakeholders to inform report content;
- advancing water reporting harmonization and convergence through utilization of both GRI Guidelines and AA1000 Principles in reporting.

The major conclusions of the study were:

- Less than 50 per cent of the companies mention the use of stakeholder input to inform their corporate responsibility reporting. Only 16 companies (15 per cent) address all three of the factors referenced above.
- Most companies report on direct operations (this is consistent with the DP Water Disclosure pilot project and the GlobeScan survey discussed in Chapter 1). The direct operations criterion most frequently reported was 'quantified water quantity data', with 98 companies (89 per cent) reporting. However, companies reported on total water use and did not provide regional or local water use (this is a major failing, as water issues and solutions are local, as we saw in Chapter 2). Companies also provided direct operations information on 'specific programs, policies, or targets for water performance' at 66 per cent, 'trend water performance data' at 66 per cent and 'Quantified Water Quality Data' at 64 per cent.
- Reporting on process-oriented criteria outlined in the CEO Water Mandate was not as comprehensive as the direct operations criteria.
- Several CEO Water Mandate elements are extremely under-reported, in particular: public policy, supply chain and collective action.
- Very few companies provided any relevant information on the three criteria addressing public policy.
- Only 10 per cent of the companies described having any role in 'water infrastructure development', which is alarming, in my opinion, considering the need for private and public sectors to collaborate on addressing water scarcity.
- The lowest percentage of companies (only three companies) reported on 'water sustainability advocacy'.
- As expected, reporting on supply-chain performance is low, with only 7 per cent of the companies reporting on 'measure supplier water performance'.

- Most companies used the GRI Sustainability Report Guidelines for reporting, with over 80 per cent of them meeting the 'use of GRI Guidelines' criteria. 18 per cent of the companies use the AA1000 Principles (www.accountability.org/aa1000series) to some degree. However, the study concluded that 71 per cent of the companies claiming to use GRI G3 water-quality performance indicators had indexes that inaccurately portrayed their actual reporting indicators, and only 53 per cent provided any information on the roles stakeholders played in informing the reporting process (also recommended practice by GRI).

Based upon the results of the study, the Pacific Institute recommended the following:

- There is a clear need to further expand corporate reporting to include common approaches to describing actions and impacts outside of direct operations.
- Water reporting would be advanced by the development of harmonized sector-specific indicators on water.
- There is a need for practical guidance on how companies can carry out water-focused materiality assessments to assist in determining reporting content.
- More work needs to be done to ensure more responsible conformity to and harmonization with existing corporate reporting guidelines.
- There is significant potential for cross-sector learning with regard to water reporting.

The bottom line is that despite commitments to the CEO Water Mandate, these commitments are only meaningful if there is robust and transparent reporting. Moreover, reporting must be not just for direct operations, but must include the entire supply chain.

Global Reporting Initiative

The Global Reporting Initiative (GRI) (www.globalreporting.org) is essentially the de facto standard for global sustainability reporting. Despite this widespread adoption, the GRI reporting framework does not provide the granularity required for robust and transparent water reporting. Its framework sets out the principles and indicators that organizations can use to measure and report their economic, environmental and social performance.

The third version of the GRI Sustainability Reporting Guidelines, known as G3, was released in 2006. The framework also includes sector supplements (unique indicators for industry sectors) and national annexes (unique country-level information). The G3 Guidelines outline a disclosure framework that organizations can 'voluntarily, flexibly and incrementally adopt'.

The G3 consists of two major parts:

- Part 1 – Reporting principles and guidance:
  - principles to define report content: materiality, stakeholder inclusiveness, sustainability context and completeness;
  - principles to define report quality: balance, comparability, accuracy, timeliness, reliability and clarity;
  - guidance on how to set the report boundary.
- Part 2 – Standard disclosures:
  - strategy and profile;
  - management approach;
  - performance indicators.

Water Disclosure project

The CDP Water Disclosure programme was initiated in 2010 with questionnaires going out to over 300 companies globally (details of the programme questions were discussed in Chapter 1). The CDP Water Disclosure programme makes up for what the GRI G3 framework lacks in granularity with regards to water reporting and disclosure. Although not directly related, the programme does tie into the G3 guidelines.

It is reasonable to expect that the CDP Water Disclosure programme will have the same, if not greater, impact on water reporting and disclosure as CDP did with greenhouse gas (GHG) reporting. In the United States, where greenhouse gas regulations have been slow to be enacted, the CDP has driven most US multinational companies to report their greenhouse gas footprint, risks and opportunities despite this being a voluntary programme.

The projected success of the programme can also be predicted based upon which companies were signatories to the WDP launch. Molson

Coors (www.molsoncoors.com), Ford (www.ford.com), Pearson (www. pearson.com) and (PepsiCo (www.pepsico.com) supported the CDP Water Disclosure programme launch and are committed to helping build water disclosure and reporting using the WDP framework (additional detail on Ford, Molson Coors and PepsiCo water leadership can be found in Chapter 9).

Ceres perspective on water reporting and disclosure

The Ceres report (Barton, 2010) not only provided benchmarking of water reporting and disclosure but provided insight on what is needed as we go forward. Ceres has been a powerful force in driving increased greenhouse gas reporting and disclosures, and now has its targets set on water. Background about Ceres and insight from Brooke Barton (the principal author of the 2010 report) provide a glimpse of where we are and where we are going, with water reporting and disclosure.

The Coalition for Environmentally Responsible Economies, or Ceres, is a national network of investors, environmental organizations and other public-interest groups that works to integrate sustainability into capital markets. Based in Boston, Massachusetts, Ceres was born out of the 1989 Exxon Valdez oil spill, in which 10.8 million gallons of crude oil were dumped into the fragile ecosystem of Prince William Sound in Alaska. Six months later, with crews still working to clean the shore, a group of investors launched Ceres to address the environmental costs of business.

This non-profit organization runs a corporate membership network aimed at helping companies integrate sustainability considerations into the DNA of their business. Companies that join the Ceres network must commit to transparent and regular reporting of environmental and social performance and impacts; they agree to enter into regulator dialogue with expert – and sometimes critical – stakeholders, such as environmental advocates, investors and public-interest organizations. Finally, member companies must set goals and targets for continuous improvement in core areas of sustainability impact.

In 1993, Sunoco became the first Fortune 500 corporation to join the Ceres network. Today, the number of member companies has grown to more than 50, including 13 Fortune 500 firms. Ceres was named one of the 100 most influential players in corporate governance by *Directorship Magazine* in 2007.

At the request of its Investor Network on Climate Risk, Ceres released a report on water scarcity and climate change in February 2009. Entitled 'Water scarcity and climate change: growing risks for business and investors' (Ceres, 2009), it outlined the wide-ranging risks companies and investors face from water scarcity, and how global climate change may increase those risks in some parts of the world. A second report, 'Murky waters? Corporate reporting on water risk' (Barton, 2010) benchmarked 100 companies on water-risk reporting and disclosure.

According to Brooke Barton, senior manager of Ceres's Corporate Accountability Program, investors responding to the report were concerned about the current 'muted' nature of water disclosure:

> *The investors in the network basically said, 'We want to get much more sophisticated in comparing companies on their water performance, but the information doesn't seem to be there.' They asked that we determine a baseline, and develop some actionable recommendations to help companies provide more investor-relevant water disclosure.*

In response, Barton says Ceres began the process of quantifying the diverse water strategies held by companies:

> *setting up a conversation about what was being done, where the gaps were, and the road ahead in terms of providing more meaningful, comparable information for investors.*

What Ceres identified most quickly was the type of water risks companies most frequently disclose. According to Barton, physical risk was the top driver for companies to take water-related action, followed by regulatory, litigation and reputational risks:

> *Only 9 per cent of companies report reputational risk related to water. That's what they report, at least; in some of the sectors where you see the most disclosure – such as mining and beverage – brand reputational risk and licence to operate are huge drivers, but this may not come across in terms of how companies are talking about it.*

Reputational risk is a bigger focus for extractive sectors, adds Barton, because companies know that their reputation for managing water resources may be a primary element in obtaining social licence to operate:

A company's access to water, whether there are growing restrictions on availability from a climate-related or hydrological perspective, is really linked to what piece of the pie it gets. If it's a shrinking pie and you're not seen as a responsible steward, then your access may be at risk.

Some companies lag behind in water disclosure, Barton says, because the executives at headquarters may not have as thorough an understanding of the problem as local managers do:

Water access may be less of a pressing issue at headquarters than in many parts of the world where a multinational's facilities or suppliers operate. It's not a challenge that people in headquarters live and breathe, but it is a challenge that facility-level managers tend to understand deeply.

Barton points out that the implicitness of water costs can also lead to a lag in action:

Because water costs are so low, it's more a question of business conti- nuity than a cost you're carrying on a quarterly basis, from purchas- ing water or investments in wastewater treatment. But that is likely to change and investors want to see that companies really understand the embedded value of water in their direct operations and supply chain, and are anticipating the price increases we're likely to see as regulatory regimes strengthen.

Barton also highlights water footprinting as an important indicator of risk awareness. While Ceres doesn't see footprinting as a water strategy in itself, the group appreciates its ability to bring companies into the conversation:

Water-footprinting exercises are really an important learning process. What we want to see are companies using tools to provide strategic information to their managers. The water-footprinting process offers very granular, detailed information that, through a lot of group as- sessment and contemplation, leads to some really interesting insights.

Insights, for example, such as the connection between water and energy. Through its work with electrical power companies, Ceres has begun to work on the transition to more sustainable electrical grids, a project which underlines the importance of water in the power industry:

> *Companies which do not produce their own energy need to start looking at the water embedded in energy, as well as the carbon embedded in the energy they're procuring.*

The water-footprinting exercise is a tool that can expose such a connection to companies just beginning to form a water strategy.

Barton notes that some of the most important strategies emerging are 'soft innovations':

> *Investors need to know how competently a company is at working collaboratively in a watershed with governments and communities, to find water solutions that meet multiple needs, are transparent, to get the prices right, and which respect key principles like the human right to water. PepsiCo is working with the agricultural sector surrounding its operations in India to reduce the water used in rice planting. The saving in water through this PepsiCo initiative will be significant. Those transfers of technology and expertise are a big part of innovation.*

Still, there's much to be done in terms of technological advancement. In many sectors, advancements in water efficiency or treatment aren't financially viable because of the low explicit costs of water. Barton says most innovation today is occurring within the chemical and home-building sectors, where physical or regulatory risks are forcing quick evolution:

> *In this country, people are moving to predominantly arid parts of the nation, and there are growing regulatory drivers for the housing sector to reconsider its tactics – from the perspective of efficient appliances, to landscaping and siting.*

In California, for instance, new regulations in some areas require developers to demonstrate secure supply for 20 years or more. 'Those kinds of requirements are really the primary driver right now, more than demand from the marketplace', Barton says.

References

Barton, B. (2010) 'Murky waters? Corporate reporting on water risk', www.ceres.org/Document.Doc?id=547, accessed 5 April 2010

Ceres (2009) 'Water scarcity and climate change: growing risks for businesses and investors', February, www.ceres.org/Document.Doc?id=406, accessed 4 October 2010

Meyer, C. and Kirby, J. (2010) 'Leadership in the age of transparency', *Harvard Business Review*, 1 April 2010, http://hbr.org/product/leadership-in-the-age-of-transparency/an/R1004A-PDF-ENG, accessed 16 September 2010

Morrison, J. and Schulte, P. (2009) *Water Disclosure 2.0: Assessment of Current and Emerging Practice in Corporate Water Reporting*, Pacific Institute, Oakland, CA

Part II
Developing and Implementing a Successful Corporate Water Strategy

Water is the best of all things.

Pindar

8

A Water Strategy Map

Success in life comes not from holding a good hand, but in playing a poor one well.

Warren G. Lester

Why a Corporate Water Strategy?

Increasingly, companies are developing strategies to address the risks and opportunities of water scarcity. And it's not just large multinationals: local and regional companies also recognize water as a critical business issue that must be managed to mitigate risk and build value. The identification of water as a critical business issue is also moving beyond the attention of the most water-intensive companies. Food and beverage companies are not alone in planning how to manage water from a physical and reputational perspective; other sectors such as manufacturing and publishing/media are paying attention, as well. The Ford Motor Company and Pearson were even signatories to the Water Disclosure Project (as discussed in Chapter 7).

These forward-thinking companies recognize that a global water strategy is only effective if solutions are implemented locally. Moreover, water is not just an environmental challenge – it is multifaceted. Successful corporate water strategies acknowledge the complexity of water and incorporate environmental, social and economic elements.

Strategy Map: The Process

Before launching into a strategy process to manage water risks and opportunities, we need to discuss broader frameworks for sustainability and reporting. Any corporate water strategy must be built within the broader context of an overall company sustainability strategy, integrate into reporting programmes such as the Global Reporting Initiative (GRI; www.globalreporting.org) and accommodate investor-driven programmes such as the CDP Water Disclosure Programme (www.cdproject.net/water-disclosure). For more information on water reporting and disclosure, refer to Chapter 7: Reporting, Disclosure and Leadership. A corporate water strategy is not just one more strategy – it is integrated into a sustainability strategy which is, in turn, integrated into the overall business strategy.

Let's start with an enterprise-wide sustainability roadmap and then examine a water strategy process. An excellent 'big picture' sustainability framework is 'The 21st century corporation: the Ceres roadmap for sustainability' (Ceres, 2010). The Ceres roadmap outlines a general strategy and framework to leverage the sustainability required for companies to thrive in the 21st century. The thesis is that businesses need to adapt to a fundamentally changed world. Sustainability provides the opportunity for companies to meet the demands of changing factors such as increased stakeholder engagement, resource constraint and climate change.

In his forward of the Ceres report, David Blood, senior partner of Generation Management, writes:

> The most progressive and forward-looking business leaders understand best-practice business strategy is about leveraging sustainability into increased revenues, profitability and competitive advantage. True sustainability means judging solutions on a life-cycle basis and considering the complete set of inputs, costs and externalities.

Mindy Lubber, president of Ceres, echoes this perspective:

> The best performing companies of the 21st century will be those that recognize this evolving new order, and invest and act now.

Water is one of the critical resource issues and externalities 21st-century companies must manage. How a company manages water-scarcity risk and builds competitive advantage is part of this new paradigm (more discussion on this in Chapter 14).

The Ceres roadmap outlines 20 expectations regarding sustainability performance for companies to achieve by 2020 (Figure 8.1):

- governance for sustainability:
  - board oversight,
  - management accountability,
  - executive compensation,
  - corporate policies and management systems,
  - public policy;
- stakeholder engagement:
  - focus engagement activity,
  - substantive stakeholder dialogue,
  - investor engagement,
  - c-level engagement;
- disclosure:
  - standards for disclosure,
  - disclosure in financial filings,
  - scope and content,
  - vehicles for disclosure,
  - product transparency,
  - verification and assurance;
- performance:
- operations;
- supply chain;

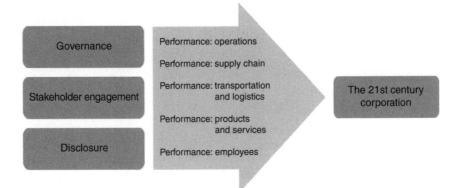

Figure 8.1 *The 21st-century corporation roadmap*

Source: adapted from Ceres (2010)

- transportation and logistics;
- products and services;
- employees.

An illustration of this roadmap is provided below and will provide context for our discussion of a water strategy and process. Any successful corporate water strategy must include the aforementioned elements of governance, stakeholder engagement, disclosure and performance (operations, supply chain, transportation and logistics, products and services, and employees). I believe there is one more element of importance in a water-strategy process: innovation.

So what does a corporate water strategy process looks like? An early example of a water strategy roadmap was developed by the Pacific Institute and Business for Social Responsibility (BSR) (2007). While that report is several years old, the basic framework remains valid – though multinationals have learned much during recent years with regard to stakeholder engagement, assessment of direct and indirect water risk, reporting and innovation.

While the process for developing a water strategy is relatively straightforward, it is *not* linear, and it requires integration with other environmental sustainability efforts such as energy, carbon and social performance (Figure 8.2). For leading-edge companies, it will include the opportunity side of the equation: innovation in new products and services.

The overall process consists of the following four major phases, each with key programmes:

- footprint/relationships;
- risks/opportunities;
- execution/management;
- stakeholder/community engagement.

Footprint/relationships

The key programmes in this phase are:

- inventory of current water programmes and projects;
- water footprint: direct and supply chain;
- water footprint: products;
- stakeholder mapping.

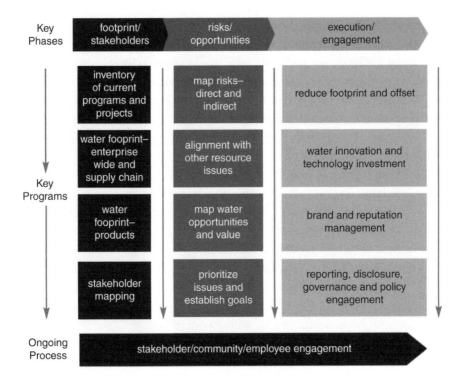

Figure 8.2 *Water strategy process map*

Source: William Sarni

Any initial phase in understanding water (or any resource) risks and opportunities begins with an assessment of current programmes and projects. Most companies have some programmes and projects in place to manage water use. However, these may not have been identified beyond the facility or business-unit level. There also may be opportunities to identify and leverage best practices across an entire company.

An assessment of a company's water footprint will provide the baseline for assessing risks and opportunities, prioritizing efforts and measuring progress. A water footprint should include the entire supply chain and information from key suppliers. Tools currently available include:

- GEMI Water Sustainability Tool (www.gemi.org/water/overview.htm);
- WBCSD Global Water Tool (www.wbcsd.org/templates/ TemplateWBCSD5/layout.asp?type=p&MenuId=MTc1Mg&doOpen =1&ClickMenu=LeftMenu).

Additional water-footprinting and water-risk tools are currently being developed, such as the Water Index from GE, World Resources Institute and Goldman Sachs (www.gepower.com/about/press/en/2009_press/120709. htm). These tools can be used alone or in combination.

The direct and supply-chain water data collected as part of a water-footprinting effort includes the following:

- water use and discharge:
  - total volume of water withdrawn by source,
  - volume and rate of water reuse and recycling,
  - total water effluent discharges by quality and disposal method,
  - water use by purpose, life-cycle stages, business functions, business units and geographic locations;
- community and environment:
  - water bodies and related habitats affected by discharges of water and runoff,
  - water sources affected by withdrawal of water,
  - annual withdrawal of groundwater and surface water as a percentage of available water from local water sources.

In addition to direct and supply-chain water-use data, companies should consider performing an analysis of the water footprint of selected products as a basis for understanding opportunities to reduce water use in the manufacturing process. Companies such as SABMiller have successfully performed product water-footprinting analyses to identify differences in manufacturing efficiencies between countries (as discussed in Chapter 4).

This phase also includes stakeholder mapping. Determining which stakeholders are critical for your company is the first step for mapping out a plan for engagement, and engaging them is a critical and ongoing process. Stakeholders include employees, suppliers, and the communities and countries in which a company operates, as well as local, regional and global NGOs.

Risks/opportunities

The next phase (which can be run somewhat concurrently to the initial phase) is an assessment of risks and opportunities. The process of mapping water risks builds on the water-footprinting assessment in the initial Phase 1.

The key programmes in this phase are:

- map risks: direct and indirect;
- alignment with other resource issues;
- map water opportunities and value;
- prioritize issues and establish goal.

The key data to map water risk from direct and supply-chain water use are:

- local hydrological conditions;
- socio-economic conditions in production regions or key consumer markets;
- business impacts on defined water resources;
- risks to consider:
  - potential scarcity risks,
  - potential flooding risks,
  - trends in regional demand,
  - deficiencies in institutional or political water governance,
  - disparities or inequities in local and regional water access and pricing,
  - impacts of the water use and runoff on the local community and ecosystems.

By this point, the foundation has been established to enable a company to understand its water footprint (though additional footprinting work is likely to be performed on additional products and operations), and the next step is to evaluate the potential water risk to business and opportunities. Mapping of water risk consists of an assessment of areas of water scarcity, water stress and projected conditions (factoring in the potential impacts of climate change). Factors such as projected increases in water demand; demands from social, economic and political factors; and disparities in water access and/or prices between large commercial users and local communities should also be evaluated.

The goal of this analysis of relative scarcity conditions and prices around a company's facilities is to enable a company to proactively identify where competition for water may become acute, as well as actions that can mitigate risk. For geographic risk areas, companies should develop plans to minimize their water use and impacts, and they should establish contingency plans to respond to water supply and related risks, such as decreasing water quality, higher water prices, extreme hydrologic events and local economic development.

It is also critical to integrate an assessment of water risk and mitigation programmes into larger ongoing efforts to reduce energy use and carbon emissions. In some cases, water-efficiency, energy-efficiency and carbon-reduction programmes may be at odds with each other. For example, a company may decide to move to air instead of liquid cooling at a facility, which would use more energy (and increase carbon emissions), yet reduce risk from water scarcity. In an integrated approach to managing energy, carbon and water, the major factor is that, while energy and carbon targets can be global, and solutions are, for the most part, fungible, water is not. Water is local, and water-efficiency programmes must be tailored to meet local needs.

One of water's great challenges is that its price does not reflect its value. As a result, when companies fund water projects, they need to account for the real value of water, including such things as licence to operate and reputational value. Companies should explore ways to place a higher value on water to ensure projects are adequately funded and meet in-house hurdle rates for investments. For example, if an impacted water-shed or water body is restored, it can provide a reliable source of water for company operations and/or the surrounding community.

The question becomes: what is this value? Ecosystems provide value through their ability to control runoff and salinity, as well as provide natural purification processes. Although quantifying this value is difficult with current economic models, semi-quantitative and qualitative assessments can be made. Organizations such as the International Union for the Conservation of Nature (IUCN) (www.iucn.org) are currently developing methodologies to quantify ecosystem value.

The next action is to prioritize issues and establish goals. It is valuable to establish water-use reduction targets, even if they are preliminary. Reduction targets can be modified over time to reflect changes in the business, such as acquisitions and divestitures (I recommend a transparent process). Knowing why water is important to the business and what challenges the business faces are helpful in prioritizing issues and goal setting.

Quantifiable goals and targets should be set for water-use efficiency, conservation and minimizing water impacts (and associated water-related risks). Efficiency programmes can have multiple benefits, including cost savings, reduced energy use and reduced regulation. As an example of reduced regulation, 'closed-loop' cooling systems can reduce regulatory costs by eliminating the need for water-discharge permits. Aggressive water-conservation programmes developed within formal agreements with water-service providers or local governments can also offer the potential to reduce reliability risks during periodic drought periods.

Execution/engagement

Now, the challenging part: effectively executing this strategy and engagement.

The key programmes in this phase are:

- reduce footprint and offset;
- water innovation and technology investment;
- brand and reputation management;
- reporting, disclosure, governance and policy engagement.

In some ways, this phase is similar to the way in which companies approach carbon-management programmes. Essentially, the process is to reduce your water footprint, drive innovation in the company, manage brand and reputational value, and engage in reporting, disclosure, governance and public-policy issues.

There are numerous technologies that can reduce water use and improve water quality, including reclaiming and reusing process water, sophisticated filtration systems, replacing water-cooling towers with air cooling, and others. Some changes involve significant capital outlays; others do not. In either case, many companies have found such technology investments can have short payback periods and generate high returns on investment. This is likely to be increasingly true as water becomes scarcer. Companies should assess the best technology available for reducing water use and wastewater discharges, and commit to using it in new facilities and retrofitting existing facilities in areas of significant water stress. These best practices can be from internal processes identified during the inventory phase of the process, or from benchmarking against best-in-class companies.

Water-efficiency programmes are not one-time initiatives. Despite increased efforts from companies and others, water scarcity and water-related business risks are likely to increase. A commitment to continual improvement in assessing risks, managing these risks and lessening impacts of the company's water use on local communities and the environment, can help protect operations from unexpected water-related business disruptions. Such a commitment should be in written form, and can be a stand-alone statement or part of an organization's overall environmental policy.

In some cases, companies may decide to invest in water-offset programmes to account for water use that cannot be reduced through water-efficiency programmes. Water offsetting is a way to invest in water conservation and development projects within a watershed.

Companies that move beyond 'greening' and effectively leverage sustainability strategy are also those that use sustainability to drive innovation. This is clearly the case with a company such as GE, which is not only reducing its water footprint and risk, but also developing innovative technologies in the areas of water efficiency and water treatment. Every company should evaluate to see if there is an opportunity side to the equation beyond just risk mitigation.

As previously discussed, one of the key value drivers with regard to water is reputational and brand value. While the price of water is low, any missteps in managing water within a watershed can limit or shut down a company's licence to operate. Investors are also taking note of how well a company manages its 'intangible value' from factors such as brand. Since many food and beverage companies have most of their value tied to their brand, managing water risk is already a key aspect in how they manage brand value.

Companies will need to tackle the issue of reporting, disclosure, water governance and public-policy engagement once a water strategy has been mapped. To meet increased expectations and demands for transparency, they should publicly report key metrics on their water use and impacts, and track how their performance changes over time. This information can help investors, customers, local communities and other key stakeholders assess how companies are managing their water risks, and it is often a useful tool for engaging employees across the enterprise in supporting water programmes.

In February 2003, the GRI produced its 'Water Protocol' to provide resource-specific guidance for organizations implementing its 2002 Sustainability Reporting Guidelines. The Facility Reporting Project is currently developing facility-level reporting metrics that are based on the GRI framework, and water is included in these.

Stakeholder/community engagement

I cannot stress enough how important it is in building a successful water strategy to identify and engage stakeholders. This is an ongoing process, not a one-time exercise. The two major elements of this process are consultation and development of strategic partnerships.

Consultation with stakeholders

Communities and employees are critical voices in the use of local water resources. While past public participation in local water policy has been limited, the public and NGOs now play increasingly important roles in water policy.

Where a company plays a large role in a community (such as in the mining sector), developing early and ongoing ties with local community groups and employees can prevent or reduce the risks of future water-related issues. In addition, proactive efforts by the company to improve water quality or availability can help build positive relations with local and regional stakeholders. These efforts may include direct participation in developing local water systems, provision of funds or appropriate technology, education and water-resource planning.

Again, water is a local issue, and local conditions vary. As a result, companies cannot make generalizations on whom to engage and how to engage. In some water-scarce regions, there is already community concern about how companies are using local resources. This will only increase as we encounter prolonged dry periods. Local issues need to be identified early, and efforts made to include the public in decisions about water, to improve company practices and to work with local groups on education and outreach. A lack of proactive engagement can lead to a loss of licence to operate.

Strategic partnerships

It has become the norm for global companies to partner with global and regional NGOs to address critical environmental and social issues. NGOs such as the World Wide Fund for Nature (WWF), Water Resources Institute

(WRI), Circle of Blue and the World Business Council for Sustainable Development (WBCSD) are partnering with multinationals to map water risk, and in offsetting programmes, stakeholder engagement and water-development projects. These NGOs operate locally and are often better able to assess the varying needs and issues of individual communities. They can serve as a company's eyes and ears on the ground.

A company's supply chain is one of its most important stakeholders. Companies should assess and evaluate water use in their supply chain, and work collaboratively with suppliers to reduce water use and minimize risks of supply-chain disruptions from water-related problems. You are all in this together.

Industry-Sector Approaches

While all industry sectors will be affected by water scarcity, it will happen in various ways and degrees. It is important to acknowledge industry-sector differences. Look at specific issues, challenges and best practices, and tailor a strategic framework accordingly.

Water-use data are available for generalized industrial sectors (agricultural, commercial, residential and industrial), but detailed data are not well developed for specific industry sectors and their supply chains. However, a recent study by Michael Blackhurst, Chris Hendrickson and Jordi Sels Vidal from the Department of Civil and Environmental Engineering of the Green Design Institute at Carnegie Mellon University in Pittsburgh, sheds some light on specific industry water use (Blackhurst, Hendrickson et al, 2010).

The authors studied 428 industrial sectors within the United States, based on 2002 data, and used economic input–output life-cycle assessment (EIO-LCA) to estimate direct and indirect water withdrawals for each sector's production, in terms of total withdrawals and withdrawals per dollar of output. Although the study is US-specific, it provides a guide for industry sectors globally.

Significant conclusions are:

- The agriculture and power-generation sectors account for an overwhelming majority of direct water withdrawals (90 per cent).

- Across all industry sectors, approximately 60 per cent of water use is indirect (supply chain), and approximately 96 per cent of the industry sectors use more water indirectly in their supply chains than directly.
- The food and beverage industry accounts for approximately 30 per cent of indirect withdrawals. The study confirms that the majority of a company's footprint typically resides within its supply chain (indirect water use).

Water risk within key industry sectors have been examined in several studies and reports, including those of the Pacific Institute, World Resources Institute, J. P. Morgan, CDP and Ceres. The majin impacts for major sectors are summarized briefly below:

- food and beverage:
  - manufacturing disruptions,
  - higher commodity costs,
  - higher power costs,
  - loss of access to sources for bottled water;
- semiconductor manufacturing:
  - production disruptions,
  - higher costs for water treatment,
  - limits on licence to operate;
- power generation:
  - plant shutdowns due to limits on access to cooling water,
  - costs to purchase substitute power;
- extractive industries (mining, oil and gas):
  - potential restrictions on oil and gas drilling (the Marcellus Shale in the United States, for example),
  - waste discharge limitations;
- manufacturing:
  - production disruptions,
  - problems with discharge of liquid wastes.

The overall impact of climate change on water scarcity and resultant impacts to industry sectors were evaluated in the report from Ceres and the Pacific Institute (2009). An overview of the water footprint of several industry sectors is summarized in Table 8.1, overleaf.

Table 8.1 *Generalized water footprint by industry sector*

Industry		Materials	Suppliers	Direct	Product use
Food and beverage	Withdrawal	High	Medium	High	Medium
	Discharge	Medium	Low (medium for food)	Medium (high for food)	Medium
Semiconductors	Withdrawal	Medium	High	Low/medium	Low
	Discharge	High	High	Low	Medium
Power	Withdrawal	High	Low	High	N/a
	Discharge	High	Low	High	N/a
Extractive	Withdrawal	High	Low	High	Medium
	Discharge	High	Low	High	Medium
Manufacturing	Withdrawal	Low to medium	Low to medium	Low to high	Low to high
	Discharge	Low to medium	Low to medium	Low to high	Low to high

Note: Relative generalized water footprint for selected industry sectors.

Source: adapted from Ceres and Pacific Institute (2009), except for the manufacturing sector

An overview of the types of water risk (physical, regulatory and reputational) is summarized in Table 8.2 below.

Table 8.2 *Generalized potential risk category by industry sector*

Industry	Physical	Reputational	Regulatory
Food and beverage	High	High	High
Semiconductor	High	Low to medium	High
Power	High	Low to medium	High
Extractive	High	Low to medium	High
Manufacturing	Low to medium	Low to medium	Low to high

Note: Relative generalized potential risk category by selected industry sectors.

Source: adapted from Ceres and Pacific Institute (2009), except for the manufacturing sector

References

Blackhurst, M., Hendrickson, C. and Vidal, J. S. (2010) 'Direct and indirect water withdrawals for US industrial sectors', *Environmental Science & Technology*, vol 44, no 6, pp2126–2130

Ceres (2010) 'The 21st century corporation: the Ceres roadmap for sustainability', www.ceres.org/Document.Doc?id=568, accessed 30 June 2010

Ceres and Pacific Institute (2009) 'Water scarcity and climate change: growing risks for businesses and investors', www.ceres.org/Document.Doc?id=406, February 2009, accessed 30 June 2010

Pacific Institute and BSR (Business for Social Responsibility) (2007) 'At the crest of a wave: a proactive approach to corporate water strategy', www.bsr.org/reports/BSR_Water-Trends.pdf, September 2007, accessed 30 June 2010

9

Food and Beverage Industries

Whiskey's for drinking, water's for fighting about.

Mark Twain

The food and beverage sectors face water risk in both direct and indirect (supply chain) aspects of their business. These sectors also face the broadest types of potential risk (physical, reputational and regulatory) across their entire value chain.

Water Use and Potential Risk

The food and beverage sectors are highly dependent on water for the production and final use of their products. To highlight the magnitude of water use in the food and beverage sectors combined, consider this: Nestlé, The Coca-Cola Company, Anheuser Busch (prior to the acquisition by Inbev) and Danone used about 575 billion litres of water, which is equivalent to the 'basic water needs' of the global population (J. P. Morgan, 2008).

The food and beverage sectors also recognize the local nature of water more acutely because of high water use within the watersheds in which they operate. Not only is the potential water impact important within the food and beverage companies because of direct water use, but these sectors are reliant on a supply chain that includes the agricultural sector. The latter is the largest global water user, and so the food and beverage sector is the most vulnerable to physical, regulatory and reputational risk.

Observations of the food and beverage sector by J. P. Morgan highlight the importance of water (J. P. Morgan, 2008). The J. P. Morgan study focused in detail on the roles of water, water risk and considerations by the investment community in the food and beverage sectors. Their conclusions are summarized below:

- Water use:
  - Water plays a key role in the manufacturing of food and beverage products. This includes direct bottling and the processing of raw food products, cooling and cleaning equipment.
  - The estimate of the total annual water use by the five largest food and beverage companies (which in 2008 were The Coca-Cola Company, Nestlé, Unilever, Kraft and Danone) is 0.1 per cent of total global industrial use, or 0.014 per cent of total global water use.
  - Direct consumption of water is a fraction of the total water footprint of water use in these sectors. For example, Unilever estimates its manufacturing operations represent only 5 per cent of total water use, with the majority from its agricultural supply chain.
  - Companies in the food and beverage sectors have focused on reducing consumption in their manufacturing operations. Their framework is to measure water usage, set targets on water consumed per unit of end product (water ratios), implement water-efficiency initiatives and report on water performance.
  - Examples of water-use (in litres per kilogram or litre of end product) consumption metrics from 2006 information provided publicly by companies:
    (a) The Coca-Cola Company: 2.4;
    (b) Nestlé: 4.1;
    (c) Unilever: 3.3;
    (d) Kraft: 6.0;
    (e) Danone: 2.8.
  - Most companies are working to reduce water use through recycling in manufacturing operations, adopting water efficiency, and increasing education and awareness of water-usage efficiency. This has resulted in an average increase in water efficiency of approximately 20 per cent.
  - The food and beverage companies evaluated as part of this study treat water risk as a global issue and, as a result, report water on a global basis. This ignores the local nature of water and the importance of reporting water use on a regional or local basis. At the time of the study, few companies were reporting water use on a local basis and highlighting operations in water-scarce areas.
- Water risks in the supply chain:
  - The most important risks in the food and beverage sectors are in the supply chain and not the manufacturing plants.

- Water-scarcity risk is an 'underestimated risk factor' for the food and beverage industries. Although they are dependent on the agricultural sector, the threat of disruptions in agricultural production from water scarcity is not well understood.
- Water scarcity may be an underestimated driver of the agricultural commodity process in general.
- Water footprinting is a more appropriate method to gauge a company's water risk; total water use (total water bills) is far too general to be useful in estimating risk from water scarcity.
- The impact of climate change on the agricultural supply chain for the food and beverage sectors is expected to be significant. Many of the world's croplands are in semi-arid areas, which are expected to become drier. An example is the High Plains (Ogallala Aquifer) in the US Midwest (primarily in Texas, Kansas and Nebraska). This aquifer provides water for 27 per cent of the irrigated land in the United States, and from 70–90 per cent of the irrigated water for these three states (Ceres and Pacific Institute, 2009).
- Climate change is also expected to raise water requirements for livestock due to increasing temperatures and drier weather.

Water-Risk Disclosure

As previously discussed, an excellent overview of water-risk disclosure in the food and beverage sectors was provided by Ceres (2010). This was based on a benchmarking of 13 food companies and 10 beverage companies. A brief summary of their findings is provided below:

- Water-use data: 85 per cent of the food companies reviewed report data on total water use, and none provide detailed site or regional data. Fewer than one-third report wastewater-discharge data.
- Reduction targets: Fewer than half the food companies report establishing water-use reduction targets; only Unilever discloses a quantified target for reducing wastewater discharges. 60 per cent of the beverage companies report water-use reduction targets; only Diageo provides a quantified wastewater-discharge goal.
- Risk disclosure: Almost all the food companies disclose some degree of physical risk from water scarcity, particularly with regard to their

supply chain. Almost all the beverage companies disclose some degree of physical risk from water scarcity, also with regard to their supply chain.

- Supply chain: Less than one-third of the food companies report addressing water risk in their supply chains. Only three of the ten beverage companies report collaborating with their supply chain to reduce water risk.
- Stakeholder engagement: Almost half the food companies disclose efforts to engage their stakeholders on issues such as watershed protection, drinking water and sanitation. The beverage companies report significant engagement and collaboration with local stakeholders on similar water issues.
- Water accounting: 70 per cent of the beverage companies disclose water-use data, but only about 40 per cent report water-discharge data.
- Differentiation by region: In the beverage sector, only Diageo reports water-use reduction targets differentiated by region (water-stressed versus non-water-stressed regions).

Company Snapshots

Campbell Soup Company

Campbell Soup Company is an iconic American brand and a producer of canned soup and other food products. Based in Camden, New Jersey, the corporation's North American division represents US$5.2 billion in sales, with another US$1.5 billion overseas. Campbell is the owner of major brands Prego, V8, Pace, Pepperidge Farm, Stockpot, Swanson and others. Sold in 120 countries globally, Campbell employs more than 17,000 people.

Grounded in innovation

Founded in 1869, Campbell's most famous product was not marketed until 1897, when Campbell was looking for a way to cut shipping and packaging costs on its soup products. The company experimentally removed water from its soups, and condensed soup was born – an early innovation! At one-third the size of other cans on the market, Campbell was the first commercially prepared soup brand affordable to a wide range of consumers – and used far fewer resources than its competitors.

Today, Campbell prides itself on this combination of business and sustainability savvy. Its 2008 corporate responsibility report states:

We recognize the connection between the long-term vitality of our business and the imperative to advance environmental sustainability

Much of the food-industry giant's business depends on a quality water supply. Vice president of corporate social responsibility, Dave Stangis, says:

It's the lifeblood of each plant. It's in the product, it's used to cook the product– it's even in the bakeries ... [so it made sense for Campbell to] ... take on water ... We've taken a ten-year goal to cut the water use in half in terms of our production. In the next ten years, we want to take the amount of water it takes to make a bag of Goldfish *or a can of soup, and cut it in half. I think some of that's going to be low-hanging fruit; some of it's going to be much harder to get.*

Stangis says Campbell's overall environmental efforts are focused on four pillars:

- promoting sustainable agriculture;
- reducing the environmental impacts of manufacturing operations (including energy and greenhouse gas emissions, water use and wastewater treatment, and solid-waste reduction/recycling);
- developing sustainable packing solutions;
- reducing environmental impact associated with the distribution of products.

All four offer opportunities for water-conservation strategy – some in terms of water-use quantity, others related to water quality. Almost every step in producing food requires water and, as a result, Stangis says, 'There is embedded water in the agricultural chain we're going after.' He also believes there is a lot of opportunity to develop creative solutions, particularly within factory heating and cooling processes.

Wastewater treatment

During the past 60 years, Campbell's water strategies have included everything from the restoration of wetlands to a 50 per cent reduction in pesticide use. Of the company's numerous achievements, however, few have received as much attention as their overland flow wastewater treatment system.

Pioneered in the 1960s as a spray irrigation method, Campbell's overland flow treatment uses the micro-organisms and bacteria that reside in soil to naturally and effectively process wastewater. The water is sprayed over a series of sloped terraces covered with reed canary and other local grasses, where microbes break down all foreign substances before the purified water returns to the local ecosystem. In early trials in Napoleon, Ohio, Campbell found the system inadequate if water flowed too quickly towards the stream site, or if water pooled halfway down, becoming odorous. Over the years, Campbell has determined the necessary slope and shaping for these terraces; overland flow is now trusted to provide proper treatment of the process wastewater and keep effluent mass discharges within regulatory limits.

The Campbell processing plant in Paris, Texas – which produces more than 1 billion cans annually, employs 1600 people and operates 24 hours a day, all year round – now treats 100 per cent of its water through overland flow. Originally an abandoned plot of cotton farmland, depleted of soil resources and ravaged by erosion, the 900-acre parcel was cleared of trees, brush, grasses and erosion features in 1964, then regraded to form uniform slopes and terraces for treatment. In Napoleon, up to 50 per cent of the wastewater is treated from June to October using a similar overland flow system. The system utilizes approximately 600 acres of land to treat the wastewater before it is returned to the Maumee River.

Heating and cooling

Napoleon's wastewater treatment is not the only feature of the plant worth noting. In 2007, Campbell engineers developed a new system to recover heat and recycle cooling water generated from the product-cooking process. Implemented at the Napoleon plant in 2008, the system uses a series of pumps, heat exchangers and water chillers to close the loop around cooker cooling-water processes.

Since the system's inception, Napoleon's water usage is down 1.5 million gallons a day, with annual steam generation dropping 151 million pounds. Because of these cuts, the demand for water-treatment chemicals has also plummeted. Since 2008, similar systems have been installed in plants in Maxton, North Carolina, and in Toronto. These three systems are responsible for reducing company water use by approximately 10 per cent since 2008. In 2010, the processing plant in Paris, Texas, will receive a similar heat-recovery and water-recycling system.

Local water-quality collaboration efforts

In 2008, officials at Campbell's Napoleon plant joined with the Ohio EPA, a local conservation organization, and private businesses in efforts to improve the quality of water within the Lake Erie watershed. Known as the Conservation Action Project (CAP), the group has implemented a series of projects to reduce nitrate–nitrogen in the Maumee River – the source of all water for the Napoleon processing plant. Most recently, Campbell funded a project to construct a water-filter strip/wetland area on a nearby piece of farmland. Coordinated by CAP and constructed by the Defiance County Soil and Water Conservation office, the wetland will act as a water-filtration system to raise the quality of water draining into Maumee. Campbell will continue to work with CAP for the foreseeable future to implement similar modifications to farmland throughout the river basin.

Investment in sustainable agriculture

Now implementing more sustainable agricultural practices itself, Campbell is committed to supporting those who are a few steps ahead of them: the researchers. In 2007, Campbell awarded the UC Davis Agricultural Sustainability Institute a US$250,000 endowment to support sustainable agriculture research, education and outreach. The grant is intended to promote preservation of farmland, advanced integrated pest management and drip irrigation.

MillerCoors

MillerCoors believes that 'with Great Beer comes Great Responsibility' – and that responsibility starts with a strong commitment to sustainable development. Taking a strategic and focused approach to sustainable development, MillerCoors identified five areas of responsibility:

- alcohol responsibility;
- environmental sustainability;
- sustainable supply chain;
- people and community investment;
- ethics and transparency.

Within environmental sustainability, water is of particular importance. Given its roots in the Rocky Mountains near the shores of Lake Michigan, and the fact that water flows through every step of the brewing process, MillerCoors takes water stewardship very seriously. It's the basis for its corporate strategy as it relates to sustainability and water. Ensuring a secure future through water stewardship is key to continued sustainability, protecting the company's reputation and licence to operate, as well as maximizing business value.

According to the company's sustainable development policy manager, Lisa Quezada:

> *Water scarcity is a reality for many around the world. With the increase of water-stressed areas in the United States, this issue is garnering greater attention, and is not just an issue for environmentalists.*

This is particularly true in the water-stressed areas in which the company operates. Quezada says:

> *MillerCoors is doing all it can to be efficient with every drop of water it uses. We want to continue to brew our great beers for years to come and share the availability and benefits of good, clean water with the communities where we live and work.*

The company strategy has evolved over time. Both its parent companies (SABMiller and Molson Coors) are signatories to the UN's CEO Water Mandate. Quezada says:

> *We have embraced and incorporated that framework into our overall strategy to become more efficient in the way we use water. In addition to our focus on water efficiency and wastewater quality and management, MillerCoors works with our suppliers to help them to do the same, engages with local communities and transparently reports our progress on water.*

Although these commitments are made at the corporate level, the focus is on local operations. Because of this, MillerCoors operates some of the most water-efficient breweries in the world. The company's success is largely due to the hard work of its energy and utilities teams in breweries across the United States. Brewery employee training encourages accountability, motivating employees to take ownership and determine methods for reducing water use and saving opportunities. Several breweries have added environmental and energy-awareness modules to training programmes to help drive awareness on water issues. Local operations constantly monitor and track water usage, as well as identify ways to improve their practices. Production facilities engage with communities on local water concerns in order to be part of the solution. This is especially critical for facilities in water-stressed areas such as southern California and Fort Worth, Texas. In addition, through contests, the company has paid the water or energy bills for employees who have submitted the best and most practical energy-saving ideas and demonstrated awareness of water and energy issues in operations.

Measurement, tracking and reporting are all key parts of sustainable development at MillerCoors. To track sustainable development progress, the company follows SABMiller's sustainability assessment matrix (SAM) model, a tracking and measuring tool based on the G3 guidelines of the Global Reporting Initiative (GRI). SAM monitors the performance of each of MillerCoors's five key responsibilities, which includes water, helping the company to focus on water efficiency, wastewater management, watershed availability, water footprinting and community investment in water-related initiatives. MillerCoors tracks its progress via SAM twice a year, helping the company establish consistent, long-term targets for continuous improvement. Results are also reported to both parent companies and publicly via SABMiller's annual sustainable development report and at www.SABMiller.com.

MillerCoors is committed to transparent reporting and to the development of best practices. The annual MillerCoors sustainable development report is a vital element in achieving these goals. The report features an external commentary by Corporate Citizenship and in 2010 will also include third-party endorsements by experts in the areas of alcohol responsibility, environmental sustainability, community social investment, and ethics and transparency. Online, MillerCoors communicates and engages with its consumers and other stakeholders about sustainable development through the website www.GreatBeerGreatResponsibility.com. MillerCoors also takes a collaborative approach to sharing and developing best practices through its participation in the Beverage Industry Environmental Roundtable (BIER), where it is currently working with other beverage-industry leaders on water-footprinting guidelines specific to the industry.

Among the most compelling aspects of the company's efforts related to water are the partnerships it has formed to help protect watersheds, conserve water, improve water quality and create awareness about these issues. Based on its commitment to water stewardship, and after researching the work of non-profit organizations in the area of water, MillerCoors decided to forge a partnership with The Nature Conservancy. Quezada says:

> *We decided our investment should align with the company's strategic priorities, which include sustainability. While water flows through every step of the brewing process, a good deal of our water footprint is in agriculture. It made sense to find a way to help barley farmers increase the efficiency of their irrigation systems and enhance water conservation. If the company could help the farmers become more water-efficient, it would be a win–win for everyone.*

The company had an existing relationship with The Nature Conservancy chapter in Georgia through its brewery in Albany, Georgia. In speaking with that group, Quezada learned they were working with local farmers on a water-conservation project independent of their activities with MillerCoors. The project involved a comprehensive plan that brought farmers access to technology to help with water-efficiency and conservation efforts. It seemed that components of this project could be brought to barley farmers.

After engaging in discussions with The Nature Conservancy, the team identified a project through which the organization's affiliate in Idaho was working with farmers in the Silver Creek Watershed. Some of these farmers were MillerCoors barley suppliers. The result was a comprehensive two-year pilot project focusing on increasing efficiency of irrigation systems and enhancing water conservation. Quezada describes the approach as holistic. Components include the purchase of land easements, streambed-enhancement projects including riparian plantings, development of a habitat-assessment tool and restoration guidelines, and education and outreach. Work will be conducted with farmers to bring about improvements in irrigation systems, including the use of more efficient nozzle sprays and energy-efficient systems such as variable-rate irrigation. MillerCoors will capture the lessons learned from this project with the goal of expanding the pilot to include more MillerCoors barley and hops farmers.

As in all its sustainability efforts, MillerCoors seeks opportunities to engage its employees. Sustainable development policy manager, Lisa Quezada, states that:

> *In celebration of our commitment to water – not only as the main ingredient in our great beer, but also as a precious resource for the communities where we live and work – MillerCoors declared September 'Water Stewardship Month'. Started in 2009, Water Stewardship Month is an opportunity for employees, their families and their friends to join together and demonstrate water stewardship in action.*

In order to make a difference in local water resources across the country, employees partnered with nonprofit organizations and volunteered more than 1600 hours on projects including river cleanups, water-quality testing, and riverbank and streambed restoration.

In addition to company-wide programmes, many MillerCoors breweries engage in local community-investment opportunities, as well as volunteer and partnership efforts. In Albany, Georgia, the company promoted a campaign to 'Keep Albany–Dougherty Beautiful' with a grant to purchase storm-drain markers, and organized an employee volunteer event to place the markers along major city streets. MillerCoors also looks to include an educational component in all volunteer activities to enhance the experience for its employees. For example, at a Milwaukee river clean-up event, the non-profit partner's executive director met with employees and shared information about the ecological health of the river and impact of the volunteer activity.

For the past two years, MillerCoors has partnered with River Network, a national non-profit organization dedicated to watershed protection and quality, to positively influence water sources in local communities through an online grant competition. In 2010, the contest awarded US$50,000 in watershed-protection grants to local non-profit organizations nationwide. Eight finalist proposals selected from a pool of applicants were posted online, and the public was invited to vote for its favourite project, more than 14,000 votes being received. The MillerCoors River Network Watershed Protection Grant Competition not only brings much-needed money to local projects, but also increases awareness about water issues, as people learn about the proposed projects and select those they believe are most effective.

MillerCoors recognizes the importance of water, both to the company and in the larger environmental context. The company is translating this knowledge to direct action through the use of innovative tracking and reporting tools such as SAM, projects to enhance efficiency in its operations, external partnerships with organizations and communities, and employee empowerment. All these strategies will be needed to achieve the goals necessary for long-term prosperity for the company and the industry.

SABMiller

Drink responsibly

One of the largest brewers in the world, since 1895 SABMiller has been making the oldest alcoholic beverage known to humankind – beer. Water, the main ingredient of beer – accounting for more than 90 per cent of the liquid content – has always been at the heart of the company. In the past decade, SABMiller has moved beyond simply acknowledging the importance of water to its business and stepped into the arena of water-awareness advocacy. With a strong presence in six continents, where more than 68,000 people are employed and countless others are part of the value chain of SABMiller and its products, this kind of step is powerful and important.

By forming meaningful alliances with various non-governmental organizations (NGOs) and industries that touch the brewing sector, SABMiller has fortified its place among the world leaders of water awareness and is constantly working towards achieving water efficiency. To that end, the company announced its own water-reduction goal: 25 per cent by 2015. Seen in terms of litres of water consumed per litre of beer produced, SABMiller is already below the industry average of 5:1. The 25 per cent reduction would mean a lean 3.5:1 ratio – saving around 20 billion litres of water annually (enough to fill 8000 Olympic-size swimming pools) – and is part of SABMiller's desire to quickly move water-efficiency measures from discussion to action throughout the world.

The strategy: 5 Rs

Water is a vital aspect of sustainable development and knits together all the other pieces of an all-encompassing vision for a company such as SABMiller, which has openly made sustainable development a top priority. A water strategy has been developed, focusing on a 'holistic, value-chain approach', built around what SABMiller calls the '5Rs of water responsibility'.

pRotect

Instead of focusing only on process efficiency at its breweries and other facilities, SABMiller is looking to all the watersheds where each of its facilities operates for information and understanding about local water issues and best practices. This goes far beyond the concept of 'water neutrality', where the goal is to replace as much water as is taken from the aquifers, rivers or other bodies of water. SABMiller's head of sustainable development, Andy Wales, says that water neutrality is 'an important start, but cannot be the end of a company's engagement in local water issues'.

One of the best examples is in India, where the combined efforts of rain harvesting to replenish the aquifers, and education of local farmers about water-efficient practices, move SABMiller's actions well beyond achieving water neutrality and into the realm of actual savings.

Reduce

As SABMiller looks to new processes, and ways to effectively change attitudes and behaviour towards water in its employee base, the company understands it cannot be effective without a baseline. A new 'water footprint' tool has become a major focus for the brewer. Early adopters of this new process, SABMiller partnered with the World Wildlife Fund (now Worldwide Fund for Nature, WWF) and joined the Water Footprint Network to see how this tool could be used, and has since been helping to make it a better process for other adopters.

Some companies have chosen to use the water footprint as a communication tool or as the peak of their contribution to water issues. SABMiller is different. Wales says that:

> The real value of water footprinting is not in a number that is put on a product, but is actually in understanding the value chain.

Tying in directly with the first of its 5Rs, *pRotect*, SABMiller uses its water footprints to understand local watersheds and the best ways to save water in those areas. For example, through this process, the brewer has found that agriculture is the largest water user in the value chain, regardless of location; however, each location has significantly different water-consumption levels due to location-specific realities that could not be helped with a one-size-fits-all attitude.

Oversimplifying water issues by using one high-level footprint number, such as with carbon footprinting, has risks. Wales says a water footprint is not the same as a carbon footprint, due to the simple fact that unlike a unit of carbon, a unit of water has very different impacts when used in different places around the globe. This ambiguity about water is the very reason SABMiller supports water-footprint use; promotes it regularly through its publication with the WWF, *Water Footprinting: Identifying and Addressing Water Risks in the Value Chain* (WWF, 2009); and plans its continued use throughout the organization. 'Water footprinting provides a very useful shared understanding of water risk', Wales explains. With this shared understanding, conversations can get started. A water footprint should be used 'as an informative basis for joint conversations, shared responsibility and shared understanding of risk, and then action', Wales says. It should be the starting point, not the end.

Reuse and Recycle

Using its water footprint as one baseline, SABMiller is working to identify as many ways as possible to reuse water at its facilities. SABMiller's Romanian subsidiary, Ursus Breweries, has seen a 15 per cent increase in water efficiency since it started implementing water reuse as part of its water-saving strategies. The main focus in this location has been to transfer recovered water from various parts of the brewing process and reuse it for cleaning.

Recycling water at a brewery occurs in much the same fashion and often requires new technology. At the SABMiller facility in India, reverse osmosis has allowed wastewater to be treated and then recycled into usable service water. While many breweries see reverse osmosis as cost prohibitive, in a country such as India, where wastewater is abundant and freshwater is not, investing in reverse osmosis makes sound business sense. SABMiller is committed to investigating and implementing this kind of technology at all its operations, where it is found to be appropriate.

Redistribute

In July 2007, SABMiller was a founding signatory of the United Nations CEO Water Mandate, which committed the brewer to implementation and disclosure of water-sustainability policies and practices. A statement on the mandate's website (www.unglobalcompact.org/issues/Environment/ CEO_Water_Mandate) reads:

> *It is increasingly clear that lack of access to clean water and sanitation in many parts of the world causes great suffering in humanitarian, social, environmental and economic terms, and seriously undermines development goals.*

It is here that SABMiller takes perhaps some of its most meaningful steps towards solving water problems around the globe. By committing the time and resources to getting clean water to local communities and treating wastewater for use in irrigation, the company is ensuring longevity in the communities it both needs and supports.

The Mozambique brewery funded an inexpensive borehole (US$30,000) and several fountains throughout the surrounding area, which provided clean water to more than 60,000 people. Fuelled by the same fire that sends SABMiller beyond water neutrality where possible, the Mozambique brewery has not stopped there. It is working to educate about water conservation, appropriate water use and sanitation. These efforts will ensure the water lasts longer and better serves the community in many ways, including decreasing the risk of water-borne illness and resulting death.

Keep the information flowing

SABMiller takes its role in sustainable development seriously, diving deeply into each community where its facilities are located, and working to find effective, local solutions to problems – with water always at the forefront. This remains true at a level outside the communities themselves, as the brewer works to raise awareness about water issues with governments and businesses around the world. 'We're trying to capitalize bigger conversations to ensure the whole watershed is protected', Wales says.

A partner in the 2030 Water Resources Group, SABMiller seeks to engage government in the conversation. Wales feels the *Charting Our Water Future: Economic Frameworks to Inform Decision-Making* report (2030 Water Resources Group, 2009) is essential for this, saying that it is:

> *elevating the water conversation from among only water administrators and the like [to] powerfully inform water strategy across government.*

Such a complex issue needs to be discussed across all sectors of government, or there will only be more problems in the long run; he says that:

If we can all work together and be water smart, we can actually tackle the water challenge.

Nestlé Waters

In 1969, Nestlé acquired a 30 per cent stake in the French bottled-water company Vittel; by 1987, the company had bought up nearly all Vittel's remaining share capital and was shaping the brand's growth. In the 1990s, Nestlé's water division – known first as Nestlé Source International, then Perrier Vittel SA – rose through the bottled-water ranks, acquiring water giants Perrier in 1992 and San Pellegrino in 1998, before launching its first multisite, international bottled water: Nestlé Pure Life. Changing its name once more to Nestlé Waters in 2002, the company became the leading player on the world bottled-water market, expanding into markets in Asia and Africa. In 2007, Nestlé Waters acquired Sources Minérales Henniez SA, becoming the leader of the Swiss bottled-water market, as well.

Since its release in 1998, Nestlé Pure Life has become the world's leading bottled water in value, selling nearly 6 billion litres worldwide in 2009. Nestlé Waters now boasts 64 brands worldwide.

In 1980, under the name Great Spring Waters of America, Nestlé Waters purchased its first springwater company: Poland Spring, in Maine. 'When we bought it, we acquired four hundred acres of surrounding natural lands as part of the purchase,' says Alex McIntosh, the company's (former) director of corporate citizenship. Knowing that the four hundred acres protected the spring, Nestlé Waters realized it would need to learn to manage the land in order to maintain its business model. McIntosh says:

> *What it forced us to do back in 1980 was to begin asking: How do you actually protect a spring? How does it work? What is the hydrogeology and the topography?*

What began as 400 acres has, some 30 years later, turned into 14,000, surrounding more than 65 spring sites in the United States and Canada. Managing its land as open space for the long-term protection of each spring, Nestlé Waters has become 'almost a hybrid company', according to McIntosh: 'Half our DNA is natural-resource management, and the other half is consumer packaged goods.' Unlike some bottled-water brands, which filter municipal water for sale, the company's springwater model tied it to particular places, and its corporate water strategy grew out of this. McIntosh says:

> *It is embedded, in many ways, in our culture. What we sell comes from real places. That's really great for us. It ties us to these places, gives us a really firm identity. On the other hand, it means that what we're doing is very much in the fabric of a community.*

Hoping to honour this tie to 'real places', Nestlé Waters began to partner with local and national conservation groups from the early 1990s, and then entered its first major NGO collaboration in 1998, when The Nature Conservancy approached it for help in protecting the iconic St John River in northern Maine. McIntosh remembers:

> *We wrote a big cheque, and our CEO volunteered a lot of his time to help lead the campaign, which is sort of Version 1.0 in corporate citizenship. The CEO wanted to create value in an important watershed in Maine, because Maine was such an important community to the company.*

Nestlé Waters's involvement with The Nature Conservancy eventually became national in scope, according to McIntosh:

> *After three or four years, we started looking at watersheds around the country together. They wanted to protect watersheds, and we had watersheds our raw material came from – so it made sense to work together for mutual benefit.*

This closer involvement, however, brought Nestlé Waters face to face with another stakeholder group: community members. During larger-scale landscape projects in Virginia, Texas and Maine, McIntosh says:

> *Some of our hydrogeologists would go to community meetings and realize that the social aspects of project siting were often far more complicated – and controversial – than the technical science or hydrology. In some meetings, there were a decent number of participants involved, often with conflicting opinions and occasionally quite vocal in their concern or anger – it was eye-opening and sometimes messy.*

As Nestlé Waters continued to engage community members and NGOs in conversation the company began to understand how it could continually improve its siting practices – and the activists sometimes came to more realistic expectations. McIntosh explains:

> *We asked them what 'better' looked like, if they had to account for x, y and z, and they thought about it and began to tell us. Our corporate leadership eventually supported some innovative – and, in some cases, challenging – community-engagement and resource-management goals based on these talks.*

McIntosh sees these collaboratively reached goals as a smart business strategy:

> *The old mindset is: 'There are companies that have a legal right to use a resource, and there are NGOs to play cop, policing the business.' I think that model is really starting to shift. Companies are now realizing that, sure, they need to make a profit – but if they don't have a water supply that works, or a regulatory regime that people trust, they really have a problem in their supply chain, not just a reputational one. And similarly, many NGOs are finding that in order to achieve their mission, they often need to engage with corporations in a realistic, solutions-based manner.*
>
> *There are NGOs that are not going to agree with you, but they frequently enjoy a greater degree of trust among the public, media and regulators. These environmental and social groups often have a specific agenda for how a resource should be managed by regulators five or six years down the road, so if companies collaborate with NGOs to solve complex issues that may not fit into a quarterly model, the companies may come up with solutions that are actually very advantageous to their business in the long run. And you can rarely do that independently, inside your own corporate board room.*

The smart companies, McIntosh says, are 'frontloading' business with good strategy: a willingness to communicate with other stakeholders, acknowledge company resource use, and examine basic environmental issues such as water management in their widest sense. McIntosh explains:

> *Leading companies are really learning from multiple venues and stakeholders. In doing that, they're learning what's around the*

corner; they're better preparing themselves for a more profitable, more successful future. That's just an element of good management that any company has to have now.

Nestlé Waters is now in the process of examining a less conventional asset: data accumulated from springs across North America, at both current and proposed bottling sites. McIntosh says the business sees these data as another value it has to offer stakeholders, from local governments to NGOs:

In a lot of places, communities don't have any watershed data of their own. It's a blank slate. That's partly why they get concerned when we show up and say, 'We'd like to test your water.' Collecting and sharing this watershed information can be really useful to a community.

Much of the data collection was simply part of Nestlé Waters' regulatory tracking and rigorous management; now, often publicly available, it is part of the company's effort to 'be a good citizen'. The data may serve even more important roles in the future, as watersheds and weather patterns shift through climate change.

Nestlé Waters continues to evolve its water-management and community-engagement practices. Recently, the company began working with Business for Social Responsibility (BSR) to establish a siting and community commitment framework. With the help of The Nature Conservancy, it completed a full pitch-pine restoration of the acreage surrounding one of its springs in Maine, transforming the habitat. McIntosh says:

The problems we face today are ones that are far too big for any one actor to take on. It's going to take a multi-sectoral effort to address them. Smart businesses understand and embrace this – particularly on water issues.

Diageo

'No water, no beer.' This slogan, adopted by the Red Stripe Employee Engagement Team, highlights the importance of water to Diageo, which produces Jamaica's internationally known beer, and is the world's largest premium drinks company. Water is an essential ingredient in all products produced by Diageo, including such famous brands as Guinness, Smirnoff,

Bushmills and Johnnie Walker. Managing this important resource is a high priority for the firm.

Historically, Diageo's focus on water quality and availability took place within the fairly traditional contexts of regulatory compliance, implementation of environmental management systems, cost containment and product quality. However, in recent years, water management has been part of far more integrated and ambitious programmes that operate in the larger context of sustainability and corporate responsibility. The real 'tipping point' for Diageo came in 2007 when the company recognized water as a broader sustainability challenge and opportunity. Interestingly, Diageo's response was driven from the supply side of the company's operations.

In January 2007, Diageo's managing director of global supply and procurement, David Gosnell, posed a challenging question to a team of corporate environmental managers assembled at the company's headquarters in London. 'What would it take for Diageo to be carbon neutral?' Global Environmental project manager, Roberta Barbieri, says, 'It was a wonderful "ah ha" moment for the company.' By the end of the day, participants were committed to moving forward and identifying key strategies. More importantly, the question inspired the blue sky thinking that would create real, meaningful change in a company tied to tradition. According to Barbieri, the thinking became much broader:

> *What are our major impacts? What would we have to do? What are our highest aspirations? [the thinking reflected] an ideal end state ... that someday Diageo would be sourced, supplied, produced and packaged sustainably, [encompassing the entire business chain] from the barley in the field to the empty bottle in the bin.*

A mere three months later, corporate vice presidents were presented with an overview of this environmental 'blue sky thinking' as they met to develop their long-term corporate strategy. Although the original mandate with which the environmental managers were challenged was climate-focused, the strategy that emerged integrated Diageo's four major environmental impact areas – water, carbon, waste and wastewater – and was driven by core values of brand heritage, legacy and pride. By the end of the session, the leadership had signed off on personal commitments and business unit deliverables to implement a shared company-wide environmental vision, which Diageo has been working towards ever since.

Numerous programmes are being implemented to move the company towards achieving its aspirational goals. As a signatory to the CEO Water Mandate of the UN Global Compact, Diageo has adopted initiatives in each of the six key areas:

- direct operations;
- supply-chain and watershed management;
- collective action;
- public policy;
- community engagement;
- transparency.

To be fair, Diageo acknowledges that some of these initiatives, such as influencing its supply chain, are in their infancy. What is clear, however, is that the company's traditional commitment to water efficiency and quality in its direct operations is now part of a larger, more integrated campaign – one that includes both corporate mandates and bottom-up dedication by employees.

The improvements made at the Red Stripe brewery in Jamaica are a perfect illustration of this inclusive approach. Great gains have been made at the facility, which had lagged behind other operations. Taking the 'no water, no beer' slogan to heart, employees have adopted an integrated approach to efficiency designed to save thousands of cubic metres of water per year.

Workers and management declared a 'Red Stripe Water Week' to mark the introduction of new, more water-efficient cleaning equipment, a water-recycling project, tighter management of leaks, and enhanced metering to monitor the water consumption of each process in the brewery. These are important first steps for Red Stripe as they move towards a more efficient use of water in their operations. This initial progress was recognized by the Jamaica Chamber of Commerce with its 2008 Environmental Award.

Diageo understands that its direct operations are only part of its impact. The next, and certainly the more challenging step, is to extend the internal commitment to the supply chain. Barbieri likens this to evolution as the company's move 'from the juvenile to the adolescent stage'. Like many of its own operations as well as those of its suppliers, Tusker, one of the leading beer brands in East Africa, is produced in an area identified as water-stressed. The company conducted a water-footprint analysis that enhanced its understanding of consumption throughout the supply chain. The results identified priority mitigation strategies that served as the basis for dialogue with suppliers.

Recognition that Diageo is succeeding in building a world-class water stewardship programme was seen in their ranking in the Ceres report on corporate water reporting. Diageo was part of a benchmarking of 100 companies by Ceres, and scored the highest of any of the surveyed companies in any of the industry sectors (Ceres, 2010). This achievement reflects how far Diageo has come in managing water as a critical business issue. At the same time, it reflects how far business in general still has to go, at least in the area of water-reporting transparency – Diageo's score, while the highest among benchmarked companies, was just 43 out of a possible 100.

I believe the most compelling aspect of Diageo's story is the Water of Life programme. This moves beyond water efficiency to address water availability in water-scarce areas in Africa, and makes a real difference in the lives of many. Linking into the UN Millennium Development Goals (MDGs), the company is focusing on providing clean, safe and sustainable drinking water to the people of Africa. The One Million Challenge has set an ambitious goal of providing one million people with access to water each year until 2015, through investments in Kenya, Uganda, Tanzania, Nigeria, Burkina Faso, Ethiopia, South Africa and Ghana. The programme is designed to ensure the efforts actually achieve sustainable results.

Several representative projects, according to Diageo, are highlighted below:

- Nigeria: mini water works. Guinness Nigeria plc completed seven projects to provide water to 450,000 people. Each project completed comprised a deep borehole, storage tank, treatment plant and distribution network to whole communities such as a mini water works installed at Iju, Nigeria, which provides water for 100,000 people from 21 fetching stations.
- Cameroon: Nature Cameroun. Over 150 employees from Guinness Cameroun joined the residents of Kassalafarm in Douala to dig a trench for a 1km pipeline as part of a water-supply project to provide clean water to over 11,000 people. Integral to the sustainability of the project, Nature Cameroun ensure training is provided to a caretaker

committee, providing them with skills to maintain the water system and educate community members on good hygiene and water-use practices.

- Ghana: Rural Empowerment and Development Agency (REDA). For many years the main source of drinking water for the Dantano village in the Brong Ahafo region consisted of a drying-up stream, which also served eight other surrounding satellite villages. With a borehole strategically situated in Dantano, all residents and those of the nearby settlements – some 18,000 people – have access to clean drinking water. Implemented through REDA, the project adopted a community-based participatory approach involving the district assembly, local community members and the traditional authorities.

To ensure the long-term sustainability of these projects, Diageo sets a high priority on measurement, evaluation and transparency in reporting. As in all of its internal and external activities, the company works with local, national and international parties including government agencies and NGOs.

Another distinguishing characteristic of the Water of Life programme is that all projects are selected and funded by local operations. This helps to ensure that the projects meet local needs and contribute to local economies, by using labour and enterprises from the communities in which they operate, while building technical and financial capacity. Taking this grass-roots commitment one step further, Diageo has established mechanisms for its employees to contribute directly and through other financial mechanisms. The company launched the 'Giving for Good' website that supports employee efforts to raise funds through individual donations, sponsorships and campaigns. One project purchased more than 4500 water filter kits, each of which provides clean water for up to 25 people over a year.

Diageo understands that its business viability is based on access to water, but even more, the company understands that the decisions it makes regarding water and other natural resources have repercussions to its suppliers and the communities in which it operates. In adopting a corporate philosophy on water and other natural resources based on the higher goals of sustainability, Diageo has set the bar high for itself – and for other companies.

Molson Coors

The family of breweries that is Molson Coors has been involved in the water business for a total of 350 years. As Pete Coors, former CEO of Coors Brewing Company and current chairman of Molson Coors says, 'without great water, we couldn't make great beer'. It is this fundamental connection between beer and water that drives the efforts at Molson Coors to create breweries that are self-sufficient, deeply involved with and working hard to inform its own employees and external stakeholders about water issues, as well as coming up with creative solutions for consuming less water each year at the 19 individual brewing locations in the business. With over 15,000 employees (including US MillerCoors, a joint venture with SABMiller) in 30 different countries, this means a detailed approach that allows for local stakeholder outreach and engagement.

Starting from within

In 2008, the same year that Molson Coors signed into the UN's CEO Water Mandate, the international brewer announced its brewery-specific operational water-reduction goal: 15 per cent from 2008 to 2012. In the three years prior to this, Molson Coors saw its water consumption drop by 5 per cent in its Canadian operations and by as much as 12 per cent in its UK-based operations. Within the United States, in MillerCoors (of which Molson Coors owns 42 per cent), where the most water is consumed annually, water usage dropped 8 per cent in the previous three-year window.

As with most brewing operations, the vast majority of water is used not only to brew beer, but also in the general cleaning of equipment, rinsing bottles and the cooling machinery. This water comes from sources local to each of the breweries, which requires a local-solutions approach to solving the larger corporate-wide water-reduction goal. In the United States operations, three out of the eight facilities are situated in areas where water is already scarce. In Canada, where the presence of water is considered abundant, issues of municipal infrastructure inefficiencies and sustainability come into play.

In order to deal with this complex subject, Molson Coors established a high-level cross-departmental/geographical team of employees called the Water Stewardship Working Group. Through the guidance of this group, groundwork has been laid for a three-year plan that closely follows the CEO Water Mandate guidelines and leaves itself open-ended, in the hope of moving forward with new, updated goals and information after

2012. The five strategic principles that guide this group have helped shape Molson Coors's global attitude and approach to water reduction for the better. These principles are outlined in the following paragraphs.

Direct operations

In beer making, water-sustainability measures are most often defined in terms of the number of water units it takes to create one equal beer unit. The industry standard has been slowly coming down over the years and now rests at 5:1. At Molson Coors the number is lower, currently 4.4:1. Part of this is due to the environmental scorecards Molson Coors breweries have been using to capture baseline data, which drive and inform how the facilities can have a smaller environmental footprint. These scorecards are based on internal information and are self-reported, and then certified independently by The Corporate Citizenship Company. The introduction of these scorecards in the early 2000s, as well as more recent efforts in conducting several local watershed risk assessments, have allowed the Molson Coors family of breweries to achieve a continual decrease in water consumption, improve awareness of water issues around the world and provide specific success stories from each of the 19 brewery locations.

One of the standouts for the brewer is the original site of Coors Brewing Company, located in Golden, Colorado. The largest single-site brewery in the world, this location is completely self-sufficient in its water use. Possessing some of the oldest water rights in the state, and dating back to the 1860s, this brewery obtains 50,000 acre feet of water annually and is then able to use it, treat it and return more than 90 per cent of it back to the Clear Creek watershed for use by other stakeholders. A few of the breweries located in the United Kingdom are also considered self-sufficient, and have become models of water use for breweries around the world.

Collective action and community engagement

As a corporation with an international focus not only on its operations but also, and perhaps more importantly, on its customer base, Molson Coors has been a leader in educating itself and others about emerging global water issues. Accomplished through collaboration with groups such as the Beverage Industry Environmental Roundtable (BIER), formed in 2006, and Circle of Blue, Molson Coors is successfully educating and engaging local stakeholders about water issues in order to promote sustainable freshwater supplies for both business and communities.

Molson Coors (www.molsoncoors.com/responsibility/environmental-responsibility/water/water-stewardship) states that BIER is dedicated to bringing together:

> *leading global beverage companies to define a common framework for stewardship, drive continuous improvement in industry practices and performance and inform public policy in the areas of water conservation and resource protection, energy efficiency and climate change mitigation.*

BIER is working to set a common ground for the beverage industry through benchmarking and sharing best practices. The working group is also researching its own water-footprinting tool and gathering information to put in a white paper that will help answer questions about the new practice and all the tools surrounding it.

Unlike BIER, Circle of Blue is a non-profit organization, and an affiliate of the Pacific Institute. The organization is focused on responding to the global freshwater crisis through journalists, scientists and community design experts, and considers itself the 'daily go-to source for global water news and data'. It is here, through collaboration, that Molson Coors has made significant strides in raising awareness about the absolutely critical state of water.

In 2009, with the expertise of the non-partisan research and polling firm GlobeScan, the team released the findings of a new global survey in a report entitled *Human Perspectives on the Global Water Crisis* (www.globescan.com/pdf/WaterViews_GlobalWaterPoll_GlobeScan.pdf). After compiling information gathered from 15,500 adults in 22 countries, one thing was as clear as glacial water: water is the most pressing environmental issue of our time. The report states:

> *people around the world view water issues as the planet's top environmental problem, greater than air pollution, depletion of natural resources, loss of habitat and even climate change.*

Truly groundbreaking work, this report highlights the very basic fact that all life on this planet, whether it relates directly to a corporate strategy or not, is affected by water and simply cannot thrive without it. Providing a voice for and pinpointing global water issues, the report highlights:

- industry and the risk of overuse in Canada;
- water contamination and a shortage of clean fresh water due to failing or absent infrastructure in China, India and Mexico;
- water pollution in Russia;
- lack of safe drinking water in the United Kingdom;
- water availability and quality issues in the United States.

This unique report also shows the distinctly human aspect of an issue that has somehow failed to gain the attention of lawmakers and vocal entities around the world. Its aim is to open the conversation worldwide and kick-start both conversation and action around the most precious of resources; and this is just what happened when it was presented at World Water Week in Stockholm, Sweden, at its release in 2009.

Public policy and transparency

As Molson Coors moves forward with the strategy laid out by the Water Stewardship Working Group, the intent is to let others know what is happening and how the global brewer is doing it. Allowing full transparency of water issues and problem-solving tactics ensures that Molson Coors is keeping the process truly sustainable. Companies that choose to keep their information proprietary are missing the point: creating a culture that moves away from collaboration in the face of global issues such as water will only do harm to themselves and additional surrounding stakeholders.

By 2013 Molson Coors will have met the CEO Water Mandate commitments and plans to continue vital partnerships with pertinent organizations such as River Network, Water for People and the Clear Creek Watershed Foundation, lobbying for water issues and using its brewing operations as examples of sound water management.

Water leadership

Molson Coors has built upon its commitment to the CEO Water Mandate, and other initiatives to address water stewardship, by committing to a lead sponsorship role with the CDP Water Disclosure programme launched in 2010 (www.cdproject.net/water-disclosure). As a lead sponsor of the programme, Molson Coors has taken a proactive role in shaping water-risk reporting and disclosure as a means to advance overall water stewardship. Just as the Carbon Disclosure Project (CDP) has moved industries to measure and reduce greenhouse gas emissions it is anticipated that its programme will result in increased awareness of the critical role water plays in businesses operations.

In closing, as CEO Peter Swinburn puts it:

> *we believe that everybody in the world should have access to water as fresh as we use to brew our beers.*

Molson Coors knows that a focus on the six core elements of the CEO Water Mandate will help minimize its own water risk, while also building partnerships and engaging local and global communities to reduce the risk for all stakeholders.

The Coca-Cola Company

The Coca-Cola Company (TCCC) is the world's largest non-alcoholic beverage company. Headquartered in Atlanta, Georgia, TCCC is best known for its flagship product, Coca-Cola, which was invented in 1886. Today TCCC offers more than 500 brands in over 200 countries, reaching consumers with more than 1.6 billion drink servings per day. It is one of the largest corporations headquartered in the Unites States, employing 92,400 people globally. With a portfolio of more than 3000 beverage products, TCCC's net income in the fiscal year 2009 was US$5.82 billion. Currently, Coca-Cola ranks number 1 worldwide in sparkling beverages, juices and juice drinks sales, number 2 in sports drinks sales, and number 3 in bottled water sales.

The birth of a strategy

In the late 1990s, TCCC began acquiring natural water brands, including mineral and spring water sites that required hands-on watershed management. Requiring a new set of skills and decisions from TCCC, these acquisitions highlighted the need to understand more fully the social and ecological dimensions of industrial water use.

The company focus on water includes becoming one of the first companies to report water quality and quantity as a material risk to its business on the US Securities & Exchange Commission investor form 10-K. Moreover, while the company had long adhered to standards regarding water quality, efficiency and treatment, a more sophisticated and forward-looking strategy was in order. TCCC assembled a system-wide team to better understand water issues and implement plans, led by vice president of environment and water resources, Jeff Seabright, and director of global water initiatives, Dan Vermeer. Over the course of several years, the team determined that existing goals to work towards conservation, lower water-use ratios, and quantify water-use targets were clear and effective. What was less clear, they suggested, was where water was coming from, perceptions of water quality and use by locals, and overall watershed stress.

Engaging with academic leaders and NGOs, participating in water-based conferences, hosting focus groups with bottlers and internal operations groups, and administering a 300-question survey to bottlers, the group developed a plant-level, comprehensive water-risk assessment to quantify risks and inform strategic responses. The assessment forms the foundation of TCCC's larger water-stewardship strategy, and highlights:

- water-resource sustainability;
- supply reliability;
- compliance with wastewater standards;
- supply economics;
- water-use efficiency;
- local/social issues related to water availability and use.

A key learning from the water-risk assessment and stakeholder engagement was that water stewardship must extend beyond the four walls of a bottling plant.

The group identified three other areas of action, beyond the boundaries of their plants and those of their bottling partners:

- Watershed protection: addresses source protection and supports the watersheds in which TCCC's plants operate.
- Sustainable communities: helps communities in the developing world gain access to clean drinking water sources.
- Global awareness and action: aims to help educate students, other industry and the public while mobilizing the international community to address water challenges.

In 2006 and 2007 TCCC focused on developing the tools its bottlers would need to manage water sustainably. Primarily, TCCC executives met with top bottlers to confirm best management practices, released a software program that provided watershed training and watershed management capabilities, and challenged bottlers to benchmark against one another. The corporation also began projects with groups such as UN-HABITAT, the International Water Association and the UN Foundation, and helped launch the CEO Water Mandate as well as the Global Water Challenge, a coalition of 24 leading organizations working to create a 'global movement for transformational change to improve access to clean water and sanitation'.

Reduce, recycle, replenish

In Beijing on 5 June 2007, Coca-Cola chairman, E. Neville Isdell, announced a new multi-year partnership with the World Wildlife Fund (WWF). Concurrent with the WWF partnership announcement, Isdell unveiled TCCC's new long-term, system-wide goal: to return to communities and nature an amount of water equivalent to what is used in their beverages and their production. Speaking at the WWF Annual conference, Coca-Cola chairman, E. Neville Isdell, said:

> *Water is the main ingredient in nearly every beverage that we make. Without access to safe water supply our business simply cannot exist.*

The strategy he unveiled followed the tenets of reduce, recycle and replenish – simple terms for a vast 'water neutrality' project.

The company's new 'Reduce' goals aim to lower the water-use ratio while increasing case unit volume. In particular, TCCC set a goal to improve water efficiency by 20 per cent over 2004 levels, by 2012. By 2008, the water-use ratio was 2.43 litres per litre of product, a 9 per cent improvement from the 2004 baseline and the sixth straight year of improvement.

'Recycle' focuses on recycling water used in beverage production so it can be returned to local communities at a level that supports aquatic life, by the end of 2010. Where needed, bottling partners are constructing treatment facilities to meet this goal. In 2008, more than 88 per cent of TCCC's facilities and over 95 per cent of process wastewater volume were in compliance with the company's wastewater treatment standards. In fact, TCCC says its own standards are often more stringent than local requirements. This is a critical aspect of the company's water stewardship programme and a best practice for other companies to incorporate into their corporate water strategies. About 70 per cent of industrial waste-water in developing countries is *not* treated before it is returned to the watershed. TCCC has recognized that in order to be a leader in water stewardship they must treat this wastewater as an investment of millions of dollars.

Perhaps the most difficult to conceptualize, TCCC's 'Replenish' goal aims to return an amount of water equivalent to what is used in finished beverages through participation in local projects. Based on actual product volume and water usage, the target will be annually refreshed to reflect increases in product volume. These projects, known as the Community Water Partnership (CWP), implement locally relevant projects in partnership with key stakeholders – from watershed protection to access and sanitation projects. In 2009 these projects replaced 638 million litres of water for community consumption and 28.8 million litres for nature, representing 22 per cent of the water in the company's finished beverages from 2009. The company aims to replenish 100 per cent of the water used in finished beverages by 2020.

In 2009, TCCC partnered with The Nature Conservancy (TNC) and the Global Environmental and Technology Foundation (GETF) to better quantify water benefits from watershed restoration and community access projects. Working collaboratively with TNC and GETF on measurement schematics, Coca-Cola is now reporting progress annually, and has achieved 22 per cent of its goal to date. Moreover, TCCC acknowledges the new, evolving nature of water quantification processes, and openly invites suggestions from outside agencies and researchers to improve accuracy. In the spirit of transparency, and to facilitate input, the company posted the results of the said research on its internet site.

Current international projects

The Coca-Cola Company works with a number of international NGOs and aid organizations to help alleviate water-related suffering and restore major water systems globally. As a long-term partner of WWF, TCCC funds and provides deep technical expertise for projects on the River Danube, Lake Malawi-Niassa-Nyasa, the Mekong River, the Mesoamerican Reef of Central America, the Rio Grande River, the Yangtze River, and rivers and streams of the south-east region of the United States. TCCC also works prominently with USAID, the Water & Development Alliance, and the United Nations Development Programme.

In common with any beverage company, the agricultural areas that supply Coca-Cola's raw ingredients are under increased scrutiny. Because agricultural production accounts for 70 per cent of society's water use, TCCC is working to better understand the full water footprint for key products. Such footprints show not only the water in the product and that which is used in its production, but also the embedded water from various ingredients, packaging and transport. Initial water footprinting of selected beverage products indicates that the largest component of the full water footprint is from the field (crops) not the factory. This awareness is enabling TCCC to place focus on engaging suppliers on sustainable water use in growing key ingredients such as cane sugar, corn and oranges.

2030 Water Resources Group

In 2008, Coca-Cola joined the newly formed 2030 Water Resources Group, a coalition of global businesses working to determine how competing demands for scarce resources can be met and sustained by 2030. Collecting the input of more than 300 specialists and public sector practitioners, and receiving guidance from a group of expert advisers, the Water Resources Group compiled a factbase that quantifies the situation for more precise strategizing. The study showed that in many areas, current supply will be inadequate to meet future needs; however, the group's central thesis asserts that meeting all competing demands for water is possible at a reasonable cost.

Initiated by the International Finance Corporation and partly managed by consultants McKinsey & Co., other group members include SAB Miller, Barilla, Nestlé SA, New Holland Agriculture, Standard Chartered Bank and Syngenta AG.

Jeff Seabright captures the approach by TCCC to water well when he says:

> *We recognize the fundamental nature of water in supporting life on the planet. Water is critical to advancing healthy ecosystems, communities, business and commerce. As a beverage company, water is absolutely critical to our business and we are working to build a truly water-sustainable business on a global basis.*

PepsiCo

All water is local

Comprising 18 brands of beverages and snacks that generate more than US$43 billion in annual retail sales, New York-based PepsiCo is a force in water stewardship or, as the company calls it, 'resource conservation'.

Water strategy is one area where the principles of trickle-down are essential. Indra Nooyi, CEO and chair of PepsiCo and chair of the PepsiCo foundation, is a firm believer that sustainability is a good business decision. A signatory to the United Nations CEO Water Mandate, she is committed to minimizing her company's water footprint.

Water as a core value

Unlike many companies whose sustainability programmes are add-ons or afterthoughts, PepsiCo made water part of not just its environmental strategy, but part of its business strategy.

As part of its social and environmental initiative 'Performance with Purpose', PepsiCo implemented a three-pronged water strategy:

- conserving water in operations;
- reducing water use in agriculture;
- working with other organizations to bring safe water to developing countries.

Water-resource efficiency

PepsiCo works to minimize its global water use through 'greater efficiency, innovative processes and new technologies'. In 2006, the company set a goal of a 20 per cent improvement in water-use efficiency for its manufacturing operations by 2015, and expects to meet that goal earlier than planned.

From 2006 to 2008, by employing myriad strategies throughout the company's worldwide operations, gains in water efficiency at PepsiCo conserved more than 7.5 billion litres of water. Utilizing waterless rinsing (or air rinsing) on all Gatorade and Propel lines in the United States saves more than 5 million litres of water per year. The Pepsi Bottling Group's reverse-osmosis recovery systems and high-recovery designs save more than 1 billion litres of water annually. The Walkers Crisps team in the United Kingdom developed engineering solutions to reduce equipment water use, and created reuse alternatives for recycled water in utility and other systems, reducing the water used to manufacture the crisps by nearly 60 per cent. These are just a few examples.

Their own backyard

Through its charitable arm, the PepsiCo Foundation, the company has made more than US$16 million in commitments to water projects around the world to support sustainable approaches to water access, conservation and usage in underserved regions.

In one of many partnerships, PepsiCo is funding the Water.org WaterCredit Initiative, which uses a microfinance programme to increase access to safe water and improve sanitation for local communities in India. The programme provides traditional grant funding to local NGOs to install pipes, taps and storage cellars in impoverished communities, reaching some 60,000 people. It also established a loan fund to help communities expand access to safe water for an additional 60,000 people during a three-year period. A 'multiplier effect' is expected to expand the impact to more beneficiaries throughout the communities.

PepsiCo also partners with the The Nature Conservancy, a large NGO that works locally on watershed measurement and monitoring, as well as on renovation and preservation issues relevant to different local communities worldwide.

Leadership and the human right to water

PepsiCo's position on the human right to water is bold and reflects true leadership with regard to water stewardship. Their groundbreaking 'Guidelines in support of the human right to water' are:

- Safety: We will ensure that our operations preserve the quality of the water resources in the communities in which we do business.
- Sufficiency: Our operating objective is to ensure that our use of water will not diminish the availability of community water resources to the individuals or communities in the areas in which we operate.
- Acceptability: We will involve communities in our plans to develop water resources, and will assure transparency of any risks or challenges to the local governments and community members in an ongoing manner.

- Physical accessibility: We will assure that our operations will not adversely impact physical accessibility of community members to community water resources and will address community concerns in a cooperative manner.
- Affordability: We will appropriately advocate to applicable government bodies that safe water supplies should be available in a fair and equitable manner to members of the community. Such water would be safe and of consistent and adequate supply and affordable within local practices.

PepsiCo's position on the human right to water is clear:

> *we at PepsiCo respect the human rights recognized by the countries in which we operate, and will not take any action that would undermine a state's obligation to its citizens to protect and fulfill the Human Right to Water and, absent of a country's Human Right to Water Policy, we commit to operate within the principles of the Human Right to Water Policy as defined by the United Nations.*

References

2030 Water Resources Group (2009) *Charting Our Water Future: Economic Frameworks to Inform Decision-Making*, 2030 Water Resources Group

Ceres (2010) 'The 21st century corporation: the Ceres roadmap for sustainability', www.ceres.org/Document.Doc?id=568, accessed 30 June 2010

Ceres and Pacific Institute (2009) 'Water scarcity and climate change: growing risks for businesses and investors', www.ceres.org/Document.Doc?id=406, February 2009, accessed 30 June 2010

J. P. Morgan (2008) 'Watching water: a guide to evaluating corporate risks in a thirsty world', www.soil.ncsu.edu/lockers/Hoover_M/html/wrkshop/Materials_for_on_web/Other_files/Shankar_Artemis_files/JP_Morgan_water_corporate_risks.PDF, April 2008, accessed 30 June 2010

WWF (2009) *Water Footprinting: Identifying and Addressing Water Risks in the Value Chain*, SABMiller and WWF-UK

10

The Semiconductor Industry

Water is the driver of Nature.

Leonardo da Vinci

In contrast to general manufacturing, the manufacturing of semiconductors requires not only very large quantities of water but also the use of 'ultra-pure water' in the production of semiconductor wafers. In Silicon Valley, semiconductor manufacturing accounts for approximately 25 per cent of all water withdrawals (Klusewitz and McVeigh, 2002). Specifically, in the manufacture of one 200mm wafer, a typical semiconductor plant (commonly referred to as a 'fab', short for wafer-fabrication facility) requires 7.5m^3 of ultra-pure water, and large facilities can use up to 10,000m^3 of ultra-pure water per day (J. P. Morgan, 2008).

Water Use and Potential Risk

The semiconductor sector faces unique water-scarcity and water-quality risk issues. Degrading water quality will result in increased water pre-treatment costs for processes such as filtration, disinfection and reverse osmosis. The location of semiconductor manufacturing in developing countries where populations may not have access to clean, affordable water potentially puts this manufacturing sector on a collision course with competing water needs. This can have an impact on a company's licence to operate and increase exposure to reputational risk.

According to J. P. Morgan (2008), water is a material risk to the semiconductor sector, and they estimate that water accounts for 20–30 basis points for the cost of goods sold for Intel and Texas Instruments. J. P. Morgan takes this analysis further and estimates that if water costs increased by a factor of two, it would reduce the earnings of Texas Instruments by US$0.02 per share and those of Intel by US$0.01 per share, using 2008 data.

It is clear that the semiconductor manufacturing sector faces increasing water risk in Asian and Pacific Rim countries, where water resources are already under stress owing to rapid population and economic growth. Currently, 11 of the 14 integrated circuit foundries (fabs) in the world are in the Asia Pacific region, accounting for more than 75 per cent of sales in this sector (Ceres and Pacific Institute, 2009).

These estimates need to be put into perspective when considering the total investment in semiconductor manufacturing. Although exposure to water risk is considered material by J. P. Morgan, the expenditures for water treatment and reuse would be about 2 per cent of the total cost for a fab, assuming its construction costs about US$5 billion.

This actually highlights the disconnect between the price of water and its real value. While the price of water is very low compared to other costs for fab construction and operations, the actual value of water to the operation is higher. Any loss of production due to disruption of delivery of adequate water quantity or quality would have an operational and resultant financial impact. This real value of water is factored into siting and operations, not just of fabs, but for any operation that is dependent on water.

The semiconductor sector has invested in water-reuse systems to ensure its reliability, while reducing the sector's reliance on public water-supply systems. This is an important illustration of how industries will mitigate risks in their operations while recognizing that the real value in water has nothing to do with actual cost. Decreasing reliance on public water supplies and delivery provides companies with increased flexibility in siting operations and assurances against business disruptions.

J. P. Morgan also states that the main risk to the semiconductor sector resides in the potential shutdown of a fab due to water scarcity or decreasing water quality, estimating that a fab shutdown could result in approximately a loss of revenue of US$100 million–200 million in one quarter, or about US$0.02–0.04 per share. We are no longer talking about the price of water, but the real *value* of water.

Water reuse and conservation is increasingly common in the semiconductor sector, with Intel as an excellent example (see 'Snapshot', below). At Intel's plant in Hudson, Massachusetts, output was doubled without increasing water use by reusing about 75 per cent of the water at the site. At its site in Chandler, Arizona, the company reduced public water use by about 80 per cent through reuse and conservation.

Water-Risk Disclosure

An excellent overview of water-risk disclosure in the semiconductor sector was provided by Ceres (2010). A brief summary of the findings, based on benchmarking of 11 semiconductor companies, is provided below:

- Water accounting data: The majority of the companies report data on water use, but few provide data on wastewater discharge.
- Risk disclosure: Nearly two-thirds disclose water-related physical and regulatory water risk, and less than one-third report on litigation risk.
- Supply-chain disclosure: Only two companies provide information on actions taken with suppliers to reduce environmental impacts, and water-specific information is considered limited.
- Stakeholder engagement: Only Intel reports on efforts to collaborate with stakeholders on water-resource management.

Company Snapshots

Intel

Based on revenue, Intel is the world's largest maker of semiconductor chips. Headquartered in Santa Clara, California, the microprocessing giant was founded in 1968 by chemist–physicists Gordon E. Moore and Robert Noyce, who in 1978 invented the x86 series of microprocessors found in most personal computers. By 2009, Intel's net revenues topped US$35.1 billion, and the company recently jumped ahead four spots on Millward Brown's Optimor rating of the world's most powerful companies, coming in 23rd.

Intel has more than 83,500 employees worldwide, with facilities in Argentina, China, Costa Rica, Malaysia, Mexico, Israel, India, Ireland, the Philippines, Poland, Russia and Vietnam, as well as in nine states in the United States. The company is known for its egalitarian office policies, including a shift away from personal offices – even top executives work in cubicles.

Now listed by the US Environmental Protection Agency (USEPA) as the largest purchaser of renewable energy in the United States, Intel has spent the past decade developing a reputation for environmental innovation. In

2007, it recycled or reused 87 per cent of chemical waste and 80 per cent of solid waste, and in 2008 the company moved to lead-free and halogen-free products. Intel has invested more than US$100 million during the past decade in water-conservation programmes at global facilities. Each year, the company reclaims more than 3 billion gallons of water instead of tapping into freshwater sources; comprehensive efforts have saved 37 billion gallons to date.

Worldwide Water Program manager, Tom Cooper, says:

> *Whether climate change is [human-made] or not, I think the experts on both sides agree this is going to affect water availability and make some areas drier or wetter than they used to be. The question becomes: how does that affect our ability to stay in business and be successful?*

Reducing at the source

Cooper says the company's real water-conservation opportunities are in technological advancements. 'As we change technologies, we are able to re-design tools', he says. 'That's where we get the real bang for the buck.' For instance, several years ago Intel increased its silicon-wafer size by several inches. Because the change in wafer size required significant changes in manufacturing equipment, engineers were able to redesign a series of previously inefficient sinks, and Cooper pointed out:

> *While converting from 8- to 12-inch wafer sizes, we've achieved a 40 per cent reduction in water use. That's just amazing.*

Cleaning these wafers during fabrication remains Intel's greatest challenge, as the wafers, hypersensitive to contamination of any sort, must be washed with ultra-pure water (UPW), which has high purity and has been deionized. It used to take nearly two gallons of regular water to produce a gallon of UPW – a high ratio for a company working to cut its water use. Committed to tightening UPW efficiency, Intel has helped lead the industry by driving that number to 1.25:1 and better. Intel also responded by installing separate drains in manufacturing facilities that capture lightly contaminated water for reuse, often in plant cooling towers and scrubbers. The overall goal is to continuously reuse water. Cooper claims the company's post-wafer UPW is clean enough for irrigation use and industrial purposes.

In 2008 and 2009, Intel linked a portion of employees' bonuses to environmental achievements – including improvements in the energy efficiency of products, environmental reputation (with both customers and external audiences) and completion of renewable-energy products and purchases – ensuring a climate that pushes towards ever more sustainable operations that reduce at the source. Cooper says:

> *It's great from a planning standpoint to get in the heads of these design engineers and say: 'Is there any way you can reduce that particular chemical? Do we really need that gallon-per-minute flow rate? Can you reduce that without affecting quality?' That's been extremely successful.*

Replenishing communities

Intel has also recognized the overall impact its high water use can have on ecosystems and communities. In Hudson, Massachusetts, the company established a US$1.5 million 'Intel Assabet Groundwater Recharge Fund' for projects that help replenish the river and its tributaries. To date, the fund has awarded more than US$710,000 in grants, including more than US$68,000 in 2008 alone. In Israel, Intel made its plant wastewater fully available for local agricultural irrigation by partnering with Numonyx BV to invest in a US$20 million advanced membrane bioreactor. And in India, wastewater from plant cafés and restrooms is treated and reused to meet 60 per cent of the community's irrigation needs.

Wastewater at Intel's Chandler plant undergoes reverse osmosis before being reinjected into the aquifer to replenish the area's groundwater. Since 1996, this strategy has put more than 3.5 billion gallons of water back into the aquifer. The Chandler plant is one of Intel's most efficient UPW treatment facilities, producing 0.85 gallons of UPW per 1 gallon of city water through advanced reverse-osmosis and brine-evaporation systems. The plant also boasts an impressive reclamation record. During the past decade, it used more than 4.5 billion gallons of treated wastewater from Chandler's Ocotillo Water Reclamation Facility, instead of tapping into potable water supplies. Millions of gallons of processed wastewater daily run cooling towers and air abatement equipment, support landscaping and irrigate nearby farms.

In 2007, the Chandler facility received the USEPA's Water Efficiency Leader Award after it had officially reduced its water demand by 75 per cent. By 2008, Intel's use was less than 5 per cent of Chandler's total non-residential and residential water use.

One of Intel's cornerstone strategies is to develop new conservation methods before being asked to do so by NGOs or governments. Cooper says:

> *We're in a space of proactive transparency, trying to keep our finger on the pulse of everyone involved, whether it's shareholders, regulators, employees or NGOs. We try to make sure we are 100 per cent aligned with what people expect of companies. And once we know what is expected, we try to go beyond that.*

One such 'stretch' was Intel's initial commitment to buying renewable energy credits.

The strategy is paying off. In June 2009, Intel's corporate environmental manager, Todd Brady, was highlighted as one of *Scientific American's* Top 10 'Guiding Science for Humanity' Leaders. Working to ensure 'the benefits of new technologies and knowledge will accrue to humanity', Brady was featured alongside innovators such as Bill Gates and President Barack Obama for his creativity, dedication and influence to ethics within industry.

Internal NGOs

> *I've worked for six other multinational corporations, and never before has an employee group been so active in environmental and safety programmes. Typically, the only emphasis would come from employees within the Environmental Health & Safety departments. That's not been the case here, and everyone seems to have a piece in it.*

Cooper refers to Intel's environmentally concerned employees as 'internal NGOs', who help channel eco-friendly ideas towards management and each other.

According to Cooper, one of the reasons Intel's employees are so engaged, is that the company is structured in a way that allows ideas to filter 'up and through', gaining review quickly. For instance, Intel operates an internal blog called 'Planet Blue', in which employees can post questions or suggest tips on living more consciously. He says that:

> *The site is full of thousands of people exchanging information – from recycling car batteries to disposing of fluorescent lights.*

Another mechanism for employee engagement is the Sustainability in Action Award, which offers motivated employees up to US$25,000 towards implementation of 'green' or human-rights-oriented projects. 'In 2009 Intel funded more than US$100,000 in cool projects', Cooper says. In Malaysia, the Sustainability in Action Award funds the initiative 'From Land to the Ocean, Our Commitment to the Environment,' which educates students and employees on ecological principals and how to protect the environment. In Ireland, Intel's fund plays a crucial role in protecting tributaries to the Rye River.

IBM

Smart business at its core

In 2009, IBM called for the 'decade of smart'. The company is pushing for a shift in vision and in communication, where intelligence is 'infused into the systems and processes that make the world work'. While this may be a new outward directive for the company, it has been working smartly on water for several decades. After conducting an evaluation of water use at its plants and labs, IBM learned that microelectronics manufacturing consumed the most water at its operations facilities. They called for a 2 per cent annual reduction in water consumption – what they got was much, much more.

From 2000 to 2008, IBM realized significant water savings at its target locations, and the process by which it has achieved these savings has taken the company to a new level of involvement with global water issues. Combining its long-standing ability to efficiently collect data with a new outlook on the importance of sharing and doing meaningful things with it, IBM has become a leader in the global discussion of water issues and, more importantly, in finding real solutions to some of the most pressing water problems.

From the inside out: IBM Vermont and water

IBM's Microelectronics Division has a semiconductor plant tucked away in rural Vermont, where amazing things are happening. It is here, in this IBM Center of Excellence, that real relationships have been formed, allowing for open and honest communication between business and government. A true understanding of water's inherent interconnectedness with all other aspects of business has been internalized, resulting in money being saved and smarter resource management. A desire for detail has led to the development of a powerful tool that can bring together the many different aspects of water in a meaningful way.

IBM Vermont, a model of sustainability, has been in operation since 1957 and has been a 'smart' facility for the past 15 years. This means it is equipped with the resources needed to examine its processes with extreme detail and care, and to come up with viable solutions for making those processes better. There may be no better place for IBM to focus its efforts on water management.

Self-described as a 'city within a city', IBM Vermont is a major player in its local water market. Water is drawn out of Lake Champlain, purified and delivered to the town of Essex Junction by the Champlain Water District, Vermont's largest water utility. IBM further purifies the water to manufacture UPW, which is 10 million times cleaner than tap water. The UPW is used to manufacture semiconductors, treated on-site at IBM Vermont, and then released back into the Lake Champlain feeder, the Winooski River. This closed-loop system allows the IBM plant to have a tight grasp on the entire water system, while simultaneously tying the company to the direct need for high water-quality standards. Janette Bombardier, site operations manager at IBM Vermont recognizes this:

> We have to provide water of the highest quality to our manufacturing client and meet the stringent environmental protections provided to the Winooski River.

Even though UPW is essential for semiconductor manufacturing, Bombardier emphasizes that water quality is only one of the goals IBM Vermont has for water once it's on site:

> Number two is reliable supply, and number three is cost effectiveness without risking quality or reliability.

Combine these goals with the company-wide goal of a 2 per cent annual reduction of water use, and Bombardier and her team have a framework that guides the business process and also allows for the key ingredient of IBM's success in water reduction: creativity and innovation.

The engineering team at IBM Vermont has come to a deep understand of the myriad ways water is connected to so many other aspects of the manufacturing facility. They now constantly examine interconnected processes that would, in general, be disregarded as not core to water use at the facility. Leveraging these connections has led them to significant water, energy and materials reductions, and, thereby, monetary savings. For example, says Jeff Chapman, senior water engineer at the Vermont facility:

> *Water has a large capacity to carry energy, so water is often used as a transport mechanism for heat energy and kinetic energy. How do we, as engineers, innovate to make the most of this water–energy connection? One example I like to use is installing a low-flow shower head in your bathroom. Yes, less water is used, which is good for the environment and your pocketbook. However, the cost savings in heat energy are typically larger than the savings from water reduction, and, of course, there are the carbon-emission reductions associated with lower energy use. It is a win–win situation.*

This kind of holistic approach, one of closing loops and purposefully connecting sometimes not obviously connected processes, is a winning tactic. One project, which captures waste heat from the manufacturing process and puts it into cold water entering the facility, saves around US$1.5 million annually in fuel costs. Chapman says:

> *It's fair to say we are constantly trying to get as much value out of water as we can. The real trick of it is being able to execute projects that allow us to capitalize on this relationship – taking understanding and turning it into action.*

This approach is especially important at the Vermont facility, because water as a raw material simply is not that expensive. At only 2 per cent of the annual budget, it barely competes with energy at 45 per cent. However, through this holistic approach, site operations manager Bombardier can clearly see the connection between energy and water, and creative thinking about one can affect the other. 'The real nugget for us is that we understand our water by value,' she says. This means that instead of simply looking to save a gallon of raw water, IBM Vermont looks to save a gallon of UPW. Chapman agrees:

> *We actually save three or four times the purchase cost of that water in other savings, such as chemicals, energy, materials, etc. We really started considering all the costs associated with that water. It's a different way of accounting.*

In fact, between 2000 and 2008, IBM Vermont had a 27 per cent reduction in water purchases, along with a 30 per cent increase in manufacturing capability, all with little capital investment in water systems. The company also saw an increase in water rates of about 30 per cent, yet still realized an annual savings of US$3.6 million because of that interconnected approach.

The cost of water varies greatly depending on where you live, and the team at IBM Vermont clearly understands that. Were they located in the south-western United States, where water is far more scarce, Bombardier and Chapman would probably have more of an emphasis on reduced use of raw water. Bombardier says:

> *We've done very little worrying about domestic water use, restroom facilities, etc. We've done a few things, but it's not something we focus a lot of our energy on, because the bang for the buck isn't there.*

To be exact, two-thirds of the water purchased goes to UPW, and one-third to other water services. Locality absolutely drives water management goals, Chapman says.

Smarter Water: interconnected intelligence

Perhaps the most exciting element of water awareness at IBM Vermont has to do with the sophisticated infrastructure created to monitor water throughout the entire manufacturing process. Comprising more than 5000 discrete and analogue sensors collecting various data in massive amounts and then putting that data into very meaningful and useful terms, this programme helps keep water quality within necessary parameters at all times. When a certain aspect of the data moves beyond an acceptable range, alarms sound – literally. 'If we lost water for five minutes, we would lose millions of dollars in production', Bombardier explains.

Chapman says it's also about risk management. Any time they look at ways of changing how they use water, they have to know if there's the potential to compromise the quality of the water or the reliability of the system. 'And in order to do that, it really is powerful to have a lot of data at your fingertips to analyse the situation', he adds.

This 'interconnected intelligence', where data meet meaningful analysis, is an extremely powerful tool. What started out as a process to avoid business disruption due to quality issues has the potential to help create positive change and avoid negative outcomes in water management far beyond IBM's walls. Data-collection programmes have been around for a while, but they lack a solid analysis piece. Chapman explains:

> As a company, we know how to manage data and extract what's important. It's a matter of gleaning more useful information from the data you already have instead of collecting yet more data, and then connecting it with other parties who have a complementary interest.

Bombardier expands the concept:

> Integrating the energy information from a municipal water district with their water information – wouldn't that be something?

Key partnerships

A major part of the success at IBM Vermont is due to partnership with the local government. The two entities are extremely dependent on each other and they have chosen to embrace it and create a trusting relationship.

The IBM plant purchases so much water that it becomes crucial to the water-pricing structure of the entire area. Should IBM conserve a few hundred thousand gallons of water, or decide to shut off equipment such as it did during the recent economic downturn, this can create a financial crisis for the water district, according to Bombardier. Water prices are predetermined based on predicted use, and that includes IBM's use. Should they consume less than predicted, the price of water is driven up for IBM and throughout the region.

The only way to deal with something of this nature is to work as closely as possible with the municipal water district. The Champlain Water District has reciprocated, working with IBM to control IBM's expenses. There is a mutual respect here: IBM is a large business in a small area and can offer insight into spending more efficiently. It also has a stake in the high quality and availability of the water, which are two things the water district works tirelessly to obtain.

This has served both parties well. It's opened the doors for impressive, cross-culture problem-solving, which was needed when IBM wanted to reduce the energy load associated with storing and pumping incoming water. The problem-solving group that was formed examined the problem, and the end result was stronger and was received better by the community than if it had simply come from IBM or the local government.

Partnering in such a manner is not new to IBM. Its Global Initiative Outlook (GIO) programme is vested in 'open, collaborative, multi-disciplinary and global' conversations, and it is through this programme that much of the water innovation from Smarter Water is being disseminated around the world. From Australia to Ireland and California to Singapore, water authorities are taking note of the insightful work coming out of IBM. They are partnering with IBM to see how they can use this new interconnected intelligence for resource conservation, sound planning and risk management. This even can be done on an ecosystem- or watershed-scale programme, not just a water utility.

One plus one equals success

For IBM, the key to success in water conservation efforts has been two-fold: valuing water and having smart water. According to Bombardier:

> When you put those two things together, you get these amazing results. You simply can't do one. You have to do both.

References

Ceres and Pacific Institute (2009) 'Water scarcity and climate change: growing risks for businesses and investors', www.ceres.org/Document.Doc?id=406, February 2009, accessed 30 June 2010

Ceres (2010) 'Murky waters? Corporate reporting on water risk', www.ceres.org/Document.Doc?id=547, February 2010, accessed 30 June 2010

J. P. Morgan (2008) 'Watching water: a guide to evaluating corporate risks in a thirsty world', www.soil.ncsu.edu/lockers/Hoover_M/html/wrkshop/Materials_for_on_web/Other_files/Shankar_Artemis_files/JP_Morgan_water_corporate_risks.PDF, April 2008, accessed 30 June 2010

Klusewitz, G. and McVeigh, J. (2002) 'Reducing water consumption in semi-conductor fabs', www.micromagazine.com/archive/02/10/klusewitz.html, accessed 30 June 2010

11

Power Generation

It is water, in every form and at every scale, that saturates the mind.
All the water that will ever be, is, right now.

National Geographic

The global power sector uses significant volumes of water for cooling purposes. Of this, a small fraction is considered consumption use. While renewable energy uses less water than conventional power generation, certain technologies, such as concentrated solar, still require significant amounts of water to generate power.

Water Use and Potential Risk

Some 89 per cent of the electricity generated in the United States is produced with thermally driven, water-cooled energy-conversion cycles, and the US thermoelectric power sector accounts for approximately 39 per cent of total freshwater withdrawals in the United States (J. P. Morgan, 2008). Although this is a significant amount of water for cooling purposes, the evaporative or consumptive use is 2.5 per cent, or 3310 million gallons per day. In addition to thermoelectric power, hydroelectric plants produce about 9 per cent of the electricity in the United States, with a portion of the water lost through evaporation (Torcellini et al, 2003).

It's helpful to look at the usage of cooling technologies in the power sector to understand better how water is used. Water cooling for thermoelectric power plants is accomplished using either once-through cooling or recirculating evaporative cooling. Once-through cooling withdraws large volumes (23,000–27,000gal/MWh) from surface waters and returns it to that source at an elevated temperature. This increase in returned-water temperature results in an increase in the evaporative body of water. Recirculating evaporative cooling uses less water (approximately

500–650gal/MWh for an equivalent plant) but consumes most of the water through evaporation.

Air cooling is fundamentally different, in that the heat generated from the steam cycle is directed to the air. A fossil power plant using this technology withdraws water only for the steam-cycle blowdown and domestic water uses, which are approximately less than 10 per cent of the consumption of an evaporatively cooled power plant (US Department of Energy, 2009).

According to the J. P. Morgan study (J. P. Morgan, 2008), coal- and gas-fired power plants typically use about 2800 and 2300 litres of water (respectively) to produce 1MWh of electricity. Nuclear power plants use about 3100 litres of water/MWh for cooling purposes. It is also predicted that carbon capture and storage (CCS) for coal-fired plants will have higher water demands.

Water is increasingly recognized as a risk in the global power sector. In 2003, low river levels shut down the 58 nuclear power plants belonging to Électricité de France, even after water temperature regulations were softened to 'guarantee the provision of electricity to the country'. In the summer of 2007, the Tennessee Valley Authority (TVA) was forced to partially shut down the Browns Ferry nuclear power plant due to the high temperature of the cooling water from the Tennessee River.

The impact of droughts on energy generation is also being felt in China. Droughts there in October 2009–April 2010 (*Bloomberg Businessweek*, 2010) resulted in 'brownouts'. China produces about 15 per cent of its power from hydroelectric plants and plans to double this capacity to 300GW of installed capacity by 2020. It is expected the drought will result in rationing of power to factories to manage the available water. According to *Bloomberg Businessweek*, if the drought persists, it will probably result in increased use of coal, with resultant increased prices for energy. This drought and its impact on energy production is part of the larger water risk in China. Widespread deforestation has also resulted in a depletion of groundwater in the south-western region of the country.

The situation in China has shown that water scarcity can force competition between public demands for water and power needs. In the United States, Dominion Power is investing US$1.1 billion in a water-recycling facility in Massachusetts to curb the release of hot water from a power plant (J. P. Morgan, 2008).

Renewable energy will also require large amounts of water. Estimates of the consumptive water use from ethanol production in the United States are approximately 4 gallons of water per gallon of ethanol produced (gal/gal). This compares with consumptive use of water in petroleum refining, which is about 1.5gal/gal. It is estimated that water use in biorefineries may be as high as 7gal/gal, although this has been decreasing over time due to improved efficiencies. It is estimated that an ethanol plant producing 100 million gallons per annum would need to withdraw approximately 400 million gallons of water per year (1.1 million gallons per day) from aquifers or surface water sources (Committee on Water Implications of Biofuels Production in the United States, 2008).

Concentrated solar plants (CSP) require water to condense steam, and provide make-up water for the steam cycle and mirror washing. A water-cooled parabolic trough CSP uses approximately 800gal/MWh. Of this, approximately 2 per cent is used for mirror washing. Dish/engine CSP technologies only require water for mirror washing (approximately 20gal/MWh) (US Department of Energy, 2009).

The regions of the world where CSP is most effective are those with abundant direct sunlight and which are also arid or semi-arid, such as the south-west United States and North Africa. Transporting water or treatment of low-quality water to support concentrated solar plants only increases the cost of power generation from these renewable sources.

As with fossil and nuclear power plants, water cooling is generally more economical than air cooling for CSP plants, because water cooling has a lower capital cost and higher thermal efficiency, and it maintains consistent efficiency levels all year round. In contrast, air cooling has reduced effectiveness when the air temperature is high.

Lately there has been much discussion of the 'energy–water nexus'. Energy and water are closely tied, and this link is further complicated by goals to reduce greenhouse gas emissions (GHGs). For example, the energy required to develop, treat and transport, and discharge water in California is estimated at about 20 per cent of the state's total energy use. In the United States, about 3 per cent of US power generation is used for water supply and treatment. Efforts to reduce energy use (and associated GHGs) and water use require an integrated approach to reconciling goals that sometimes conflict. For example, in water-stressed areas, it may be necessary to use air-cooled technologies in power plants, resulting in higher capital costs, in order to conserve available water for other public or private use.

The relationship between energy and water is illustrated in Figure 11.1.

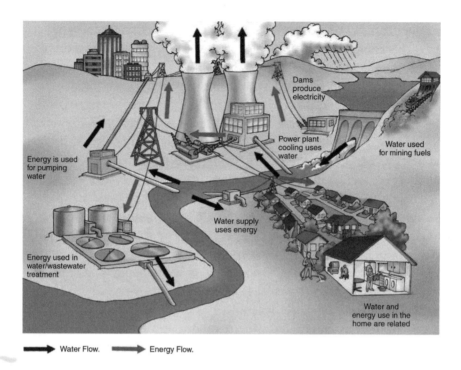

Water Flow.   Energy Flow.

Figure 11.1 *The energy–water nexus*

Source: adapted from US Department of Energy (2006)

Water Risk and Disclosure

An excellent overview of water-risk disclosure in the power sector, with 13 companies being benchmarked, was provided by Ceres (2010). A brief summary of the findings follows:

- Water accounting: Fewer than 50 per cent of the electric power companies provide data on total water withdrawal, and only American Electric Power provides site-level data; less than one-third reports wastewater discharge data.
- Risk assessment: Almost all the companies disclose some degree of physical risk from water scarcity, and all report exposure to water regulatory risk.
- Wastewater-reduction targets: None of the companies disclose targets to reduce contaminants in wastewater discharges from power plants.

- Supplier engagement: None of the companies disclose efforts to engage or evaluate fuel suppliers on water impacts and risks.

Company and Industry Snapshots

EPRI

Founded in 1973, the Electric Power Research Institute (EPRI) is an independent non-profit organization that conducts research on issues of interest to the electric power industry in the United States. Focused primarily on electricity generation, delivery and use, EPRI also tackles power challenges such as reliability, efficiency, health, safety and the environment. EPRI has offices in California; North Carolina; Tennessee; Washington, DC; Massachusetts; and Texas, as well as in Tokyo and Madrid.

EPRI's membership currently represents more than 90 per cent of the electricity generated and delivered in the United States, and spans 40 countries.

Water concerns in power generation

All thermoelectric power plants create waste heat energy as a by-product of the useful electrical energy produced. For most plants, discharging this heat requires the use of cooling water. Many plants utilize the *once-through cooling* system, in which water is extracted from a river, lake or ocean, run once through the plant and returned to the original body. Most new plants, according to regulation, must use *closed-cycle cooling*, which recycles water many times, then evaporates it as a means of cooling.

Tina Taylor, director of environment at EPRI, says each method has its own set of environmental concerns. Although once-through cooling uses less water overall, there are concerns about potential temperature increases in surface water. Concerns also exist about organisms being entrained or impinged as the water is withdrawn from lakes, rivers and oceans. Closed-cycle cooling does not create the same ecosystem concerns, but it does use more water and fuel overall. Taylor explains:

> *Almost all new plants being built right now are required to use closed-cycle cooling, and it's less efficient, both in terms of fuel and water. But the lower rate of withdrawal created less impact on fish and larvae. As the industry looks forward, we may have limited options for cooling, because even closed-cycle cooling does still use water.*

In response, she says, EPRI has been researching options such as *dry cooling* – a method in which air is blown over water flowing through tubes, much like a car radiator. Dry cooling is more expensive, less efficient in terms of energy production, and requires more land – but because it does not use evaporation, it is an attractive option for water-scarce locations. Some plants in the American south-west already use air-cooled condensers. Taylor comments:

> *The industry is looking at decreasing the cost and increasing the efficiency of that technology. Right now it's probably not a viable technology for nuclear plants; but we are exploring hybrid systems that might allow dry cooling some of the time with closed-cycle cooling as a backup.*

Other plants are experimenting with using treated wastewater in cooling operations. Palo Verde Nuclear Generating Station, 55 miles west of Phoenix, Arizona, recycles more than 20 billion gallons of treated effluent each year, drawing from several municipalities.

EPRI has also worked with companies willing to use wastewater from the oil and gas industry. According to Taylor:

> *The challenges of that approach are proximity to a high volume of available water and the need for pretreatment that may be necessary to prevent fouling or scaling of plant equipment.*

Water-quality trading

To EPRI, water-use concerns are inherently local. A plant in California may need to focus its attention primarily on fish protection, while a plant in Phoenix is going to be most concerned about total water usage. Taylor explains:

> *There are different issues with water for power companies: water quality, water-temperature considerations, the availability of water in the first place, the impact of physically pulling water into the plant. Yes, companies are concerned about water, and the reasons they are concerned will be very specific to the geography and local concerns in that area.*

One locality in which EPRI has been particularly active is the Ohio River Basin. It is a major contributor to the Mississippi River, and as much as 35 per cent of the water emptying into the Gulf of Mexico each day originates there. The basin spans 14 states and is a major source of the nitrogen- and phosphate-laden runoff that is causing hypoxia – a dead zone the size of New Jersey – in the Gulf of Mexico.

In 2008, EPRI netted a million-dollar targeted watershed grant from the USEPA, in support of a proposed water-quality trading programme that would facilitate lowering the nutrient loading in the Ohio River and potentially aiding the gulf hypoxic zone. The programme creates a market that pays participants to reduce their emissions by allowing regulated industries to purchase water-quality credits. In particular, it may give farmers incentive to optimize their fertilizer use.

Taylor says:

> *We're bringing stakeholders together into a marketplace to achieve faster, more efficient cleanup by working together – and by encouraging the cheapest, best practices that can be implemented.*

Water and carbon

Tina Taylor also stresses that water strategies must co-evolve with other environmental concerns:

> *One of the greatest trade-offs in the industry right now is: What's more important? Water or CO_2? Almost anything you can do to use less water, for a coal or gas plant, is going to result in higher emissions of CO_2.*

She points out that a number of new biomass facilities have opted for dry cooling, despite the cost and inefficiency, so water will not be a limiting factor in the future:

> *Many of the things you do to solve one environmental impact create another one. When you think about water strategies for the energy industry, the options you have may reduce the amount of water you use, or the temperature you put it back at, or the flow you extract it from, but in all cases we're working on, it produces some other result. And we don't really have a good way, scientific or regulatory or financial, to weigh those impacts in a way that's globally appropriate.*
>
> *Carbon is easy, compared to water.*

A goal to reduce carbon by a particular percentage is generally translatable to all facilities within a company. A goal to reduce water use, however, can have a wide range of impacts. She notes that:

> *In one area, it may be increasing the cost of electricity in an area that can't sustain a higher cost, and it may not even matter that it uses less water, because there's plenty of water there. In another area, where the water is very scarce and needed, there's a higher environmental value in using less water. We really need to move toward a holistic approach, understanding the complex interactions of our impacts on the environment.*

Part of this holistic approach is consumer education – making sure individuals understand the ties between water and energy, and Turner says:

> *In California, 19 per cent of the energy used in the state is related to water. It's moving water to where people need it, purification of the water and cleanup of wastewater. Any time you can save water in California, you're saving a significant amount of energy, as well, and thereby saving CO_2 emissions. The same is true for energy: 40 per cent of the water withdrawn in the US is related to energy use. So anytime you save energy, you're saving water use, as well.*

Some utilities are starting to incorporate this idea into their CO_2 reduction strategy. The Salt River Project (SRP), an EPRI member utility in Phoenix, has been running public campaigns to raise awareness that a fluorescent bulb is a water-saving device, and a low-flow showerhead is an energy-saving device. SRP's website includes links to the homepage of *evolve*, a showerhead that offers 40 per cent water-usage savings by monitoring the temperature of water while it is warming up, then reducing the flow to a trickle when it is ready (consumers can restore full water flow by pulling a small cord).

SRP also recently unveiled a brand new solar thermal plant in Peoria, Arizona, in collaboration with Tessera Solar. The Maricopa Solar Plant will operate with low cost, no water use and an efficient sun-to-grid conversion ratio, helping to diversify the utility's desert holdings in a manner conscious of both water and carbon.

Exelon

Focusing energy on water

It is no secret that producing energy requires the use of water. Exelon Corporation realizes that for continued business success, defined in terms of both getting centralized power to 5.4 million homes in the eastern United States as well as continued profits, the relationship between water and energy production cannot be taken for granted. Exelon is taking serious steps to ensure the company's longevity despite issues in the areas of climate, regulation and finances.

Through the use of an employee committee focused on water-use issues, water footprinting and a site-by-site approach, Exelon has gained excellent knowledge of the power generator's water use across its region and pinpointed areas for higher efficiency. By acting quickly and using a holistic approach that includes partnerships with various entities, Exelon is also able to withstand external factors, many of which seem to be out of the company's hands. Exelon remains a leader in the field, and understands that addressing water strategically now will serve everyone better in the long run.

The interconnectedness of water

In 2008 Exelon announced its business and environmental strategy, 'Exelon 2020: A low-carbon roadmap'. While focused on reducing annual GHGs by more than 15 million metric tonnes per year by 2020, nearly the equivalent of their 2001 carbon footprint, measures to reduce GHG emissions also have a direct relationship to the power company's water footprint. In order to reduce environmental impacts in one area, Exelon understands the linkages to reducing impacts in other areas and the financial benefits that can accrue. To this end, the company has been an adopter of water footprinting, using a comprehensive water-balance approach that it developed to measure consumptive and non-consumptive water use and water recycling. Exelon completes the water footprint exercise every three years, providing the company the opportunity to routinely evaluate water-reduction opportunities.

Through this process Exelon determined that 99.6 per cent of the 39 billion gallons used daily to operate their nuclear, hydro and fossil-fuelled power generators is considered non-consumptive. Hydroelectric energy generation is responsible for the vast majority of this amount, followed by nuclear generation, with fossil fuels using a relatively small portion of water company-wide.

It is here that Exelon finds itself at a crossroads in understanding just how interconnected water is with everything else. While the power generator is working to reduce its GHGs in an effort to slow climate change, climate change is having an effect on the very bodies of water that keep Exelon running.

According to the USEPA (2009), hydroelectric may be the form of energy generation most susceptible to impacts from climate change. Its effectiveness requires knowledge of water amounts, temperatures and flow patterns, all of which are subject to the impacts of climate change. Much of this is unknown at present, but it will most likely have some effect on Exelon's hydroelectric generation. Maintaining fish populations and other riparian life will also be required as climate change impacts water quantity and quality. The company understands that if it can start working on ways to use water more efficiently and to identify alternative sources now, it will be prepared for the time when the water-quality characteristics of the rivers it depends on begin to shift.

Changes in regulations will also impact water availability. Phase II of the Clean Water Act mandates that better care be taken with the quality and temperature of water exiting a power plant, which means potentially significant infrastructure investment. Exelon is also seeing an increase in various fees related to water and watershed management. If it can use less water in its operations overall, the company will be in a better position to weather any changes in water availability.

Surging forward

Not surprisingly, Exelon has announced that water is a top-tier issue. With climate change the main focus of the company for the next few years, having to move less water around will mean a reduced need for using pumps and other equipment that require energy, thereby reducing GHGs. By continually learning about the ways in which water and energy intersect, Exelon is already creating new methods of managing water resources.

The employee-driven Water Use Working Group serves as the hub for conservation efforts and awareness. Its objectives include updating water footprints, identifying ways to save water and money, including regulatory risks, and developing a corporate water strategy. At the end of 2009, this group of Exelon employees had gathered information across the board and presented the case for water savings and awareness to the executive team.

The company is now actively seeking water- and money-saving measures where these are most appropriate. This includes a site-by-site approach, where each location is examined and water-saving activities are based on the specific needs of that facility. Commercial facilities are being addressed through the company's efforts to achieve LEED (Leadership in Energy and Environmental Design) certification. At the power plants, the company is looking into actions that could be taken to reduce water use, and is identifying alternative sources of water. Several local factors are taken into account, including the price per gallon of water, the type of energy being produced, local and federal regulations and social issues.

Exelon also recognizes that by partnering with other organizations it can obtain its goals in a more holistic way. For example, the 2008 partnership with scientists from the University of Maryland to remove nitrates and phosphates from water in the Susquehanna River led to the use of naturally occurring cleaning processes already present in cultivated algae. This low-carbon process goes beyond simply cleaning water, as it ties together GHG reductions and supporting the local entrepreneurial spirit.

Exelon is in a unique position to see just how intertwined and important water issues are becoming. With water at the heart of much of its activities, the company is aware of its responsibility not just to shareholders, but also to the community at large, for being proactive in reducing water use and consumption. Baselines have been set and localized actions are in hand. Other energy companies would be wise to take note of Exelon's keen awareness of water issues.

References

Bloomberg Businessweek (2010) 'Drought in China hits the energy sector: hydroelectric power shortages mount in southwestern China', *Bloomberg Businessweek*, 26 April–2 May 2010, pp20–21

Ceres (2010) 'Murky waters? Corporate reporting on water risk', www.ceres.org/Document.Doc?id=547, February 2010, accessed 30 June 2010

Committee on Water Implications of Biofuels Production in the United States (2008) *Water Implications of Biofuels Production in the United States*, The National Academies Press, Washington, DC

J. P. Morgan (2008) 'Watching water: a guide to evaluating corporate risks in a thirsty world', www.soil.ncsu.edu/lockers/Hoover_M/html/wrkshop/Materials_for_on_web/Other_files/Shankar_Artemis_files/JP_Morgan_water_corporate_risks.PDF, April 2008, accessed 30 June 2010

Torcellini, P., Long, N. and Judkoff R. (2003) *Consumptive Water Use for US Power Production*, NREL/TP-550-33905, National Renewable Energy Laboratory, December

US Department of Energy (2006) *Report to Congress on the Interdependency of Energy and Water*, US Department of Energy, December

US Department of Energy (2009) 'Concentrating solar power commercial application study: reducing water consumption of concentrating solar power electricity generation, report to Congress', http://www1.eere.energy.gov/solar/pdfs/csp_water_study.pdf, accessed 30 June 2010

USEPA (2009) 'Energy production and use', www.epa.gov/climatechange/effects/energy.html, October 2009, accessed 17 September 2010

12

Extractive Industries

Between earth and earth's atmosphere, the amount of water remains constant; there is never a drop more, never a drop less. This is a story of circular infinity, of a planet birthing itself.

Linda Hogan

Extractive industries – the mining, oil and gas sectors – use water for a variety of purposes. In many instances, extractive industries are faced with the challenge of having to operate in arid to semi-arid environments, as they need to go where the ore, oil and gas reserves are located.

The oil and gas sector uses water for well drilling, well completion and fracturing. While water demands are not significant in conventional oil and gas drilling, water use in the development of tar sands is intensive, with about 4–5 litres of water to separate out each litre of oil sand. Water use in metal mining is about 100–8000 litres of water per ton of ore extracted.

Water Use and Potential Risk

The mining sector relies on high volumes of water, and mining operations cannot be relocated based on water availability. Therefore, the mining sector is potentially challenged by water scarcity and, in some instances, competition with local communities for water resources.

Water Risk and Disclosure

An excellent overview of water-risk disclosure in the oil and gas and mining sectors was provided by Ceres (2010), based on benchmarking of 13 companies in the oil and gas sector, and 13 companies in the mining sector. A brief summary of their findings follows:

- Water accounting data: About two-thirds of oil and gas companies report total water usage data, and less than half provide wastewater-discharge data; 77 per cent of the mining companies report water-use data, and four mining companies report site-level data.
- Risk disclosure: More than half the oil and gas companies report some degree of physical risk. All but one company discloses some regulatory risk. Litigation and reputational risk is limited to three and four oil and gas companies, respectively. All the mining companies report physical and regulatory risks, about two-thirds report litigation risks, and more than 25 per cent report reputational risks.
- Reduction targets: Only two oil and gas companies (both oil sands operators) disclose water-use reduction targets, and only Total reports a wastewater-reduction target. Six mining companies set quantitative targets to improve water efficiency.
- Supply-chain engagement: No oil and gas companies disclose engaging with suppliers on water management or water risks.
- Stakeholder engagement: More than 50 per cent of the oil and gas companies report stakeholder engagement with local communities on water-management issues; 77 per cent of the mining companies report collaborating with local governments and communities to address water-related conflicts and manage local water resources.
- Direct operations: Six mining companies have 'strong' reporting of water-management efforts in direct operations, with eight mining companies providing information on water-specific management systems, strategies or policies.

Company Snapshots

Encana Oil & Gas (USA) Inc.

Like other natural gas companies, water management for Encana Oil & Gas (USA) Inc. may be different from most other industries. Put simply, a natural gas company can have too little or too much water. The company's goal, where feasible, is to achieve a 'water balance'. This includes trying to reuse water produced as a by-product of its operations. According to Jill Cooper, the environment group lead for Encana's US Division:

> *Recycling as much water as possible is good for the company and good for the environment.*

Producing natural gas requires water both to drill the well and to hydrauli-
cally fracture the rock, which is deep underground. The water used for
drilling and fracturing (flowback water) is recovered from the well and
stored or disposed of before gas begins to flow. Water that is found with
the natural gas is called 'produced water'. This is often not hydrologically
connected to surface water and would not otherwise have come to the
surface.

To protect groundwater, Encana uses fresh water to lubricate and cool
the drill bits. Recycled flowback and produced water is used in hydraulic
fracturing, a process that maximizes the amount of natural gas produced
by a well. A mixture of water, sand and chemicals is injected into the
ground at high pressure to create small cracks in the rock and allow gas to
flow more freely to the surface.

Natural gas operators face regulatory and financial challenges in acquiring adequate water resources and managing produced and flowback
water at the surface. As a result, Encana manages water at all its operations carefully. As Cooper explains:

> *Water is integral to our processes. We manage water as we manage*
> *natural gas – very carefully. Whether or not we maintain a water*
> *balance, we are always managing the resource.*

Like other companies, Encana values and works to strengthen its corporate reputation. Commodity companies have a different perspective on
this issue from businesses that operate in the consumer market, as natural
gas companies sell product to utilities and other businesses (business-to-
business marketing).

Reputation is important to Encana. Cooper says:

> *Our reputation matters to us and our stakeholders, which includes*
> *our shareholders; the communities and landowners in areas where*
> *we work; the local, state and federal governmental entities we work*
> *with; and nongovernmental organizations. Because of the impor-*
> *tance of water management in our stakeholders' perspective, it is*
> *critical we manage water responsibly.*

Regulators and communities in which Encana operates can have very
specific concerns. A primary concern is often the protection of groundwater, as Cooper explains:

Stakeholders are concerned about water quality down hole. When we drill a well and use water to conduct hydraulic fracturing, stakeholders want to know we are protecting against the release of natural gas or any other product into the water system.

According to Encana, natural gas operations are primarily regulated by state government:

Each state has regulations designed to protect soil and groundwater, how companies drill a well and well integrity. It is the responsibility of companies to ensure natural gas wells are constructed, drilled and operated appropriately, and [of] state regulators to provide oversight and enforcement of the standards. Encana and the industry in general have a strong economic incentive to do it well.

Cooper explains that the company invests in partnerships that produce substantive results for the communities in which Encana operates. This involves a strong educational component:

If Encana is going to partner with a NGO in a meaningful way, we want them to know more about our industry and operations.

The company and its stakeholders share the benefits of these partnerships. Recently Encana entered into a partnership with Xcel Energy, the Environmental Defense Fund, Environment Colorado, Western Resource Advocates and the State of Colorado. Together, the partners successfully worked on legislation to convert existing coal plants to natural gas. The resulting bill, signed by Governor Bill Ritter of Colorado in April 2010, will reduce air pollution and greenhouse gas emissions (GHGs), while creating greater demand for natural gas. The result is a win–win–win for the public, the environment, and utilities and energy companies.

The company's focus on 'water balance' plays an integral part in all these efforts. Encana considers the entire life cycle of a well, from 'bare land to bare land', in water management. This allows for a long-term and holistic approach to water management in its operations and in the type of relationships it fosters with stakeholders. In a very tangible way, it also is emblematic of a larger and more sustainable business and environmental philosophy.

Rio Tinto

The Rio Tinto Group: investing deep within

For the past decade, Rio Tinto Group has continued to be a leader in industrial materials supply and science, and a staunch practitioner of sustainable development. Water is an essential aspect of sustainable development – something Rio Tinto Group is well aware of. Whether in the mining process itself or water issues surrounding the communities in which they are mining, water touches everything the company does.

With approximately 65,000 employees at more than 110 operations globally, ranging from climates rich in water to those highly parched, the Group realized it was important to bring a unified vision and understanding to water. To that end, Rio Tinto released a water use and quality standard in 2003, accompanied by a five-year target calling for a 10 per cent reduction in freshwater gallons per metric tonne of product. The five-year target resulted in a 6.3 per cent water reduction and created a huge amount of awareness among employees. It was the first step in an important long-term process, and another five-year target is currently being set. To aid in that, the Group relies on a water strategy it released in 2005.

Rio Tinto Minerals

There are five operational businesses of the Rio Tinto Group, each with its own unique focus. Rio Tinto Minerals is based in the United States and mines borax and talc, both of which are in primarily arid locations such as California's Mojave Desert and the Andes in Argentina. This makes Rio Tinto Minerals an operational business especially aware of water issues and a model for the rest of the group in this area.

According to Rio Tinto Minerals's sustainability and environment director, Gregg Wagner, the company has always had water-reduction targets in place; water-reduction measures are even a factor in employee performance metrics. This sets Rio Tinto Minerals ahead of other competitors. By way of example, Wagner says, during the five-year goal set between 2003 and 2008, the business achieved a 23 per cent reduction in freshwater gallons per metric tonne of product – 16.7 per cent more than the combined Rio Tinto Group.

Wagner and his team were able to do this through assigning different relative values to water. In the dewatering wells around the borax pit and in the upper aquifer, where water is pulled to depressurize wells, there is a very high total dissolved-solids content. This makes the water undesirable for certain types of reuse, such as steam applications or drinking water. Instead of viewing this water as waste to be immediately discarded, Rio Tinto Minerals decided to use it for road watering, screen washing and other off-spec applications. Higher-quality water coming from steam applications is also recycled. 'Every gallon is reused as many times as we can before it's used on road watering', Wagner says.

This subset of the larger group has been able to create a deep-seated awareness and knowledge in its employee base, something for which the larger organization is striving. Wagner explains:

> *Many of these water-use reduction ideas are coming from our employees. They aren't from the top down; they're from the bottom up.*

Rio Tinto needs its employees to understand all the embodied costs inside water and the role it plays globally for the company. It needs them to view it as the 'significant business asset' it is. As Wagner puts it, 'In some regards, water is just as important as the ore we're digging out of the ground.'

To that effect, and after much consultation and conversation both internally and externally about managing long-term risks and opportunities, Rio Tinto developed its water strategy, consisting of three areas: improve, value and engage.

The strategy

Improvement is seen as higher efficiency and preventing potential impacts on water quality and quantity. The aforementioned five-year targets are very important in this area. 'We've found targets are very good at keeping people focused', Wagner says. Given Rio Tinto Minerals's history of excellence with this type of short-term goal setting, it seems fitting the group would adopt the same focus.

A water-risk assessment, which has already been used by roughly 40 operations, encourages new ideas and allows for many aspects of water to be viewed on one sheet. Using the water standard developed in 2003 is also part of improving water efforts. Each operation is required to follow the standard, which mandates that water balances and a water-management plan must be used; there must be skilled water personnel on the staff; and water infrastructure must be appropriately designed. Given the varied locations of Rio Tinto operations, the tactic of implementing broad-stroke frameworks such as this standard allows each operation to create successful water plans specific to its location.

Valuing the unique nature of each operation's location is important to Rio Tinto, and communicating with those potentially affected by the operation is part of the water strategy. At Rio Tinto Minerals, Wagner says, they have always held community meetings:

> We share information, let the communities know what we're doing and explain what effect it will have on them.

Water also has its own values within each operation. According to the company publication, *Rio Tinto and Water*, a value-based assessment tool has been developed in partnership with the Sustainable Minerals Institute at the University of Queensland in Australia. This will help identify some of the qualitative values of water, such as the cultural and social thoughts that persist on a truly local level.

Considering that many of the employees live within the community right outside the facility – in the case of Rio Tinto Minerals, about 35 per cent – engagement is hugely important. In the water strategy, engagement is also considered through internal collaboration and working with government on water-management issues.

Placing value beyond the strategy

The Rio Tinto water strategy and sustainable development approach are as much about respecting the local people and their customs as they are about mining. This is sound corporate social responsibility, which always equates to smarter business practice. Wagner says:

> They're not making any more of the product we're pulling out the ground, so using our resources as efficiently and effectively as possible is really important to us.

As water becomes scarcer and the ability of industry to use it becomes less of a priority over issues such as drinking water, companies such as Rio Tinto, which have already been conserving water and working with local communities, will be more likely to have a licence to operate. Wagner is aware of this:

We could end up having water reductions forced on us. We want to be ahead of the curve and be using less water than we were historically, so we have enough water to continue operations.

References

Ceres (2010) 'Murky waters? Corporate reporting on water risk', www.ceres.org/ Document.Doc?id=547, February 2010, accessed 30 June 2010

13

Manufacturing

If there is magic on this planet, it is contained in water.

Loran Eisley

Global water use in the manufacturing sector (excluding the semiconductor sector) is increasing, primarily due to expansion in emerging economies. Although most of the water is used for cooling water (non-contact), the volume of water required in this sector is significant and increasing.

Water Use and Potential Risk

Not only is water quantity important, but it can also be a critical factor for certain manufacturing requirements. In most cases, cooling with brackish water will suffice, but for other manufacturing processes quality is an important factor. The timing (availability) of water is important for manufacturing requirements, as well.

Water efficiencies within subsectors such as steel manufacturing can vary significantly. For example, steel companies in India require approximately 10–80m^3 of water, versus approximately 5–10m^3 for steel manufacturing in the United States (J. P. Morgan, 2008).

Company Snapshot

Ford Motor Company

Ford Motor Company, a global automotive industry leader based in Dearborn, Michigan, manufactures or distributes automobiles across six continents. With about some 176,000 employees and about 80 plants worldwide, the company's automotive brands include Ford, Lincoln,

Mercury (production of which has been announced by the company to be ending in the fourth quarter of 2010) and, until its sale, Volvo. Ford's environmental initiatives can be traced back to founder Henry Ford, who experimented with bio-materials and alternative fuels for the vehicles the company began producing more than 100 years ago.

Today, the concept of sustainability is integrated throughout the company in the belief that economic and environmental goals can and should be aligned. Chairman William Clay Ford Jr notes that the business case for sustainability has been proved repeatedly:

> *In fact, we believe that the best way for us to be more profitable is to make our business and products more sustainable.*

Environmental goals

Ford sets environmental goals in several key areas: worldwide energy consumption, worldwide water usage, fleet fuel economy and fleet CO_2 emissions. Progress towards meeting and exceeding those goals has been recorded every year for the past decade. Ford fully understands that it has the opportunity to work with others in finding creative solutions to environmental challenges, including climate change and resource conservation.

Turning to water

Ford first launched a voluntary Global Water Management Initiative in 2000, which focused on conservation of water, the reuse of storm and process water, and management of water quality. The initial goal set was to reduce water use by 3 per cent per year. As part of the commitment, Ford conducted several pilot projects at a number of different plants worldwide to identify more precisely all processes that use water, seeking the best opportunities to reduce its use.

Progress in cutting its global water use has been significant. Between 2000 and 2009, Ford's global manufacturing operations reportedly reduced water consumption by more than 62 per cent (10.5 billion gallons). That would equal the amount of water used by 575,000 people in a year (based on average consumption of 50 gallons a day in the United States). To date, Ford has concentrated on improving water efficiency in its plants in order to reduce overall usage. Key performance indicators for Ford include overall water consumption and gallons per vehicle.

Sue Cischke, Ford group vice president, Sustainability, Environment and Safety Engineering, says the company has made it a priority to conserve water during the past decade:

> *Now we are ready to take another important step in our commitment to this issue. It is clear that water scarcity is quickly becoming a critical global issue. As such, it carries with it significant social and environmental implications, and we will all need to be part of the global solution.*

When the Carbon Disclosure Project (CDP) extended its reporting approach on carbon emissions to work towards management of the world's water resources, Ford became the first car-maker to join CDP Water Disclosure. As a founding responder, the company will be able to help shape the Water Disclosure questionnaire, which will serve as the protocol for water reporting. Ford believes CDP Water Disclosure, like the reporting on greenhouse gas emissions, will increase the availability of high-quality information for those who want to understand the risks and opportunities of water-related issues. That information will also be useful for Ford to both encourage corporate responsibility and to reduce the environmental impact of the company's facilities. Not only is it a strategic issue for business, it is also a human rights issue, as Cischke recognizes:

> *There is much more discussion these days about learning to live in a water-constrained world. This environmental issue has become increasingly important to our stakeholders, including customers, business partners and investors.*

While water is a more immediate issue for companies that use it as an ingredient in their products, such as food and beverage manufacturers, other companies, such as Ford, do need to be mindful. Ford understands the relative risks to water availability at its manufacturing facilities around the world, and these include watershed conditions, the water in raw materials and supply efficiency. Clearly, in some regions, water issues are primarily community issues and, as a corporate citizen, Ford is an integral part of those communities where it does business.

Ford's decision to sign up to the CDP Water Disclosure is based on the understanding that it will provide a globally harmonized method of water reporting, critical to developing solutions to water challenges.

How Ford does it

Ford uses a corporate Global Emissions Manager (GEM) database to track several key environmental concerns, including energy use, carbon dioxide emissions, waste sent to landfills and water consumption. As Cischke explains:

> *Managing risk begins with measurement to deliver a deeper understanding of where and how much water is used. Through comprehensive tracking, the company is able to set more effective environmental-management targets.*

Key performance indicators for Ford

Water use and availability remain important to Ford's global operations. Water is used at every point in its supply chain and is a critical component in some of the company's manufacturing facilities. The company has launched a new strategy to view water use both from the environmental and the social perspectives. That will include assessing the consequences for water availability and quality that could result from increased production of battery electric vehicles.

In 2010–2011, Ford expects to identify additional opportunities for water-use reduction, even as new water targets and goals are set. Engagement with stakeholders will play an important part in deepening understanding of how water issues will impact the company. That will include evaluating opportunities with the UN General Assembly CEO Water Mandate, the US State Department Global Water Solutions Center, and local stakeholders in all regions, including India, Mexico, China and South Africa. It may also mean building new relationships with outside stakeholders.

Ford Motor Company's Hermosillo Plant

Ford's Hermosillo Stamping and Assembly Plant (HSAP) is located in the Sonoran Desert of north-west Mexico, south of the Arizona border. There, an extended drought that began in 1995, coupled with population growth, created a severe water shortage. At Hermosillo, Ford has cut water use despite a doubling in the production of vehicles. This unusual feat has been accomplished through the addition of innovative water-treatment systems that allow extensive recycling of water within the plant.

As one of the area's largest water users, the HSAP responded to the drought conditions by cutting water usage by 43 per cent between 1995 and 2000, but when the plant was selected for expanded vehicle production in 2003, water use was projected to double.

To accommodate the growth in production without increasing water use, the plant installed a biological water-treatment system known as a membrane biological reactor, now also installed at other Ford plants in Chihuahua, Mexico; Chennai, India; and Chongqing, China. The system uses an ultra-filtration membrane process followed by reverse osmosis to make 55 per cent of the plant's wastewater suitable for high-quality reuse within the plant's processes. The treated water can also be used for irrigation, bringing to 65 per cent the amount of wastewater that can be recycled.

As a result, Ford's water consumption per vehicle unit at the plant has dropped by more than 34 per cent since 2000.

Overall, Ford's worldwide facilities have been able to reduce water consumption by tracking water use during plant downtimes, by optimizing cooling-tower operations, and by investing in advanced technologies. Ford's GEM database helps track their efforts. Sue Cischke says:

> As we look ahead, we will be developing ways to integrate a water strategy throughout all elements of our operation, including engaging our employees on community volunteer efforts geared toward water protection and conservation. We will be focusing on water issues, because, while we have made impressive gains, there is more we can, and should, do.

Water volunteers: integrating a water strategy on a local scale

For ten years, Ford volunteers supported efforts to restore stream banks, remove log jams and re-energize the Rouge River watershed – a local tributary in south-east Michigan that is important to Ford's manufacturing history. In 2010, in support of the corporation's attention to a water strategy, conservation became the focus of a Ford Accelerated Action Day. Janet Lawson, director of the Ford Motor Company Fund & Community Services, explains:

> The members of the Ford Volunteer Corps embraced the call to show their support of a water strategy. Some 600 Ford employees and retirees joined with nonprofit partners to tackle water projects in more than a dozen locations. Their efforts ranged from installing an

educational garden of native plants that would improve a watershed,
to installing a rain collection system at a local nature centre.

In Ghana, a Ford vehicle dealership, Mechanical Lloyd Co. Ltd, hired a professional well driller for a local project. With the help of 20 volunteers, the driller installed a well for the 3000 villagers living near Apirede, who now have access to clean drinking water.

References

J. P. Morgan (2008) 'Watching water: a guide to evaluating corporate risks in a thirsty world', www.soil.ncsu.edu/lockers/Hoover_M/html/wrkshop/Materials_for_on_web/Other_files/Shankar_Artemis_files/JP_Morgan_water_corporate_risks.PDF, April 2008, accessed 30 June 2010

Part III
The New Water Paradigm

Children of a culture born in a water-rich environment, we have never really learned how important water is to us. We understand it, but we do not respect it.

William Ashworth

14

Seven New Rules of 21st-Century Thinking

Executives are constrained not by resources but by their imagination.

C. K. Prahalad

The old paradigm for how we manage water resources is being replaced. We have a set of new rules for how to become water stewards and manage water risk and opportunities.

For a view of enlightened 21st-century water stewardship, look at Singapore. It is a model for developing diversified water sources, water reuse, water pricing and water efficiency. This island city-state, which receives, on average, 93 inches of rain per year, is officially classified as 'water-stressed'. (According to the World Business Council for Sustainable Development, water stress is defined as less than 1700m^3 of annual water use per capita, which is where countries begin to experience periodic or regular water stress. Water scarcity is defined as less than 1000m^3 of annual water use per capita.) In part, the water stress is a result of urbanization: a population of 4.6 million occupies less than 700km^2 (Water-Technology.net, 2008).

What makes Singapore a leader in water stewardship? Necessity.

Singapore has relied on Malaysia for water for much of its history, especially since Singapore became a separate nation 43 years ago. While these two countries have water agreements in place with regard to price and supply, there have been occasions where the water supply has been in jeopardy. Therefore, though Singapore is not in an arid or semi-arid climate, it has decided to manage a precious resource wisely. The high urban density of Singapore makes water management a priority, and the island is divided into 55 urban-planning areas and two water-catchment areas.

Singapore is committed to being self-reliant in water, and this has resulted in a rethinking of the most basic aspects of water: sources of supply, treatment, reuse, public policy and pricing. The country recently announced an investment of US$1.47 billion in water infrastructure during the next five years, as part of its overall goal of water self-sufficiency. A cornerstone to Singapore's approach to water stewardship is what the Public Utilities Board (PUB) terms its 'four taps strategy'. The four taps are:

- water reclamation;
- desalination;
- water efficiency;
- importation.

This strategy also captures the best thinking on source diversification, catchment harvesting, importing of water from Malaysia, water reclamation and desalination.

The two new 'taps' are water reclamation and desalination. Reclaimed water is marketed as 'NEWater'. This recycled water is successfully integrated into the national water supply, initially for non-potable uses, and then blended with reservoir water for potable purposes. Singapore has three PUB-built plants that recycle nearly 90 million litres a day using membrane ultra-filtration, reverse osmosis and UV treatment, before the water enters reservoirs. A fourth facility has been built by Keppel and, by 2010, when a fifth is complete, recycled water is expected to provide some 30 per cent of the state's supply. Singapore has taken recycled water a step further, selling bottled NEWater to increase consumer confidence in recycled water.

Singapore is also investing in desalination, its fourth 'tap'. Opened in 2005, the SingSpring SWRO (seawater reverse osmosis) plant is Singapore's first desalination facility, and one of the most energy-efficient in the world. Water was priced at US$0.48/m^3, which was a record low for desalinated seawater when the plant opened. This plant has the capacity to produce approximately 136 million litres a day, which represents approximately 10 per cent of the national water requirement.

While desalination could increase to provide 30 per cent of the country's needs by 2011, the cost of desalinated water is about double that of recycled water. As a result, there will be greater investment in water recycling than in desalination and diversifying water supplies. Singapore is also looking to diversify sources of imported water and plans to pipe water from Indonesia's Rhio archipelago.

In addition to the investment of US$1.47 billion in infrastructure, US$20 million has been spent on research and development projects. Individual plants, such as the SingSpring SWRO and Ulu Pandan reclamation facility, cost US$200 million and US$380 million, respectively.

In 2007, PUB won the Stockholm Industry Water Award as an example not only of integrated water management encompassing sound public policy, but also of innovative engineering solutions. This award reflects how well Singapore is moving towards its goal of being water self-sufficient by 2061.

For Singapore, water is not just a risk; it is also a business opportunity. The country is promoting water-technology development: Nanyang Technological University has three water-related research units, and Singapore's water industry now has more than 50 companies.

What does Singapore's forward-looking water stewardship mean for local businesses? They now have the ability to grow. Make no mistake; industry will be constrained by water shortages if the public sector does not manage the resource wisely. As environmental strategist Andrew Winston puts it:

> *If you think about the three main uses of water – person/sanitation, agriculture and industry – which one will be short-changed in a crunch? No matter how influential businesses are, local and regional leaders will be very unlikely to turn off the taps to homes or for growing food. Industry will bat last. This fact makes water a completely unique resource.*

In Singapore, industrial use of water is increasing, as the city is running at about 4–6 per cent growth annually. While the PUB efforts have been government-funded, the private sector has capitalized on government research and development initiatives, and is translating technology solutions to meet individual industry and company needs.

Singapore has successfully brought innovation into its water industry and illustrates the 'new rules' of 21st-century water stewardship. The combination of diversifying water sources, water reuse, water pricing, public–private partnerships and innovation are addressing the challenges of water scarcity and supporting economic growth.

Let's expand on the 'new rules' of 21st-century water stewardship.

The Seven New Rules

Water risk is the best-kept business secret. While multinational companies have moved forward in addressing energy use, carbon emissions and material use (waste reduction), a focus on water has lagged.

As discussed in Chapter 6, the world is moving from 'hunting water' to 'water cultivation'. This is driving increased efficiency in how we use water, diversification of water sources (beyond just surface water and groundwater) and water reuse. There is also increased engagement and collaboration with stakeholders to reduce competition for water resources.

In general, there are seven major shifts in how we need to think about water (Table 14.1). These new rules will form the basis for creating true water-stewardship strategies to manage risks and opportunities.

1 All water issues are local, and the watershed is the building block

All water issues *are* local and, as a result, the key building block of a global water-stewardship strategy is the watershed. This is fundamentally

Table 14.1 *The new water paradigm*

	Old paradigm	New paradigm
1	Water is a global issue with global solutions	All water issues are local, and the watershed is the building block
2	Water is like carbon	Water is unique
3	Water is reliable through public infrastructure systems	Companies can no longer solely rely on public water source
4	Water is priced according to value	The value of water far exceeds its price
5	Direct water use is the only thing that matters in managing water risk	Water use in the value chain is typically much greater than direct water use
6	Water risk can be managed internally	Water risk can be managed effectively only with stakeholder input
7	Water scarcity is only about managing risk	Water is a significant business opportunity

different from energy and carbon, in which global strategies can be translated into global actions.

Since the watershed is the focus for any water-stewardship strategy, the water-efficiency goals and stakeholder-engagement efforts at the facility level become critical. Global targets for efficiency can be established, but they must be tailored to meet the individual capabilities and capacity of local operations to implement global goals.

2 Water is unique

Water is not like carbon, because attributes such as geographical location and timing are important in managing water. Therefore, frameworks used for energy and carbon do not translate well to a global water strategy – unless the importance of the watershed is included. While the basics of footprint evaluation and resource use remain the same, options for offsetting water use and 'neutrality' do not.

Despite the unique aspects of water, the concept of 'peak water' (adapted from the peak oil concept; see Chapter 2 for more detail) can be a valuable tool in managing water within a watershed, and can be used to better understand water scarcity and response actions.

3 Companies can no longer rely solely on public water sources

For companies to ensure business continuity and maintain their licences to operate, they will need to develop the capacity and capabilities to provide a reliable supply of water. In view of the increasing competition for water within a watershed, companies can no longer assume public infrastructure will provide an uninterrupted supply of water. Companies have no choice but to develop core water-stewardship competencies, as the absence of water for a business can be 'show stopper'.

It is also reasonable to assume companies will, to the extent possible, move 'off-grid' with water, just as they are developing on-site renewable energy strategies to manage energy supply and price volatility. Off-grid water will include diversification of water supplies (such as rainwater harvesting), water reuse and cost-effective treatment options.

4 The value of water far exceeds its price

Water is cheap and is expected to remain an insignificant part of a company's operating expenses for the foreseeable future. Despite the potential for increases in water pricing and tiered pricing models, the cost of water is not likely to have a significant impact on the cost of goods sold. This may change over time, but for the foreseeable future, it will be the other characteristics of water that hold the most value for companies.

Water issues can impact on companies in relation to their licence to operate; physical risk (disruption); and reputation/brand value; and can potentially damage companies or their supply chains operating in water-stressed and water-scarce areas. Decreased availability of water for direct and indirect (supply chain) use, along with potentially increased competition for water with local communities, can disrupt a business and/or cause a company's licence to operate to be revoked. The way to capture the greatest value from water is to proactively engage with stakeholders to ensure business operations are not disrupted due to lack of water, and reputations and brand value are maintained (or increased). Taking this further, the more a company can reduce its dependence on cheap water, the more it will be able to ensure greater resiliency as water becomes scarcer.

5 Water use in the value chain is typically greater than direct water use

As with carbon, the largest portion of a company's footprint is typically elsewhere in the value chain, both upstream and downstream. This is particularly true for the food, beverage and apparel sectors, where the upstream agricultural component uses a large amount of water. Downstream water use includes consumer products and residential appliance use. Increasingly, companies will be examining their water supply-chain footprint, just as they now are measuring and evaluating how to reduce their carbon footprint. This is challenging; although companies such as Wal-Mart are succeeding in this area, most companies can only *influence* their supply chain.

Water supply-chain risk resides in potential disruptions and reputation/brand value. No longer are companies at 'arm's length' from their supply chains due to outsourcing of manufacturing. Potential disruptions from a lack of water can impact a company even if they do not have much direct water use, their supply chains may use a lot of water and represent the majority of their water footprint. This is evident from the nature of the questions posed in benchmarking studies such as the Ceres 'Murky waters?' report and the Water Disclosure Project questionnaire. In addition, most companies have less understanding of water use and risk within the supply chain than of direct water use.

6 Water risk can be managed effectively only with stakeholder input

Water cannot be managed as an internal issue alone. Increased competition for water resources within a watershed requires companies to proactively engage stakeholders with a goal of developing mutually beneficial water-stewardship strategies. The reliability of water delivery to businesses can only be ensured through public–private partnerships and long-term planning.

More than any other issue, water requires proactive engagement with diverse stakeholders, including investors, who are increasingly aware that water can represent a material risk to a business. How a company mitigates this risk and, if possible, develops business opportunities, should be communicated to investors. New reporting and disclosure frameworks, such as the Water Disclosure Project, are emerging. If one uses carbon as a guide for reporting acceptance and adoption rates, it is anticipated these will only increase over time.

7 Water is a significant business opportunity

With business risk comes opportunity. Just as sustainability is a driver for innovation, so is water – 'watertech' is a business opportunity. Companies are recognizing that water scarcity is driving innovation in water treatment, storage, distribution and new sources of water. Historically, innovation in the water industry has been underfunded and adopted slowly. This is changing as venture capital investment in 'water tech' increases and organizations such as ImagineH2O (www.imagineh2o.org) are fostering innovation through prize competitions. Others, including HydroPoint Data Systems Inc. (www.weathertrak.com) and Aquasciences Inc. (www.aquasciences.com), are emerging to solve challenging issues such as water efficiency and new sources of water (such as water moisture capture from air), respectively.

Current Trends and Conclusions

The water industry is in a rapid state of flux, as awareness increases of the business risks and opportunities posed by water scarcity. This is driving the creation of new stakeholder partnerships, new water-pricing models, new businesses and an overall reconsideration of how we manage water.

Some observations on rapidly evolving trends in the water industry include:

- Water footprinting is a nascent 'technology' and is evolving rapidly. No standard is currently in use, and it remains to be seen which water-footprinting approach becomes the global standard. Companies may elect to use multiple approaches to better understand enterprise-wide and product water footprints. Currently, the real value in water footprinting is in increasing awareness of water use along a value chain, to influence business decisions. This is not about 'eco-labelling' for consumers, but about using tools to identify opportunities to reduce water use and mitigate water risk, and to create business value.

- Water is a driver for economic development. Remember Diageo's 'no water, no beer' quotation? The bottom line for businesses is: without adequate water to run their operations, there are no products. Therefore, water can be a driver for economic development, or it can undercut economic growth.

- The human right to water is important and will not go away. Expect more and more companies to follow PepsiCo's lead on acknowledging the human right to water (as discussed in Chapter 9). Increased competition for water will drive new stakeholder partnerships in an attempt to ensure water is available both for the public and private sectors.

- Water prices will increase, and tiered water pricing will become the norm. Expect water prices to increase, to reflect the real value of water. In turn, this will affect the cost of products and track the amount of embedded water in a product. Tiered pricing structures also will be increasingly common, to promote water efficiency.

- Off-grid water solutions will compete with centralized water supply and treatment. Companies will consider off-grid water solutions to insulate business operations from water-disruption risk, as well as competition with other stakeholders. Off-grid treatment solutions, such as point-of-use (POU) technologies, will be deployed in an attempt to improve the reliability of treated water for business operations.

- Embedded water in products is essentially embedded risk. No longer will the amount of embedded water in a product be taken for granted; water will be managed in a similar manner to carbon footprints. In addition, expect trade policies to be influenced to some degree by the movement of embedded water in products (virtual water), as countries recognize that such a precious resource (water) is being exported.

- Investment in water technologies will continue to increase. Despite previous interest in the water industry, it appears the time is right for investment in water technologies to address water supply, transportation, storage and treatment. The investment community is paying attention to the water market, in part due to current investment in energy and the clean technologies used for managing carbon.

- Water solutions will drive new types of partnerships and collaboration. It is currently the norm for multinational companies to partner with non-governmental organizations (NGOs) to solve pressing environmental and social problems jointly. Collaboration on water issues is no different. While multinational and NGO partnerships are helpful, they are also optional. Not so with water, for this represents a complex environmental, cultural and social challenge. No one company can tackle the challenge of water scarcity alone.

- Water solutions will be integrated with energy and carbon solutions. 'Silo thinking' on water issues and solutions is a flawed approach. Although companies are just beginning to develop frameworks for addressing multifaceted resource issues with 'systems thinking', it remains a challenge. Integrated energy, carbon and water management is becoming an essential aspect of forward-thinking resource management. Expect to see more academic research – and trial and error – in balancing competing resource objectives and valuation.

  Integrated resource management will also drive the development of cross-functional teams to address water-stewardship issues. This will include IT, investor relations, communications, operations, R&D and, of course, 'C-level' management.

- Water strategies require better data to inform business decisions. In general, companies are moving quickly to identify, collect and interpret both direct and indirect water data. This is, essentially, where industry was several years ago with energy and carbon data. Increased need for water data will drive increased adoption of IT solutions to monitor and interpret it on a real-time basis. Also, expect to see increased standardization of water-performance metrics, such as water per unit of production.

- Current water and reporting frameworks are inadequate. This is changing rapidly with the release of the recent Ceres 'Murky waters?' report and the CDP Water Disclosure programme. In contrast, The Global Reporting Initiative's water-use questions are too general to be of much value, and new reporting standards will emerge. However, companies will view the voluntary programme in the same manner they view the voluntary Carbon Disclosure Project (CDP): it will, essentially, be mandatory.

The New Water Industry Ecosystem

Historically, the water industry has been highly fragmented. This is changing, with a rapidly evolving 'ecosystem' of water investors, entrepreneurs, NGOs, private sector initiatives, 'think tanks' and water-stewardship industry leaders. New partnerships are being formed to tackle the challenge of water scarcity, risk and opportunity. This is a positive development, as collaboration will be the only way to address the water, energy and carbon challenges in an integrated manner.

Although this is by no means a definitive illustration of the network of entities and relationships of the water-industry ecosystem, a current view of the ecosystem is provided in Figure 14.1. It is intended to provide examples of the various stakeholders.

A Call to Action

While water scarcity represents a significant business risk to be managed, it also represents an opportunity to create business value. Those companies that proactively build and implement a forward-looking water-stewardship programme will create a more resilient company and increase reputational and brand value.

I believe the companies profiled in this book understand the true value of water, and are working in good faith towards solving the challenge of water scarcity and 'closing the water gap'. They are also moving beyond just resource efficiency, and are building innovative thinking into their core businesses.

The call to action is not just for companies to develop a water strategy. It is for the public and private sectors to understand the real value of water and to manage this resource in an integrated fashion with other resources, such as energy, and issues such as climate change. Moreover, there is urgency in taking action. Currently there is a general lack of political will

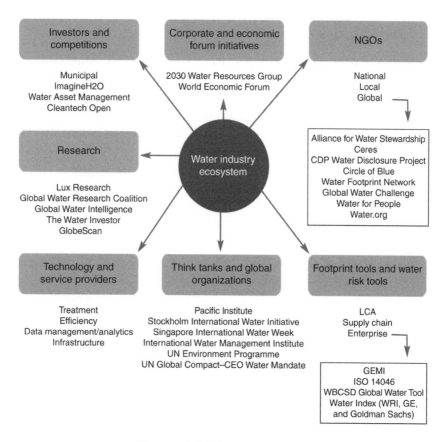

Figure 14.1 *Water ecosystem*

Source: William Sarni

to reduce greenhouse gas emissions and address climate change. I antici-
pate actions to address water scarcity will not drag on as climate change
begins to alter weather and hydrologic patterns. This reality was captured
well by Paul Dickenson, the CEO of the Carbon Disclosure Project, when
he stated, 'If climate change is the shark, then water is its teeth and it is
an issue on which businesses need far greater levels of awareness and
understanding' (Irbaris, 2009).

It would be unwise to wait until the tap turns to a trickle. The time to
manage water and all of our resources as if we truly valued them is now.

There really is no other alternative.

References

Irbaris (2009) *CDP Water Disclosure: The Case for Water Disclosure*, Irbaris, http://www.capinnovations.com/uploads/CDP_Water_Disclosure_PDF.pdf, accessed 4 October 2010

Water-Technology.net (2008) 'Singapore's self sufficiency', www.water-technology.net/features/feature2026, 10 June 2008, accessed 30 June 2010

Index